Divorced with Love

Our journey through heartbreak and separation into forgiveness and friendship

Michael Schiesser and Neelama Eyres

For Kai,

Our one and only sweet prince.

Without you this book would not exist - without you we wouldn't have made it to where we are NOW. This book is dedicated to you our beloved son, teacher, healer, and bringer of such exquisite joy.

Thank you for teaching us what it means to love.

Acknowledgments

We'd like to thank Jennie Nash, our writing coach, for without your diligent support, encouragement and weekly deadlines we would never have finished this project! Many people read and reviewed our memoir along the way. Your support and feedback were invaluable: MeiMei Fox, Alix Madgrigal, Katherine Hample, Louise Klein, Craig Sweetnam, Leslie Traub, Michelle Cole, and John Groff. A huge thanks to Mark Coleman, for your feedback, inspiration, and unbelievable support. To our dearest friend and colleague, Howard Ross: a thousand thanks for being our best friend and rock as we traveled the treacherous 'divorce terrain' and for your inspiration, support and love in writing this memoir. To our dear friend Judith Alexander, you are the best kind of editor and ghost writer, because you not only brought meaning and grammar to Michael's G'English (German-English), you went above and beyond by pouring your eyes and heart onto every letter of this book, and believed in us and our story and kept us going through many valleys of doubt. This book would never have happened without you - Danke - Merci - Thank You, dear one. Marilyn Damiano, aka Neelama's Mom, librarian in heart and soul, lover of books-- you inspired, coaxed and loved us through each and every line of this book. Your encouragement helped us to keep going and make this book a reality, and we're forever grateful for your support. To all our friends -- too numerous to name - your love and support is deeply felt and appreciated, Thank You All. To all of our students - you are also our teachers - and your lessons are a part of our hearts and this book, Thank You All.

Michael:

To My family: Hugo and Katarina Schiesser, Hans and Christine, Guenter and Kriztina, Johannes and Christian. To my teachers: Pfarrer Ort, Father Heimler, Maria Hippius,, Graf Duerkheim, Osho, C.G. Jung, Sigmund Freud, Santosh, Sri Poonja, Chokyi Nyingma Rinpoche, Kalindi, Gourasana, Faisal Muquaddam, Sri Amma Bhagawan, Adyashanti, Ken Wilber and the mystics of all traditions.

Neelama:

To my partner David, your incredible love and support mean the world to me. To my family: Marilyn Damiano, Bob and Peg Eyres, Marc Hample, Langdon, Katherine, Gracie & Lowell. My Gigi Ruth, Grandma Cavallaro, and my late Grandma Eyres. Aunt Heidi, Aunt Judy and Uncle Dan. Lolina, Totono, Covi y todo mi familia de Espana. To my teachers: The Lady, Osho, Brahma Vedant, Faisal Muquaddam, Sri Amma Bhagavan, Adyashanti, Richard Rohr, Father Thomas Keating, Cynthia Bourgeault, and the mystics from all traditions.

iv

We bow in gratitude and hope as your students we are doing you honor by attempting to live your teachings.

Lastly, with the lines from a devotional song we want to express our deepest gratitude to that Mystery which ultimately can't be named, but loved and worshipped:

"All I have you gave to me,
the eyes to see,
the heart to feel,
Now there is only one thing left to do,
I give it all back to you - I give it all back to you"

May you, dearest reader, benefit from our hindsight's, so that you journey through the human 'sea of separation' be with the least amount of suffering and the greatest amount of healing, transformation, and love.

Praise

"Michael and Neelama offer a vulnerable, poignant, wise, and ultimately redemptive story that takes us beyond romantic infatuation into the deepest kind of love - a spiritual partnership in which both are committed to serving God and humanity (plus a special child). Given our high rates of divorce, this book should be mandatory reading so that the inevitable tumult of separation can serve our ultimate freedom."

Stephen Dinan, CEO The Shift Network, Author Sacred America, Sacred World

Contents

Introduction

"For one human being to love another, that is perhaps the most difficult of all our tasks—the ultimate, the last test and proof, the work for which all other work is but preparation."
— *Rainer Maria Rilke*

This quote was on the front page of our wedding invitation.

We were married in June 2002 in an incredible explosion of love in Marin County, California. Almost everyone in attendance told us our wedding touched them deeply and opened their hearts like none other. Two years later we became parents of a special needs boy named Kai.

Four years after our wedding we separated, and in December 2008 we were legally divorced.

Today we live together as friends (with no benefits!), co-parenting our son in Woodstock, Georgia. One of the greatest gifts of going through our divorce differently, with the emphasis on personal growth and healing, was the resurrection of our 'family relationship.' Our son is the greatest beneficiary of this, and his joy is made palpable when he sits in between us, wrapping each of his arms around one of our necks, pulling us close, and beaming with delight. Those moments are the most precious—and make our entire journey worth it. Our family eats and plays together—especially charades—one of Kai's favorite games, or races around the perimeter of our home, an event that usually ends in squeals of joy. Even after all of these years, due to his special needs, one of us stays in his room each night until he falls asleep, and remains on duty throughout the night. It's been a blessing that we're able to share this load. The major difference to traditional family life, is that we each retreat into our own bedrooms at the end of the day, and share the romantic side of life with other people.

You might ask, "What the heck happened?" What sparked our love, what ended it, and what made it possible for us to move across the country and live together?

We'll get to that in the story you are about to read. But before we begin, we want to share a little bit about who we are and why we wrote this book.

We are spiritual teachers who own a company called The Inner Journey Institute. We have been facilitating transformational workshops across the United States and Canada since 1999. Our work bridges the worlds of psychology and spirituality, and in its essence, serves to connect the individual to his or her true nature and potential. Although it might sound cliché, we love people and feel extremely grateful to support and witness their healing and transformation, and growth into their fullness.

What do we mean by spirituality? For us, spirituality means a connection to a force greater than ourselves—a force, or presence, that has been called so many names, and for us is ultimately nameable. We do not adhere to any specific religion, but we respect and have been inspired by the deeper truths inherent in all major religious and wisdom traditions on the planet.

We believe that being a teacher carries a huge responsibility. Our experience has shown us that we can only take people as far as we ourselves have gone. Inner growth has been a priority for most of our adult lives, and has deeply influenced us as human beings, parents, students, and seminar leaders. It is the underlying thread of the journey we are about to share with you.

We have made every effort to share that journey as authentically as possible. For us, being a spiritual teacher does not mean being "above it all" or being a perfect human being. Many students search for a teacher who has "attained" something. We believe that the best teaching we can offer is our own humanity. Our work and our teaching is not about *getting beyond* our humanness, but rather recognizing it with compassion, and learning how to own and accept *all* of who we are. In our work with ourselves and with countless others, we have seen that when people rejects parts of themselves in the pursuit of a spiritual ideal, they suffer greatly and feel even further away from the all-embracing presence of God. We have come to realize that acceptance itself *is* the doorway to spiritual transformation.

Why are we writing this book? We have witnessed—over the past eighteen years of working with thousands of people from different backgrounds, classes, races, religions, sexual orientations, age groups, and education levels—that relationships are *the* greatest source of both joy and pain in people's lives. Participants in our workshops usually share with us the more painful side of their relationships. We have seen that people are often burdened by guilt, by blame, by the inability to forgive themselves and others, and unfortunately have not been shown a way to mend a broken heart. For years we have facilitated people through these challenging obstacles, and have become experts in helping others transform.

It came as a big surprise when, suddenly, we found ourselves in the same ditch we had helped our participants climb out of so many times. What follows is the story of how we navigated through the heartbreaking terrain of divorce, and what we found on the other side.

Even though this book is a personal memoir, the divorce process has many universal elements. As you walk with us through our journey, you will be shown how to walk through a collaborative divorce. At certain points in the book, we will pause our personal story and address the overarching human elements at play. We know, embedded within our personal story, is a collective experience, with collective life lessons that can lead to healing, forgiveness, compassion, greater self-awareness, and to all of us becoming bigger, better, brighter human beings.

Even though we've been in the field of transformation for many years, we are just like any other human being—and when faced with our own divorce—we confronted the darker sides of ourselves and each other. We faced the hell of divorce. We intend to tell our story as a roadmap—so that others can learn how to transform the pain and anger of divorce into a profound opportunity for growth. Our story is designed to teach others how to uncouple peacefully with a productive outcome.

This story is told with both of our voices. In each chapter, there is a "hers" and a "his" section. In our experience, there are *always* two sides to every story. Yet, in most books about relationships, and in almost all books about divorce, the reader hears only one side. So many of us enjoy a book with one starring character—the hero or heroine who steals our heart and inspires us. That's the one we side with, root for, and defend inside our head. In this book, we hope to show you that there is no hero or heroine, nor is there one objectively true viewpoint. The same "story" is remembered differently by each person—not objectively as "truth," but rather, like all memories, subjectively as "perception." In our book, we consciously expose the incongruities between our perceptions—to reflect the reality that, as humans, each of us has a unique perception of events. Where most of us get into trouble with each other is in believing that our own perspective is *the* truth.

Our writing is also influenced by the conditioning of two very different cultures. Neelama was born and raised in upstate New York, while Michael was born into post-war Germany, and therefore punctuates his writing with occasional German expressions or quotations.

Our story is told from both a woman's and a man's perspective, with the vision that our two genders can come to better understand and respect each other's differences. This is also reflected in our different writing styles. Neelama writes primarily from an "I" perspective, emotionally-based and poetically animated, while Michael writes in a direct and masculine style, which is often more analytical—and sometimes quite blunt.

We have found, in our work with others, that when people can open themselves up to different viewpoints, their capacity for compassion and forgiveness grows exponentially. This kind of understanding creates an opportunity for tremendous healing and is, we believe, what will transform the world one person at a time.

We have written two very different, yet honest, accounts of what happened on our journey—a journey through love, marriage, divorce, business partnership, and co-parenting a special needs child—and how the intensity of those experiences forever changed our lives.

This book exposes the truth of what happened inside of each of us. It's not always pretty, and may even be shocking at times. Being leaders in the field of personal transformation, it was humbling to be faced with our own human flaws so directly and brutally. We made the decision, however, even risking detriment to our image as teachers, to stay in integrity and tell the truth. The cornerstone of each of our life's work has been a deeply held belief that honesty and authenticity are both the foundation of, and the path towards, freedom itself.

In closing, we acknowledge that we are two human beings, just like you, who got thrown a myriad of curve balls by this beautiful and excruciating thing called Life. We believe our story can give insight and support to those who are currently in relationships, going through a divorce process, parenting a child (especially a child with special needs), or anyone who is unresolved in matters of the heart.

You may say we are dreamers, but there is nothing more fulfilling to us than witnessing people open up and connect—to themselves, to others, and to their unique spiritual source. May this book make you a dreamer too.

Chapter One:
A Shock in the Bathroom

(Hers: Please, NO!)

I stared down at that little blue plus sign as if I'd been given a death sentence. My body trembled, and a deep ache filled my bones. It was an anguish I'd never before experienced. My husband, Michael, and I stood there in shock, looking down at the white stick, and the tiny yet immense result staring us in the face. We ran out of the house as if it were on fire and, finding the nearest drugstore, bought six more of those damn sticks. Test after test, and what seemed like a million plus signs later, my body revolted. I cried, I screamed, I protested: *No NO . . . no NO . . . not this . . . this cannot be happening to me*. It was too soon for morning sickness, but I felt nauseated. Thoughts raced through my head as I looked for a way out, a backdoor, some kind of escape from the reality staring back at me. I came up short every time.

That day had started as any normal day; I got up, meditated, and went jogging. I then decided to take a pregnancy test, because my period was a couple of weeks late. I had been late before, and knew that my anxiety about possibly being pregnant often prolonged my period unnecessarily. In the past, taking a pregnancy test and seeing that I wasn't pregnant often did the trick. Earlier that week, I'd bought a test kit, and I now decided to set things right and help my body to get back on track. That strategy had always worked in the past, and I expected today would be no different.

I was 32 years old at the time, and had never been pregnant. My husband and I were using condoms and the rhythm method as our form of birth control, and most of the time I'd been careful. Never in a GAZILLION years did I expect to see that little plus sign. To me, it appeared out of nowhere, like a tornado. All I could muster in response was sheer defiance: no way, Life, I don't accept you; I don't want your terms; I hate your brutal, insensitive terms; this doesn't work! Let's just rewind: take me back to yesterday—that's when I liked you, that's when you were pretty much how I wanted you to be. Life gave no response to my tirade, save for the blue plus sign, which did not flinch.

From within the eye of my own personal storm, I barely noticed Michael, who sat mere inches away from me on the edge of the bathtub. I remember him looking stunned, yet it seemed simply the initial surprise that I'm sure many guys experience when faced with the prospect of becoming a dad for the first time. My reaction was in an altogether different category. More like: *I can't . . . I won't . . . PLEASE God, don't make me!* And in our different reactions, we were immediately and forever separated. That day in our little bathroom was the beginning of our end.

(His: Oh Mein Gott!)

Oh mein Gott! Neelama pregnant? I was startled, shocked, disconnected, and just stood there in our bathroom, frozen in disbelief. A jumble of thoughts raced through my head in rapid succession. *How can this be? No, it isn't true! Didn't Neelama tell me that she had already ovulated three weeks ago? There's no way she can be pregnant. The test results must be false! Us, having a baby? A child? Me—a father?* My mind could not stop racing.

A few tests later, I could no longer deny it. My beautiful and beloved wife of a year and a half was pregnant. I had never even imagined myself being married, let alone having a child! The sensation of shock set in. I was stunned, scared, and in the face of the biggest decision that might ever confront me, I suddenly felt an urge to run. The question came into my mind, *what are we going to do?* Like billions of couples before us, I realized we had only two options: to have the child or to abort. To my own surprise, the notion of the second alternative was only fleeting, and didn't evolve into a thought train.

While still dealing with my own fear, I suddenly became aware that Neelama was in an even more distressed and agitated emotional state. In my homeland of Germany, it was known as *usser sich sein*—she was literally *outside of herself,* freaked out, and almost crazed with confusion and doubt. Her reaction only added to my own uncertainty and angst, leading to another thought train of inner questioning. *Am I ready to be a father? At 48 years of age? Oh Lord, help me,* I pleaded, the power of my early Catholic conditioning kicking in, as it often did in a crisis, my confused mind seeking refuge, advice, help. Stuck somewhere between *Oh Lord, help me,* and *Ach du lieber Gott* (Oh my dear God), I felt cornered by life, and, to be honest, dismayed.

Chapter Two:
Retracing Our Steps

(Hers: My Life is About God, Not Kids)

I never thought I'd become a mother in this life. From a very young age, I had decided that the kid route was not for me. I was eight years old when my brother Langdon was born. The day my parents brought him home from the hospital, I peered with excitement into his bassinet, thrilled to meet my little brother, and even more delighted to become the "big sister" and the "little mommy." When he saw me, he belted out a scream so loud that everyone ran in to see what happened. Needless to say, he hadn't warmed to me, at least not initially, and my great fantasy of becoming a mini-mom never came to fruition. If anything, the opposite occurred. I was struck by the sheer amount of work and sacrifice it took my mother to juggle everything already on her plate, while now caring for an utterly dependent newborn who seemed to cry *all the time*. Many nights throughout Langdon's early years, I'd lie in bed, trembling, afraid of the screams coming from the tiny creature across the hall. I couldn't understand what on earth could make him cry that way . . . and for so long. But what scared me even more was watching my mom unravel at the seams, when her frantic attempts to stop the crying failed miserably. I'd cringe as she desperately pulled her hair, screaming, "Jesus, Mary and Joseph" in a way that, even then, I knew wasn't spiritual. From my eight-year-old vantage point, the whole parenting thing pretty well terrified me.

Perhaps because of this early experience, I never felt that gut feeling so many women describe, as if their very body was endowed with a knowing: I am meant to be a mother. This inner yearning to have a child was a stranger to me. I chalked it up to motherhood simply not being my calling in life. And for the most part, I felt reconciled with that truth. Michael and I had loosely discussed the possibility of children over the past several months and, ironically, just a few weeks before getting pregnant, I had arrived at clarity on the matter once and for all: no, I was definitely not interested.

I'd announced this decision to my mom during a road trip, as we headed down the coast from Marin, where I lived, to Santa Monica. We found ourselves on the most beautiful stretch of Highway One, right around Big Sur, where the ocean and sky meet in a way that takes your breath away, and commands you to believe in something greater than yourself. It was one of those majestic California days: a clear blue sky and shimmers of light dancing on the water, proclaiming nothing but joy. In the power and beauty of that moment, I found the courage to tell my mom what I thought would be devastating news for her. With some trepidation, I began shakily, "I need to share something with you, Mom. After a lot of contemplation, I have decided that I don't want children. I can imagine this will be a disappointment to you, and I'm really sorry for that. I know how much you love children and wanted to be a grandma. And yet I cannot find a real pull in me to have kids. I've never felt that, and still don't feel it. Michael and I have been looking at the idea and pondering it since getting married, but I really cannot find a *yes* in my heart for this . . . so I want you not to expect any grandchildren from me."

I slowly exhaled and noticed it was easier to breathe, like a weight had been lifted. I sank into the car seat, relieved that it was out in the open—truth revealed in its nakedness. What came next was rather surprising to me. I had thought there would be some protest, or at least a few tears coming from my mom's side of the car, but her reply was so easy, so simple. She began to talk in slow motion, her voice filled with compassion, "To be honest, honey, I am really okay with that. This is your life, and your choice. And I totally understand and respect your decision. I really do. Langdon will probably have children, so I will likely get to be a grandma someday." As I gazed out onto the ocean, I felt a sense of peace come over me, as if I'd somehow been let off the hook.

I'd made a similar declaration to some of my closest girlfriends during a women's camping trip. We were sitting around a bonfire one hot night, drinking wine and confessing our truths to each other. Many of them knew that Michael and I had been vaguely pondering the child question for some time. Suddenly, I stood up and declared that I had arrived at a decision: my life, at least for now, was about "birthing *myself,*" and until that passage was complete, I didn't feel prepared to give birth to another. The notion of birthing myself symbolized my journey of spiritual growth, which, although admittedly selfish, was the only life I knew at the time. My friends raised their glasses of wine and nodded their heads passionately, indicating their support. These women had been my closest friends for almost ten years, and during that time they'd seen how my spiritual quest had become the centerpiece of my life.

I believe the intense focus on my spirituality stemmed largely from a pivotal event in my upbringing. I had been raised as a Catholic, but when I was nine, my mom and my stepdad, who was Jewish, decided to give me the choice between continuing to go to church or joining them at temple. They sat me down at our kitchen table and made their declaration: "It's up to you—you can do whatever you want. Whatever you decide will be just fine."

Looking back at it now, this was a pretty big decision for a nine-year-old: choosing a religion!

"Well, where is Langdon going to go? I asked, referring to my little brother, "Temple? What do you guys think I should do?"

"Langdon will be raised Jewish; he will go to temple. But you can do whatever you want—it's *your* decision," they replied, "Take some time to think about it."

Think about it? That didn't really happen. I was only nine, after all.

Ultimately, like many of my most profound decisions, this one was made in an instant . . . and influenced by a very cute boy. That summer, I was enrolled in the Jewish Community Center's summer camp, where I met Saul. My heart took up residency with him immediately. He was all I could think about, and I created countless fantasies about our future—all revolving around the same basic plot: Saul thinking that I was the most amazing person on the planet, followed by a public declaration of his eternal and undying love for me. In those fantasies, we were married—a thousand times. But wait, I forgot—*I wasn't Jewish.* In the end, the decision to convert was an easy one. The following weekend I was at temple instead of church.

Yet, in all seriousness, the conversion did something to me. Even though both religions exist within the same Judeo-Christian stream, converting at the age of nine felt like I was entering an entirely different world. Where were the little wafers, the holy water, and Jesus, for God's sake? Why did my mom look traumatized whenever I knelt down or tried to cross myself? And then the deeper questions began. How many Gods are there? And if there is really only *one* God, then why does this feel so foreign? The whole thing sent my system into deep confusion. I think it's what propelled me on my relentless search to do whatever it took to find this thing called God. Years after my conversion, I was given the opportunity to have a Bat Mitzvah. The word "bat" means "daughter" in Aramaic, the common spoken language of the early Jewish people. The word "mitzvah" is Hebrew for "commandment." The Bat Mitzvah ritual symbolizes a significant coming-of-age within the Jewish faith, and it was through this process that I began to take Judaism more seriously.

I attended classes each week to learn Hebrew, because it was important that I read in the original language of the Torah for the ceremony. It took over a year to prepare—attending special classes, and writing out my speech. When the day came, I stood up in front of a couple hundred people—members of our temple, most of my family, my junior high friends—and proclaimed myself a faithful Jew. I still wrestled with the God questions in my heart, and occasionally wondered about church versus temple. I tried to reconcile it with the notion that there could only be one God, just different ways to access Him. My search continued, and by the time I got to college, I'd decided to pursue God via the academic route. This turned out to be an interesting intellectual endeavor that taught me much, but still failed to answer the deeper pull of my heart, which longed to know God directly.

Shortly after college, I moved to San Francisco's Bay Area, which was a Mecca for spirituality. It was like being at a huge buffet—so many choices. And finally, what I had always longed for—an *experience* of God versus a mental understanding—began to unfold. In the Bay Area, a dear friend introduced me to a spiritual community that focused on opening people up to a mystical and embodied experience of the Divine. Their form of prayer and meditation was through music, emotions, and dancing—and it rocked my world. It was within this community, at the age of 25, that I met Michael. He was fifteen years older, and had been around the spiritual block that much longer. I was attracted to his maturity, and respected his overt dedication to personal growth. Our first few dates were full of deep and heated conversations about God, over beer and Thai food in San Rafael. Our early relationship lasted just under a year, at which point my spiritual quest took me on a year-long sabbatical around Southeast Asia and India, during which time Michael and I had very little contact, and only by email.

When I returned from my trip, it was to my hometown in upstate New York—to give my body time to heal from the various intestinal bugs that are often acquired when one visits the Third World for any length of time. I was in culture shock—simple things felt like too much: driving a car, standing in the grocery store amidst all that toothpaste, and being perplexed that one little item could warrant so much choice. I felt lost as to my life's direction. After such a profound year of seeking, I couldn't fathom how I should now proceed. I reached out to Michael—I knew he had travelled extensively on a similar quest, and hoped he could help me regroup.

He himself had just returned to California from a three-month trip to Burma, and we spent many nights talking on the phone about our discoveries, our confusion, and our endless questions. In Michael, I felt I had someone who could really understand me.

He wanted more—that was made clear. But I didn't feel the same—I wanted a friend. He was persistent, and after many months of phone calls, he figured out a way for us to come together that wouldn't seem too threatening for me. I had just begun dabbling in teaching my very first workshops on yoga and meditation. By that time, Michael was an experienced workshop teacher, and he was going up to Canada to teach a weekend course. He offered to let me be his assistant and to teach the yoga/meditation portion of the workshop. The offer was too enticing to resist—I was sold, and off I went.

What happened on that trip was interesting, to say the least. We arrived in Ottawa late at night, and because our hosts assumed we were a couple, they put us in the same room—with one bed. At first, I was taken aback, but as it turned out, we had some great days (and nights) together in that room. Yet I still regarded Michael more as a friend than anything else, and didn't feel that "falling in love" feeling I'd come to rely on in prior relationships. Towards the end of the week, I told him that I couldn't feel my *yes* to really be with him—that this had been a great experience, but it wasn't going any further. The rest of that day was difficult, with very little talking and lots of awkwardness between us—until the workshop got underway.

Then something pivotal happened. In those amazing days of the workshop, something fundamentally changed in my feelings towards Michael. Up until that time, I'd never seen him teach—I'd only known him as a peer, a fellow student in our meditation community. Sitting quietly in that workshop, watching him facilitate, I think two things occurred. First, I got a glimpse of his essence: I saw and experienced his soul in its magnificence. And second—perhaps because of that, or perhaps not—I began to experience the missing piece: that unmistakable sense of falling in love. I found myself suddenly and irrevocably enraptured by him, and it was clear to me that he was no longer just a friend. I had fallen head over heels into deep admiration and love for this man whom, at times, I even idolized.

Of course, the initial period of enchantment eventually faded, and yet the bond of love between us deepened and matured. Together, we spent the next four years building an incredible life. Michael had become so many things to me: a teacher, a mentor, a fellow seeker, a lover, and a very best friend whom I looked up to and trusted with my life. Our time was spent building our business, teaching workshops together, forming a wonderful community, traveling, and focusing on our inner growth. We had shared ideas about living a simple life, and had chosen different priorities than mainstream couples, so that our resources could be spent on what mattered most to us. We had both lived communally most of our adult lives; we both drove used cars; we didn't go on typical couples' vacations but, rather, sought out opportunities to immerse ourselves in third world cultures where we could afford to spend several weeks or even a month. We studied with a teacher in the East Bay, named Faisal, whose beautiful combination of spirituality and psychological work had presented a roadmap for our own inner paths. Our shared life was very full and rich, and my plan was to continue down this road of ever-deepening growth with the man I loved. Children? No, I couldn't see how *children* would fit anywhere into our beautiful life.

(His: With Her, I Could Do It)

Neelama and I had loosely explored the possibility of having children, even as recently as a few months before the fateful "bathroom discovery." I had played with the idea of becoming a late father, but we had never considered deliberately moving in that direction. For most of my adulthood, children had been out of the question. I had lived an unusual and somewhat nomadic life, pursuing a spiritual journey. It started out with a unique career choice which ran contrary to the dreams of my father, who wanted me to be an engineer: my youthful and naively adventurous spirit had me join the Bavarian police force. After five years of trying hard to fit into an economically safe but very restrictive structure, my rebelliousness pushed me out of the world of law and order and into the pursuit of a degree in philosophy and in pastoral counseling. I felt I had come home, and that my inquisitive mind had finally found the environment it needed to thrive. After successful completion of my studies, the intellectual undertaking turned into a spiritual quest that, over the next twenty years, led me to many exotic places in the world. I had lived in a Zen monastery in Japan for a while, been a Buddhist monk in Burma for many months, and made frequent travels throughout India—all part of my exploration of several Eastern spiritual traditions. I had even left my homeland of Germany to immigrate to the United States, just to be close to my spiritual teacher. In those years of seeking, I participated in many courses, seminars, and trainings led by preeminent teachers in the field of human and transpersonal psychology. In all this, I was driven by my life's single quest to know God, expressed in Eastern terminology as to awaken and become enlightened, and in Western language as to experience union, or to be filled with His/Her/Its presence. This quest originated all the way back in my early childhood.

I was born on January 1 in 1956, in a small rural village of 950 people in the Franconia area of Bavaria, Germany. Our elder village priest, who was my mother's spiritual mentor, sensed something in me which, as my mother later told me, led him to suggest that she encourage me to become a priest. So when I was a toddler, she took me along when she visited her little "Mother Mary Chapel" in the woods. Sitting in that tiny chapel, at the top of a hill overlooking our village, I had my first exposure to devotional practice. I watched as my mom and some of the other women from our village gathered to pray. The women knelt down on primitive wooden footrests, their fingers moving over their rosary beads, as they repeated words of praise to the divine Mother. In that little church, a seed was planted in me that bore fruit in the form of a life-long yearning: I longed to understand the mystery that these grown ups were praying to.

One of my most striking memories was of myself at the age of five, walking home alone from kindergarten and stopping, out of curiosity, at our village church. Barely able to reach up and pull down the black iron handle, I managed to open the huge wooden door and was suddenly transported into another world. As I walked towards the altar of what felt like a giant cathedral, the smells of incense, the statues of angels, and the shimmering gold light opened a door inside me. I felt something in that moment which can only be called a numinous, or otherworldly, presence. I was in awe, filled with the deepest sense of wonder and joy. I wanted to experience this again and, fortunately, was to have more of these moments throughout my childhood.

I always questioned why it was I, but not my two brothers, who were exposed to the same environment, who had this longing. I often wondered why I was the one child from this idyllic little village who was destined to be catapulted out into the world in search of God or spirit. Why me? Why did I not follow the norm like everyone else: find a career, get married, settle down, and raise a family? Many years later, one of my spiritual teachers had a word for it: fate. That was my fate.

Fate did indeed knock loudly on my door on a warm October night in 1996. I was a student in a meditation group in Marin County, California. At the conclusion of one evening's meditation, the members of our group were asked to partner up with someone. I made a beeline for a young woman who I'd seen for the first time in the group. Several others were heading towards her too, but I got there first! When we hugged for the first time, oh wow—she was so juicy. As our bodies melted into each other in that hug, I started to fall in love. It was Neelama. Over the next few months, we saw each other at other meditation events and parties. The leap into a romantic relationship happened on her twenty-sixth birthday. In a way, our connection was the last birthday gift of the day, and I felt it was I who'd received the gift. Neelama was fifteen years younger than I, yet way beyond her years in presence and depth, and I felt she met me on many levels. For the next six months, we were absorbed in a passionate romantic relationship, until our respective spiritual journeys caused our paths to part.

During the following two years, we were able to connect only by email and phone, until we finally reconnected during one particularly magical night, on August 15, 1999, in the countryside near Ottawa, Canada. Neelama and I had just returned from eight wild and wonderful days and nights together in romantic Quebec City. This summer night was to be one of the most amazing experiences of my life. After finishing our first workshop together, Neelama surprised me by announcing she would not be leaving right away as she had originally planned. Following a wonderful dinner with our new found Canadian friends, we cocooned into the tiny guest bedroom, which was to become our "Temple of Love." We were up all night, sharing our innermost feelings, ripping our hearts open, laughing, crying, making love, and diving deeper and deeper into each other. Lying in each other's arms, naked on all levels, a true intimacy occurred. Our vulnerability had opened the door and our two hearts merged. By the time the sun rose the next morning, we had said *yes* to each other. It was crystal clear to me that she was my woman and I was her man. Uncharacteristically for me, I had absolutely no uncertainty or doubts about this commitment.

Now, in 2003, four years since we had committed to each other that August night, Neelama was pregnant. After the initial shock, and some waves of doubt and fear—*Oh my God, my life as I know it will be over*—I found myself warming up a little more each day to the idea of us having a child together. During the three previous years, my life's calling had come together. Working with a team, I founded a transformational company called Inner Journey Seminars, into which I brought Neelama as a business partner and co-facilitator. Our company was blossoming: we enjoyed success, our transformational seminar was taking off in several cities, and we passionately loved our work of assisting people in their life journeys. To top it all off, we were living in gorgeous Marin County, had a wonderful circle of friends, and for the first time in my life, I was growing real roots in the material world.

At some point during the first week of contemplating the pregnancy and the hard decision we had to make, a clear thought formed in my mind: *With her, I could do it—I could have a child and start a family.* I knew Neelama would be an amazing, caring, and nurturing mother. To me, our relationship was like a strong and beautiful boat that could weather any storm. And I was fully committed to sharing our lives together for the long haul, which for me was a prerequisite for raising a child.

Chapter Three:
Pro-Choice Meets Pro-Life

(Hers: A Decision to be Made)

The day after the shock in the bathroom, I went to see my OB/GYN to get an official report, hoping against hope that this had all been some big mistake. But no, the doctor came into the room announcing with joy that I was indeed pregnant. Seeing the fear and concern on my face, she slowly lowered herself into a chair and encouraged me to share how I felt. As I poured out all my anxieties, she just listened—occasionally nodding her head, in a way that indicated she'd heard this countless times before. How many other women had sat in this sterile office, discovering they'd become mothers? How many of them had looked into her eyes, releasing their innermost feelings and deepest fears in the privacy of this modern-day confessional? She listened with an absence of judgment and a wealth of compassion that allowed me to open the floodgates and share my plight.

When I'd finished my tearful monologue, she told me that the important thing to remember was that I was very newly pregnant—this meant I had time on my side. She also reminded me that I had a choice in this matter and suggested that, while I was making up my mind, I could at least make an appointment to terminate the pregnancy. Yes, an abortion! I didn't have to go through with it, she emphasized, but she felt it might relax me to know this was an option. It was the first time since the moment of terror in the bathroom that my mind and body were able to calm down—at least temporarily. When I got home, I went into our bedroom to find Michael, who was anxious to hear about the appointment. "Well, it's official," I said, " I'm pregnant. I also spoke with the doctor about all my ambivalence, and she suggested I make an appointment for an abortion just so that . . . " I couldn't even finish my sentence. As soon as the "a" word was uttered, Michael came at me like a freight train.

"What? You did *what?*" he screamed, turning beet red as he continued. "How could you do that? You didn't even ask me how I felt; you didn't consult me. You went ahead and decided this by *yourself?*" He paced around the room as he spoke, throwing his arms up in the air. "I am the father . . . we are married . . . don't I have a say here? How can you keep me out of this? It's not fair . . . I can tell you right now, our marriage will not make it if you do this!"

This adamant outburst hit me like a cannonball. I couldn't believe this was my husband. Of course, I'd seen Michael get angry before, and we'd had our share of heated arguments over the years. But the severity of this reaction sent me reeling. We'd never had this conversation before—the possibility of having a child had never been on the table in any real way—and I had no idea he was so profoundly against abortion.

"Wait a minute," I yelled back, "how dare you? How can you say that— how do you *know* that this would lead to the end of our marriage? So this is it? I either do what you want, or I get an abortion and a divorce? That's what it boils down to? Our marriage is over? Screw that! What about *my* feelings, what about my body, what about what matters to me?"

He replied by quoting from a study of a famous psychotherapist, who had observed that couples who have gone through an abortion have a much higher percentage of separation and divorce. At that point, I was already raging inside and couldn't listen. This was the first of many arguments that went like that, back and forth, defending our points of view as if our lives depended on it. Nobody ever won these battles. We screamed *at* each other but couldn't find a way to really listen *to* each other.

Within a few days, we agreed to seek help from our spiritual teacher, Faisal. As we pulled up to his house in El Cerrito, I noticed my palms were wet with fear. Sitting in the session room waiting for him to arrive, I fidgeted in my chair for what seemed like an eternity. I wondered what he might think of me, how he might perceive my negative reaction to the pregnancy, or if he would judge the abortion appointment the way Michael had. When Faisal came into the room, I could feel my stomach tighten, as if preparing for an attack. I felt guilty about this, because Faisal had been nothing but a brilliant and open-hearted teacher to me over the past few years. He was a short man, with warm brown eyes, and a nice little belly that somehow rounded out his wisdom with some humanness. He spoke softly, yet with the weight of truth on his lips. And within minutes, I realized he was not going to judge me—it was I who was doing that to myself. In the session, he held a space of incredible neutrality between Michael and me, which opened the door for a powerful exploration. He let each of us share our feelings about the pregnancy, while periodically asking pointed questions that challenged both of our positions.

I hoped Faisal could get Michael to see that some of his indignation came not from "truth," but from his own egoic reactions. Then, as any good teacher would do, he asked me to put my own point of view under scrutiny as well. "Neelama," he said, "at least be curious, and explore what is causing your huge reaction. What is going on underneath this big *no* of yours? The pregnancy is triggering a huge fear inside of you . . . what is that all about? I ask that you be willing to explore whether, underneath the surface resistance, there *might* be another part in you that is a *yes*—a part that wants the child."

This concept was so hard to get my head around. Yet there was a tiny part of me, my "professional side," that could put on the "counseling" hat and understand him. I knew, from all the work I'd done on myself and with others, that whenever we have such an intense resistance to something, there is usually an underlying trigger worth exploring. Something beyond the present day situation is usually involved. But it was only one tiny part of me that knew this; the rest of me was taken over by a freight train of resistance which dominated—taking center stage, belting out its loud and clear operetta: *NO. No no no NO.* From this place, I couldn't imagine that there would be a *yes* somewhere underneath, but I trusted Faisal's suggestion and made a commitment to myself that I would try my best to understand the *no* in me, and look at whether, however deeply buried, there might also be a *yes* in me somewhere for this pregnancy.

(His: Fighting for the Unborn Child)

When Neelama got home from her doctor, and mentioned that she had set up an appointment for an abortion, I instantly freaked out, and a wave of hot anger took over my body. I got up and stomped angrily around the room. I felt pissed off, hurt, and helpless because I had not been consulted. I screamed, "Hey, I am involved here, too! I am the father. Talk to me first! Let me have a say in this." As we argued, I paced around our bedroom, triggered and agitated. Over the course of the argument it became increasingly clear to me that I was holding the smaller end of the stick— ultimately it was her decision. What could I do? I couldn't physically stop her. All I had was fervor and persuasion. I was in a state of desperation, and felt I was losing the battle. From my perspective, I felt like I needed to fight for the life of this unborn child. In a last-ditch effort, I desperately declared, "If we have an abortion, we will not make it as a couple." This statement was based on observations from one of my teachers, the psychotherapist Bert Hellinger. He had done inner work around the world with thousands of people, and had observed that quite a high percentage of couples that go through an abortion eventually separate. This finding had stuck with me, and now surfaced in response to Neelama having set a date to terminate the pregnancy. Looking back, something of even greater significance was behind the intensity of my reaction.

I had already been through two abortions and didn't want to be part of another. In the fall of 1986, I was in a new relationship with a wonderful Brazilian woman named Chandra, who was eight years older than I. We had traveled to Japan, and after some time it became clear that, while I really liked being there, she didn't, and decided to leave. A few weeks later, she called me from Hawaii, telling me that she had just gone through an abortion . . . with our child. I was shocked, upset, and relieved—all at the same time. A few months later, we resumed our relationship and moved to Anchorage, Alaska. The following spring, Chandra found out that she was pregnant again. This time both of us wrestled earnestly with the decision of whether or not to have the child. Our relationship was loving and solid, but ultimately, after a series of long talks, meditations, and prayers focused on taking the right course of action, we decided to end the pregnancy. This was a heart-wrenching decision, and one that neither of us took lightly. We went to the abortion appointment together, but she had to go through the procedure alone. Afterwards, we had a farewell ritual for the fetus and wept in each other's arms. Chandra recovered quickly, at least physically. Three years down the road, we finally separated, as good friends whose lives were taking us in different directions.

Sixteen years later, while participating in a workshop called Family Constellation, the issues around the two abortions from that relationship re-surfaced. In Constellation work, other participants act as "surrogates" to depict people from one's past. Towards the end of the Constellation session, the facilitator placed two people in front of me on the floor, representing the two aborted fetuses. As I looked down at the two beings in front of me, I was stunned at the immensity of what I felt. Seeing them, and realizing that if they were alive they would be around fifteen years old, opened the floodgates. I held on to both of them tightly, wailing in a mixture of pain, guilt, and loss. Although it hurt, at the same time it felt so good to finally grieve and weep. I hadn't even realized, until that moment, that I was carrying such guilt and pain; it had been buried away all those years.

After this unexpected but welcomed catharsis, I was invited to plainly state the facts that had led us to the decision to have the abortions. Seeing those beings represented in front of me, and being able to take responsibility for having aborted their opportunity for life, was a very freeing experience. The liberation I felt has stayed with me to this day. I know abortion is a huge and serious topic, and I want to be clear in saying that I believe and honor that this is a choice that every person needs to make for him or herself. Based on my own experience, I personally didn't want to terminate a pregnancy again.

All this was the backdrop that came crashing into our bedroom that day, just hearing that Neelama had set a date to terminate the pregnancy. We were stuck and couldn't find a way to end our standoff.

We reached out to our teacher, Faisal, knowing he could be counted on to help us explore the intensity of our reactions to each other. I secretly hoped that he would agree with my position that the abortion should be avoided at all costs. But, he didn't take sides. Rather, he challenged me to look at my own righteousness, saying, "Wait a minute, Michael, how do *you* know what is best for that soul, or what's best for Neelama? Who are you to claim you know what's right? When you say you know what is right and true, you are playing God." His direct words shook me up, and made me question my belief about what was "right." I felt as if I'd been smacked, but in a good way—as if awakened from an unpleasant dream. He also asked Neelama to make the same inner inquiry, which helped relieve me. By the end of the session, we had both softened a bit, and I was able to make myself vulnerable. I looked into Neelama's eyes and shared that, for the first time in my life, with her, I could imagine having a child—that's how special our relationship was to me.

Chapter Four:
Having to Choose Twice

(Hers: The Body Speaks)

A few days later, Michael went away on a work trip to Canada. I think we were both beyond ready to have a break from each other. After our session with Faisal, I had decided that I was going to spend a week delving deeply into my *no,* and another week exploring the possibility of a *yes*—even though that was impossible to imagine. The *no* was easy— that's what I was feeling, and I could readily access all the cons regarding motherhood. During my *no* week, while having tea with a girlfriend, who was herself a mom, I expressed all my concerns about having a child, especially the things I feared giving up most: my freedom and independence. Throughout my life, I'd had a thirst for exploring new places and cultures, and had learned how to travel on a shoestring budget. I was so afraid that, with motherhood, this would come to an abrupt end, and somehow result in a boring and meaningless life. After I had rattled off the rest of my rather lengthy list of concerns, I realized how egotistical I must have sounded to Britta, since she herself had raised two kids.

Cringing inside, I said, "I hate admitting this to you, but a part of me is just plain selfish, and has no desire to give up my life for someone else. I'm not proud of this side of myself, but it's there." I looked down at the ground, ashamed and afraid of what she might think of me.

Her reply couldn't have been more compassionate, "I understand how you feel," she said, "that's exactly how I felt many years ago, and sometimes even now! It's so hard to imagine giving up your independent life, especially when it's the only life you've ever known."

I exhaled, relief washing over me to know I wasn't alone in feeling this way. "So what should I do?" I pleaded, hoping she could somehow just give me a solution, a clear sign as to whether or not I should have a child.

She smiled, reaching out to squeeze my hand in reassurance, "That, my friend, is a question only you can answer."

The more I contemplated my *no*, the more I had to face reality; if I decided not to go forward with this pregnancy . . . then what? And as I seriously began to consider having the abortion, things became even more difficult. The more I contemplated it, the more I couldn't imagine actually *doing it*. It was a great idea, in theory, and knowing I had a choice did give me a sense of freedom: abortion was available as an option. But when I delved deeper into the reality of how the whole thing would play out for my body, and that of the being inside of me, I couldn't bear the thought of it. As the week wore on, the certainty of my *no* began to unravel in a way for which I was not prepared.

Then it was time for the *yes* week. I visited a few friends who were parents—to watch them interact with their babies or young kids, hoping to somehow be able to see myself in their shoes. I was trying my best to understand something just by "peeking in," but it was nearly impossible. It was like watching someone eat Chinese food, and trying to imagine what it might taste like, without ever putting the food into your mouth. Seeing it and tasting it were two entirely different things. What *was* most helpful were my conversations with these parents. In talking with them, I heard of their challenges—the blood, sweat, and tears that this "job" required. But the stronger message I got was that the good outweighed the bad. They described their parenting experiences as something so very precious and magical, and over and over again assured me that the hard work and sacrifice were more than compensated for—by the gifts they'd received in return. Another help was their consensus that being a parent gets easier over time. This relaxed me a bit, especially knowing that some of my friends had similar interests to mine—that life for them was not *only* about being a parent. This was important; as there was a big fear in me that everything I loved was going to be taken away forever. I had a couple of girlfriends in particular who assured me that a certain amount of their independence had returned over time. And while this was helpful to know, it did not make me an instant convert.

During my *yes* week I also went to see a movie about parenthood. I emerged from the theater in a state of despair, balling. I was beside myself, and couldn't find my car. It was pouring rain, and my clothes were soaking wet by the time I reached a covered island in the parking lot, ducking underneath to get my bearings.

In the midst of my emotional meltdown, there was only one thing to do: call my mom. With fingers dripping, I dialed her number and prayed she'd be at home. Hearing her voice on the other end unleashed even more emotions but, somehow, between sobs, I managed to get out my fears. "I'm terrified. I'm scared to death of going forward with this pregnancy. I just can't do it . . . but I can't even imagine the alternative either. Oh mom, what am I going to do?"

My mom listened patiently and then asked me if, perhaps, there was something else contributing to my intense fear.

"What do you mean?" I asked.

"I've been thinking a lot about this," she began, slowly and with trepidation, as if not to knock down a very fragile me. "Ever since that incident with Dr. Ellsworth, you have always feared doctors. I wonder if, on some level, you are afraid of the medical aspects of pregnancy and childbirth."

As I paused to think about what she'd said, I was suddenly overcome with a flood of memories from that dreadful day. My mom had always said I was just a tiny baby when this happened, but I recalled being older, perhaps four or five, lying on a table in a cold and sterile office with Dr. Ellsworth, a very large man who exuded zero warmth. I didn't know it at the time, but I was there for some sort of shot, maybe a vaccination. All of a sudden, he lunged towards me rather hastily, with what looked like a giant dagger in his hand. Realizing the dagger was meant for me, I freaked out, screaming and flailing all over the table. Soon there were a few other people in the room holding down my arms and feet, and crushing my body on the table to restrain me. I felt suffocated by the weight and I totally panicked, screaming as loud as I could. Dr. Ellsworth yelled at me to "shut up and hold still" as he jabbed the needle into my arm. His job done, he turned and left the room, with not a word of apology or understanding. I was shaking when my mom came to me. That traumatizing event left me with a fear of doctors that I'd carried my whole life.

I could still feel the residue of that memory in my body as I began to consider whether some of my fears of pregnancy went much deeper that I knew. Even a natural pregnancy involved tests, blood-work, and routine visits to the doctor—all of which I dreaded. But as my mom and I continued to talk and the rain continued to fall, I felt my body giving up the tension it was holding, and a sense of calm descending. She ended our conversation in her usual way, with a loving reminder that whatever decision I made, it would all work out just fine. Even though I was a grown woman, this was my mom, and I was still her little girl, and in the middle of that inner and outer storm she was still able to calm me down. I could breathe again. I found my car and drove home.

When Michael returned from Canada, we didn't speak about the "issue" again, and yet the tension between us was palpable. The month that followed was excruciatingly difficult, as I continued to feel caught between my deep ambivalence and a sense of pressure coming from him. I felt confused, and wanted out of this scenario, but still couldn't imagine actually *having* an abortion. I prayed for a clear "sign." I wept and prayed, and waited for God to descend with a great big piece of white paper bearing a big bold YES or NO. I prayed for nature to take its course if this pregnancy wasn't meant to be. I begged for clarity—a simple black-and-white answer. I prayed, and waited, and prayed some more. That answer never came, at least not in the form I wanted.

I woke up one morning and lay in bed, feeling my body and looking out our windows at the trees, their leaves glistening with the rays of the sun, announcing the day had begun. I thought about getting up to start my day, but my body would not cooperate. The bed felt so soft, and the warmth of the sun relaxed me. I wasn't ready to be vertical. My hands found their way to my stomach, which, to my surprise, did seem like it was already growing. As my palms touched the skin near my belly button, I couldn't help but sense that a life was growing inside of me. In that instant, I remembered that today was the date of the abortion appointment. Lying there, I realized that nothing inside of me was moving in that direction. As I tried to imagine myself going to the procedure, my body gave its final protest, mounting a resistance so huge that I could not even get out of bed, let alone get in the car and drive to the doctor. My hands remained on my belly, and with a gentle tapping motion, confirmed to my mind what my body already knew: I was not going to end this pregnancy. I was keeping this baby. And so it was in the *not going* that I began to consider that there must be a *yes* living somewhere inside me for this child. For the first time since that fateful day in the bathroom, a peace descended over me. It was a quiet and subtle relief. Its presence was quite different from the excitement I'd seen in the eyes of so many new mothers. It produced a calm versus a "happy."

Out of fear of being different from other newly pregnant women, and wondering whether something was indeed wrong with me, I didn't share my decision with many people at first. It was as if it were taboo to even admit how I was feeling. I imagined that many people wouldn't be able to relate to me, and I imagined being judged, especially by the mommies in Marin County, many of whom seemed determined to be *the* best mothers on the planet. These were women whose true calling and fulfillment came from being full-time moms—women who used the best organic cloth diapers, natural soaps, and homemade lotions, who spent hours in the kitchen making baby food from scratch, and who probably wouldn't even dream of ever hiring a babysitter. These women were the crème de la crème of mothers and in my little head, just six weeks pregnant, I knew I could never measure up to them.

In the months that followed, Michael and I largely recovered from the huge rift that had taken place regarding the pregnancy. We had always been a great "team" and this partnership returned as we prepared for our new arrival. Our closeness and affection came back, and along with that the ease in being together. One of our favorite activities during those months was lying in bed together reading *Harry Potter*. I would stick my head under Michael's armpit and we'd curl our bodies close together, book in hand. We would alternate reading chapters to each other, changing our voices to depict the different characters. We laughed so hard that our bodies' shook, and tears spilled onto the pillow. It was in those sweet moments that we felt our love for each other again, and it soothed most of our bruises like a healing balm.

There was a turning point around the fifth month of pregnancy. We received the results of an ultrasound indicating that the lateral ventricles in the brain of the fetus were enlarged. This led to a series of tests to get more information. It was at this point that we found out the gender of the baby. When I heard it was a boy, I must admit my heart sank for a brief moment. Since moving forward with the pregnancy, I had felt, and secretly hoped, that I was carrying a girl, and had even created some fantasies about having a little "me." Hearing that I'd be having a boy brought up some disappointment, but it didn't last long, and my fantasies switched rather quickly to a little boy "me." The additional tests showed that there was a small chance that something could be wrong with the baby's brain. They didn't know for sure, nor could they confirm what might be wrong, but because of this, I was eligible for what was called a "medical abortion." This was where you give birth to a dead fetus. There was no part of me that could even imagine doing this, but it was interesting to me that, in this way, Life/God gave us yet another opportunity to look at our choice. Another pause. Some might even say another "way out."

Michael and I decided we would try to calm our minds and find clarity through a meditation retreat: to be in silence and contemplation for a few days in our home. On one of those days, while meditating in our bedroom, it struck me that I was sitting just a few feet away from where our child had been conceived only a few months prior. I remembered that night vividly: August 15th, 2003. I only knew it with certainty because, at that point in our relationship, sex had become more of a rarity than the norm. That date happened to be our anniversary—not our wedding anniversary, but the anniversary of that pivotal night in Ottawa, Canada in 1999, where we'd finally said *yes* to each other. To commemorate this, we'd planned a special ritual, which ended in a beautiful act of lovemaking on the floor in front of our altar. Looking at the altar now, and feeling our son growing in my belly, it gave me great comfort to remember that he'd been conceived in sacredness and love, even though it had not been my conscious intent to create a child that night.

During the remainder of the meditation retreat, I began to feel the life inside of me, and each time I sensed him, I was immediately ushered into an experience of great calm and peace, which felt almost "oceanic" to me. When Michael suggested the idea of the name "Kai" for our son, I discovered that the name meant "ocean" in Japanese, and that is one of the reasons I agreed immediately. Often, when I closed my eyes, I saw an image of a triangle, which to me represented the three of us. I had the distinct sense that we three souls were here to help each other, to teach each other, and to heal together. And very quietly, the inklings of a deeper *yes* began to emerge. This did not arrive in the way my mind had hoped all those months back. There was no direct thunderbolt from God, delivering that right or wrong "answer." It wasn't given to me, but rather, much like the life in my womb, it simply grew inside of me and was slowly but surely revealed.

(His: From Fear to Excitement)

As Neelama's decision-making process continued, I felt she was avoiding me. She talked with great frequency to her friends, and I felt an ever-increasing loss of control on my side. Being helpless was a difficult feeling to endure. For millennia, I said to myself, men have made the decisions in situations like this, leaving the women without choice. Even now, in many countries and societies, men are still the decision-makers, with no regard for the woman who actually carries the baby in her body. But for my generation of men, in this culture, things had changed dramatically: we were now the ones with no choice. My desire to have the child could be overridden by Neelama, and most of our friends in our little subculture would side with her. I found myself part of an historic irony: I remembered the huge pro-abortion protest in Germany at the beginning of the '70s— women carrying posters with signs like *Mein Bauch Gehoert Mir!* (My Belly is Mine!) and me wholeheartedly agreeing with them. Now, as a potential father who wanted a say in the matter, I was on the other side. Looking back, I realize that it was that helplessness which drove me to utter the fateful words, *"With an abortion we might not make it."* The impact of this statement, or subtle threat, didn't show itself for a few years, but it set events in motion of which I was totally unaware.

There followed many heavy days and restless nights—the atmosphere tense between us. We were, for now, on two different sides. To a degree, I understood Neelama. While I had a deep yearning for this child, I was also scared out of my mind at the prospect of parenthood. At every crossroads in my life, fear and doubt had been my companions. This decision was no different, and in fact, it trumped them all. I was worried about having to provide for a family and commit to a helpless being that truly depended on me. Up to this point, I had neither owed nor owned anything that could "tie me down." I had always wanted to be "free" which, for me, had meant being able to pull out stakes and take off whenever and wherever I wanted, to pursue my spiritual journey—my quest to find the Divine. With a child in my life, that would be over. After our emergency session with Faisal, I returned to do more work with him to confront my own issues regarding fatherhood.

I had been Faisal's student for about three years, and saw him twice a month for one-on-one inner work. Neelama and I were also part of Faisal's ongoing group, which met weekly and on one weekend each month. The most unique element of the body of work that he called the Diamond Logos was a process called Inquiry: guiding the individual within themselves. The job of the Diamond Logos teacher was to hold space for the student to be present with whatever might arise inside—emotions, sensations, memories, insights, thoughts. That's the role Faisal played in our sessions, and I faced and experienced my fears about having a child as they manifested in my physical body. I also looked at the other side of my psyche—the part that wanted the child. I saw my desire to be a father, to have a family, to play soccer with my son, to leave a legacy, and I acknowledged in me the simple but powerful biological urge to procreate—to pass on life.

When the session concluded, and over tea with Faisal in his downstairs kitchen, I asked him a question, "I want to hear your personal experience, not as my mentor, but as a father of two children. How did that impact you?"

In response, Faisal walked me over to a picture of his daughter and his son, and pointing to them, said, "It has expanded me a lot; it has made me grow in areas where I would not otherwise have challenged myself; it has made me a more human teacher. That has been my experience. *And* you should also know that it will be okay if you decide not to have a child."

Two incidents occurred to help me in my decision, which might have been pure serendipity—or fate. On the way back from Faisal's house, while stopped at a traffic light in Berkeley, a young African-American couple crossed the intersection in front of me. The woman was very pregnant, and her partner was carrying a young girl. This couple was laughing joyfully. As I observed them, something in me relaxed regarding my own worries of whether I would be able to provide for the child in Neelama's belly. Watching their joyful innocence in the middle of that sunlit intersection inspired me to trust life.

A few weeks later, I flew up to Ottawa, where I regularly taught an ongoing transformational workshop, called the "Essential

Pilgrimage." I learned that one of the members of the group, Brian, had two of his children later in life, the last one when he was fifty-two. When I asked him about his experience, all I needed was his joyous smile to give me the answer. All this contributed, in those first weeks of uncertainty, to solidifying my decision of a *yes* to the birth of our baby.

While I was traveling, I knew Neelama was in deep exploration of her inner conflict. We avoided discussing the abortion again, after the terrible fight in our bedroom. I breathed a sigh of relief when the date for the appointment passed. Shortly thereafter, upon returning from another couple's session with Faisal, Neelama called one of her dearest girlfriends, Suzie, who lived in Australia, and shared excitedly with her that she was going to have the child. She laughed and cried, and for the first time, I heard a spoken *yes* from her mouth. I recorded this scene on our video camera, because I knew it was a turning point for us. I was so relieved and happy. We were in for the "great unknown" which, in its human form, seemed to be doubling in size daily inside Neelama's belly.

Many weeks later, we hit the first big reality check of parenthood, when we learned that an ultrasound had produced some worrisome images. While waiting for the next ultrasound results, we did a lot of online research on possible complications. During this anxious period, I added to my usual meditations the spiritual practice of my childhood: prayer. I started to pray again—for the unborn child, and for guidance for ourselves as parents. During this second period of decision-making, I shared with some friends that I was willing to take the risk to move forward, even with the chance that there might be slight developmental defects in our child. Looking back, I see this statement as both wonderfully heroic and incredibly naïve. I had no idea what was coming . . . which was a good thing.

The further the pregnancy progressed, the more excited I became. I felt that Neelama was on board, and we were a team again. Yes, we had endured three rough months, and had fought and challenged each other, but we had made it through.

The last four months of the pregnancy were a beautiful time for me—attending prenatal classes, reading books about birthing and childrearing, kissing Neelama's growing belly, talking to the little one inside, and savoring many sweet and nourishing moments with my wife as we worked together to prepare for the great shift ahead.

Chapter 5:
Contractions, Expansions, and the Miracle of Life

(Hers: Climbing Everest)

My first contraction came at 6:30 in the morning. I woke up to go to the bathroom, and noticed a mild menstrual-like cramp. About fifteen minutes later another cramp came, and then I realized that the waiting was finally coming to an end. I told Michael, and we continued to lie in bed, excitedly noticing and writing down each mild contraction that appeared over the next couple of hours. Later that morning, we got out of bed and called Chandra, whose midwifery skills and loving presence had been a great support to us through the pregnancy. After listening to our report, she confirmed that this was indeed early labor. She urged us to go for a gentle walk on the beach, but to remain relaxed to conserve energy.

Around noon, we arrived at Muir Beach, in Marin County—a lovely beach we had visited together countless times before. The wind was wild, but we found shelter on the far side and were fortunate to discover we had the tiny beach to ourselves. In those hours, the contractions became more intense, but the sounds of the ocean soothed me and took me inward. As I walked under the great open sky, feeling the support of the warm sand under my feet, I felt connected to the energy of Mother Earth and to the ebb and flow of life. Michael, on the other hand, was like an excited little boy, calling tons of people to tell them "it was happening!"

Around four o'clock that afternoon, the gap between contractions became shorter and the pain grew more intense, alerting me that it was time to return home. As soon as we pulled into our driveway, I headed downstairs to our bedroom, where the contractions now took on a life of their own—each one making me sweat with nausea. The only way I found to bear the pain was to walk around every time a contraction came . . . so for the next few hours, I continued to pace up and down our oblong bedroom. At eight o'clock that evening, our midwife arrived and checked me. Given that I'd been in labor since early that morning, I thought for sure I'd be ready to go. But, to my extreme disappointment, I was only three centimeters dilated.

I thought I would die when she told me this news, and a moment later I asked her for the pain medicine. She smiled, and reminded me we had decided to do a home-birth with a natural labor. She had once told me that there were two kinds of pain: pointless pain, and pain for a purpose—childbirth was the latter. She explained that the biological act of the body doing what it was naturally designed to do, give birth, would far outweigh any fear I might have of physical pain. Yes, I had agreed to a medication-free birth, but now I couldn't remember what on earth had made me do so. I grimaced, pleading,

"Don't you have anything, even a homeopathic remedy, that could help with this pain?" She smiled lovingly and said, "I don't have any medication at all in my possession. This is the time for you to find the resources within yourself to make it through." I was so angry I could have punched her right there.

The contractions were becoming unbearable. It was as if someone had stuck their bare hands inside of me and was ripping apart my uterus—pulling, twisting, and yanking it right out of my body. Around me were my two midwives, a few of my dearest friends, and Michael—all of whom were silently loving and supporting me with their palpable presence. And yet I knew that, on this journey, I was ultimately alone. I got into our big bathtub, and the warm water gave me the essential nudge to forge on. I discovered that this was where all my spiritual training over the past decade was finally being put to the test. In that tub, feeling the most intense pain of my life, was where the rubber hit the road. I could see how my mind's reaction to the perceived intolerable sensations created a mental idea of what it thought was my "edge." In the moments when I could stay in my body, and just *be with* what was happening, it was still absolute hell, but, to my surprise, bearable. The process pulled me into a depth I had never reached on any meditation cushion.

After four hours in the tub, the midwife checked me again and said I had finally reached ten centimeters—I was ready; I could get out of the tub and push my little heart out. I wound up on the floor, with Michael and my birth team cheering me on. Those final pushes and screams were so guttural; it felt like they came from some ancient part of my soul. After about an hour of intense pushing, at 1:48 a.m. on May 20th, 2004, I felt a huge pop and release, and our son Kai was born.

I couldn't hold him immediately—they had discovered that there was meconium in the amniotic fluid, which meant that Kai needed to be suctioned immediately after birth. The little guy was so shocked from the entire experience that he was screaming bloody murder. It was excruciating to watch his rough entry into our planet, and to know I was helpless to change it. After what seemed like an eternity, the crying stopped, allowing Michael and I, drenched with the sweat of sheer desperation, to finally exhale. With both of us lying on the floor, just a few feet away from where Kai was conceived, we relaxed into our new experience of this tiny precious being. He looked like a little Buddha, a newborn, and a wrinkly wise old man, all rolled into one. It was something truly remarkable.

The next morning, I woke up with an inner knowing that something awesome had taken place. Up until the birth, I was very pain averse, popping a pill at the first sign of any ache. Something happened to me through the natural labor that was more powerful than I could ever have imagined. It was as if the labor itself was a profound process where I had burned through many layers, many perceived limits, and found places of strength, courage, and surrender inside that I never knew existed. I felt like the most powerful woman on earth—as if I had climbed Mount Everest. Looking out on the broad expanse of life from the peak of that mountain, I knew with unwavering certainty that I could do anything.

(His: Her-oism, the Stargazer, and the Shock)

We walked a lot in those weeks before the birth, all over the still green hills of Marin County, wistful reminders of the hills of my Bavarian childhood. One of the many recommendations of our midwives was to do a lot of walking, to prepare mother and child. The due date came and went. After waiting nearly three weeks, becoming a little more worried each day, we decided we needed a change in environment. We took a day-trip to Harbin Hot Springs, our honeymoon spot, and a favorite place for retreat and relaxation. In a meditation hut high in the hills of Lake County, we wrote a "welcome letter" to our baby, inviting him to come out and be with us—we were ready for him. Lo and behold, the next morning Neelama woke up with contractions . . . it had begun.

As in many of the tales one hears about mothers who are about to give birth, Neelama went on an energetic cleaning spree that morning. Interrupted by occasional contractions, she vacuumed, dusted, and reorganized the already orderly-arranged cupboards of our home. We bought some flowers, and then proceeded to walk and rest beside the wild waters of the Pacific Ocean. It felt like the perfect place to "hang loose" with an unborn baby boy whose name, Kai, means ocean in Hawaiian and Japanese.

Later that afternoon, we arrived back home and were greeted by some of our housemates and Neelama's best friend, Jen—all of whom were very excited to be part of the welcoming committee. We had planned a water birth in our large bathtub, but this changed drastically once the midwives discovered there was meconium, a baby's first stool, in the water. At that moment, the two midwives, who worked as a team, urged Neelama to come out of the tub, because of the danger that a water birth could pose to the newborn. As I watched her throughout the entire birthing process, I felt both awed by and afraid for her many times. Seeing her in this state, I experienced the toughest of feelings—helplessness. I wanted to take her pain away, or at least share some of it. But, beyond holding her gently and offering comforting words, there was nothing I could do. In that room were hours of raw humanness, unfiltered behaviors, uncensored utterances and naked emotions. Natural birth seems like a great idea—until the process is in full swing.

In our culture, there's a lot of talk about heroes, but being there with Neelama I really understood that any woman giving birth, particularly without drugs of any kind, is a true heroine. The intense level of pain that I witnessed her endure was excruciating just to watch, let alone bear. After many hours of labor, she was exhausted and our little boy still hadn't made much progress. The tension in the room grew, because we knew that at a certain point we had no choice but to take Neelama to our "backup" hospital, ten miles away. The midwife signaled me discretely that we had only thirty minutes until that became an imperative. In response, I felt anxious and worried.

As the midwife examined Neelama one more time, she found that Kai was pushing his forehead against the pubic bone and so his head hadn't tilted forward enough to slide through the pelvis. Later, she told us that this is called a "brow birth." In Germany, a child born in this manner is called *Sternengucker*, meaning stargazer. At this point, all of us in the room became cheerleaders, encouraging Neelama to push a few more times. With all the will and energy she had remaining, and the help of the midwife, who was able to turn the baby's head slightly, Kai slid through the birth canal. Seeing the midwife catch Kai in her hands brought immense relief and joy to my heart. Yet it wasn't to last long. No sooner had he arrived than the midwife put a tube down his nostril to suction him—our precious newborn was so startled, and screamed so hard that, for me, those were actually the hardest moments of the whole birthing process. Even now it pains me to think that our little prince experienced this shocking start to his life. Finally the procedure was complete, and the midwife handed the screaming new arrival to me. I carried him to Neelama, who tenderly held him on her chest. Speaking softly in his ear, we both welcomed Kai to our family and to the world, hoping our calming voices would help him to relax too. It didn't, and soon the joyous high we'd felt upon his birth gave way to feelings of utter desperation. We looked at the midwife for support, but she couldn't help either. Kai just screamed and screamed with all the life force he had in his little body.

About two hours later, he finally exhausted himself and fell asleep. At about 5:00 a.m., the midwife left. I will always remember that moment—Neelama and I looked at each other, and at the tiny sleeping bundle in the bed between us, in a shared feeling of having been abandoned by our midwife. We found ourselves on our own with a newborn. Since the beginning of time, most parents must have felt something similar with their firstborn—*What do we do now?*

Being intimately present for Kai's birth taught me two important lessons. The first was a real understanding of what a mother goes through to bring a new life into the world. Witnessing Neelama giving birth was scary, awesome, primal, and raw—a rare experience in life. The second lesson was *der mensch denkt, Gott lenkt*, or "man plans and God steers." Knowing how impactful and traumatic the birth experience can be, we did everything possible to have our child born naturally, without drugs, in a quiet, loving and welcoming environment—and, still, there are some things one cannot control. Thus the stargazer, Kai Schiesser, was born.

Chapter Six:
Stretched to the Max

(Hers: How Precious Sleep Is)

Our first week with Kai was magical. We three co-existed in a dream-like state, spellbound by each other. Michael and I spent most of our waking hours in our bedroom, staring at Kai for hours on end (and he at us), falling in love with this treasure. We were explorers discovering a new world—the first look at his fingers and toes, the first eye contact, the first time he drank from my body. Every moment contained a miracle that felt specifically designed for us. Reluctant to leave our oasis, we didn't set foot outside of the house. People visited and were temporarily ushered onto our island, where they slowed down with us and drank the nectar of what can only be described as the preciousness of new life.

Our little bubble was alarmingly burst when Kai was just two weeks old and we took him to his very first doctor's appointment. We had asked our friend, Lindy, who was a pediatrician, to become Kai's doctor once he was born, and she'd happily agreed. At our first appointment, expecting to hear normal, routine news, Lindy dropped the bomb after measuring Kai's head. "His head measurement is very small . . . *too small*," she said. This indicated that his brain hadn't grown to the proper size in utero, and was a huge concern. I stood there, frozen to the floor, my mind flashing back to that abnormal ultrasound reading we'd had when I was five months pregnant. I remembered how we considered at that time that something might have been wrong. But *might* have been wrong was altogether different than definitely *was* wrong. I found myself unable to process what I was hearing and what it all meant. Lindy, noticing my shock, said she wanted us to come back in a couple of weeks so she could measure Kai's head again. As we walked out of her office, with me holding Kai in my arms, I burst into tears. Michael, bless his heart, tried to be the voice of reason, helping Kai and me into the car with encouraging words, "Let's not go too far down this road until we know more; this might not be as bad as it sounds." Wiping my eyes with Kleenex, I nodded, trying so hard to make myself agree with him, wanting so badly for everything to be okay.

"You're right, let's wait," I said. "Let's see what she finds in a few weeks." On the ride home, my body went limp against the back seat, as if it had taken a physical and emotional beating.

It's funny what we humans do to try and cope with bad news. A few days later, Michael went out and bought his own tape measure, and whenever he could get Kai to lie still, tried measuring our son's little skull himself, as if to prove the doctor wrong. He never could get a consistent measurement, and I lived in a suspended state of anxiety before the next appointment. I couldn't shake the notion that something was seriously wrong with our son. Two weeks later, we returned to Lindy's office, where she carefully took measurements of Kai's head again—only to find that it still measured way below normal. Lindy referred us to a neurologist, who encouraged us to get an MRI that could reveal more information. However, we couldn't bring ourselves to put a tiny newborn through such a procedure, especially when the findings, while they might bring more clarity, would not make a difference to how we would support Kai at this early stage. The neurologist used words like *developmental delay, therapies,* and *special services.* I just stood there, dumbfounded, as if staring at a movie that was playing in fast forward. I couldn't make out the picture, let alone understand the plot. Having postponed the MRI, we wouldn't know the extent of our son's condition for almost a year.

Our family fairy tale had been rudely interrupted at our very first doctor's appointment. In the weeks that followed, we were inundated with information about testing, the resources available to us, and all the different kinds of support that Kai might need. Michael and I were slowly emerging from our state of shock, and beginning to realize that we had a baby who would have special needs.

Ironically, I was becoming painfully aware of my needs too, namely sleep. Nobody can prepare you for the *hell* that is sleep deprivation. I knew about it, I'd read about it, and Michael and I had even devised some strategies when I was pregnant to try to prepare for it. But the closest experience to sleep deprivation I'd ever had were the all-nighters I'd pulled in college. After one or two of those endless nights, I used to drag myself into bed and sleep, and sleep, and sleep some more. In motherhood, however, one does not have this luxury.

Kai, perhaps because of his brain condition, would cry inconsolably during the day and wake up in twenty- to thirty-minute intervals every night, screaming. We were still living communally, but had moved into a bigger house, and Michael and I now occupied the master bedroom—a large room with floor-to-ceiling windows that looked out onto the picturesque, serene marshes of Novato. Kai slept in a crib-like apparatus in the corner. Throughout the nights, we took turns picking him up and pacing up and down our bedroom. The crying seemed relentless, and it rattled my nerves to the bone. Some nights, out of sheer desperation, Michael and I would lie in bed and scream at God, each other . . . and, unfortunately, sometimes even at Kai. Between the days and the nights, we just wanted the screaming to stop. My whole body ached for sleep and quiet. It was in those moments, in the darkness of our bedroom, that I came face-to-face with a helplessness that terrified me. As the sleepless nights continued, I felt raw and devoid of energy and strength. Pushed to my wits' end, I finally understood how a mother could lose it with her child. I thank God that I never did. Yet those nights brought me to my knees and showed me I was breakable. It was a raw and painfully humbling time.

Then there were the diaper changes. Thank God for communal living. Sometimes it took four adults to change a diaper the size of our hand. Kai screamed bloody murder, as if we were mutilating him. The baby books never talked about this. Doing those diaper changes was like going to battle, and I'd come away like a wounded warrior. Kai also hated baths, getting dressed, and (this was the worst) his car seat. Car seats have been the saving grace of many parents since they were invented, but this luxury eluded us—just to drive to the grocery store was such an ordeal that we needed to be entirely out of food for me to attempt it alone. Kai would scream bloody murder during the entire ride, and I would grip the wheel and pray out loud to drown out his voice. There's something about your child's screams that unravels you like nothing else. I barely went anywhere alone in the car with him for that first year. When the three of us did go out, I usually stayed in the backseat, holding Kai in my arms or breastfeeding him, while Michael drove. I knew it was illegal, and maybe even dangerous, but all that logic doesn't hold a candle when you're trying to stay sane.

We didn't find out until a year later that Kai's brain had great difficulty processing certain stimuli. This explained his aversion to certain things (baths, diaper changes, the car seat) as well as his need to be constantly held in a vertical position while in some sort of motion (in the Baby Bjorn, pacing around our bedroom, or bouncing on the huge green ball). Perhaps this soothed his nervous system . . . we'll never know.

As the year progressed, we couldn't help but notice that Kai hadn't met any of the developmental milestones for rolling over, sitting up, or even crawling—all of which should have been happening within that time frame. We tried to keep a positive outlook, but just under our terribly thin skins, we were seriously worried.

Despite the challenges, there were many precious moments that year too—many beautiful experiences of being with Kai, and sweet times with the three of us together. We took long walks—often in the early morning hours, as that seemed to be his favorite time of day. I loved the special connection that came through breastfeeding, and like so many new parents, could get lost in just looking at his face. I was present to the miracle of life and was often overcome with a sense of wonder that this little being, once the size of an almond living in a pool of dark liquid inside me, was now living life on the outside—growing, changing, and responding to this new world around him.

One night, while Kai and I were in the bedroom, he was lying on one of those baby blankets that have an attachment going from corner-to-corner with colorful things dangling down above him. He was looking up at those little objects as if he were staring at God

Itself. I was amazed at the way he looked at them, lingering on each one with a freshness that indicated he was not thinking about what he saw—rather, he was experiencing it directly. Then, out of nowhere, he made a sound that sounded like "I." You would have thought I'd won the lottery. Who knew one teeny tiny sound could produce such ecstasy in a person? Every cell in my body had its own private dance party whenever he made that sound. I must have sat there with him for two hours, coaxing him to say it again and again, delighted each time it came out of his mouth, as if I were hearing it for the first time. It was sheer bliss. I entered his world that night, the world of awe and wonder. There were many touching moments such as these, but I'd be lying if I said this was only a wonderful time for me. Like so many things, it was a time filled with equal parts joy and pain; heaven and hell; gain and loss.

One of the greatest losses was loss of freedom. Kai needed to be "on the body" all the time, and in virtually constant motion. This meant I was standing and carrying him: walking . . . moving . . . rocking. It was shocking to me how difficult it was to have someone physically attached to me almost every waking hour, even if it was my own son. During that first year, it became abundantly clear that my body was no longer my own. At times it felt like Kai's body had burrowed itself deep inside me, and taken possession of my flesh, my muscles, and my very self. A voice from inside screamed out, "For God sake, he is *your child* . . . why does this HURT so much?"

I did not know. My thirty-three years of independence had given me countless hours of time and space alone, and I wasn't used to being around *anyone* that much. I felt terrible that I was so challenged in this way, and judged myself for it. At the same time, the constancy of it all ground me down and frayed my nerves. I needed some help.

Britta and Maria, two of my housemates, who were also dear friends, sat me down at the kitchen table one day when Kai was around ten months old. Their faces showed real concern as they proceeded to share, "Neelama, you look like a walking ghost. Kai's demands are really taking a toll on you. Many days you don't even shower, let alone get out of your pajamas. This is not a normal situation, and we really think you need to get some help, to get a little break. It's really wearing on you, and we are worried." I broke down in tears right there, in the middle of our sunny kitchen. I was a new mother, in one of the most beautiful places on earth—I was supposed to be happy. And yet I felt so beaten down. They squeezed my hands and I felt their love and care. I took their advice to heart, especially since they were both mothers themselves and they helped me to realize that what I was experiencing was more extreme than the norm.

After the conversation, I began to think about how I could take better care of myself. One of the challenges of getting a break was due to the breastfeeding schedule. Because Kai was not yet eating food, I couldn't really leave him for more than an hour or so. I thought putting him on a bottle would help sustain him a bit longer; unfortunately Michael wasn't supportive of this idea. Many times he'd indicated that he wanted his son to have the real deal: mommy's breast. I could sense Michael's resistance whenever we talked about testing out the bottle, as if his body cringed at the very idea. At the end of my rope one day, I pumped my milk, handed Michael the bottle, and left the house, hoping against hope that this would work. I returned a couple of hours later to a crying baby and a frustrated dad.

As I came into the bedroom, Michael got up from the rocker and handed Kai to me. In a righteous tone that immediately made me feel guilty, he said, "He is *really* hungry; the bottle thing didn't work."

I fired back at him with an accusatory voice, "What was the problem? Did you try different nipples on the bottle like they said to? Did you try putting Kai into different positions?"

"No," Michael yelled, "It just didn't work. This is not my fault—he just didn't want it. I tried. Don't get so pissed at me!"

But I *was* pissed, and somehow I didn't believe that he really *had* tried. Staring at them both, I felt the first hints of resentment start to boil inside. Bound by the food in my breast and the needs of my son, and frustrated with my husband, who I felt was not on board with helping me find reprieve, I was deeply conflicted. I loved breastfeeding, but was starting to feel imprisoned by that too. I longed for the day when I could leave the house for hours, accountable to no one. I wanted to get lost in a store, or sit in a café luxuriating over a huge cup of coffee—to read a newspaper cover-to-cover, or to simply feel my own body with nothing attached to it. I longed for myself.

(His: Pacing and the Bouncing Ball)

Within two weeks of his birth, it was clear to us that Kai was what pediatricians call a "colicky" baby. He cried for more than three hours a day, pretty well every day of the week, and very often at night. We were told that between 5 and 25% of infants begin life this way, testing the nerves of their parents to the max. Way, way back I had been a policeman in Bavaria and often worked the nightshift, so while sleep deprivation wasn't new to me, the cumulative effect of months of sleep loss was.

The frequent crying and screaming of our baby boy, whom I lovingly nicknamed "the little prince," pushed me to the edge like nothing else in my life ever had. I desperately wanted to help him, but there was nothing to be done. We lived, on and off, in a state of despair and exhaustion. As the weeks of sleeplessness turned into months, Neelama and I devised a system of alternating night shifts, so each of us could get some sleep. While we made a good team relieving each other this way, each of us also tended to use the other as a target for venting the frustrations, irritation, and anger that go along with caring for a colicky baby.

The nights were particularly tough in this period, and in all honesty, I lost my temper a few times. To allow Neelama to catch a few hours rest alone in our bed, I would often spend nights with Kai in the guest room. Many nights, feeling that I just couldn't stand his crying a moment longer, I found myself understanding how child abuse happens. More than once during those early months, I heard myself screaming at him to "shut up," and a few times I actually shook his little body to get him to stop screaming. Each time this acting out was immediately followed by a guilt-inducing voice in my head that I call "the inner judge." That voice told me what a bad father I was to treat an innocent and helpless child this way. A painful memory came back to me from my own childhood—an image of my own father screaming in rage at us, his three young sons: "I should have thrown you against a wall when you were little." For years I had judged him for uttering those words, and accused him of abusing us. During some of those nights with Kai, I found myself in exactly the same inner constellation of despair, helplessness, and rage that my father must have found himself in. At some point I spoke a silent apology to him: *"I'm sorry, Papa, for having judged you. I fully understand how we three young boys could sometimes have driven you quite literally mad."*

On top of the challenge of Kai's colic, we found ourselves facing a new and worrisome situation. What had seemed like a slight possibility during pregnancy was now a confirmed reality. Our little prince was different from other babies. To what extent was not clear, and I was still optimistic that all would work out with time. The challenges we confronted had to do with *waiting*. We waited for Kai's crawling phase to happen, which never really *did* happen—he went more or less from lying down to sitting up, but way behind the usual timeline for that. He was way below the percentile curves physically, both in height and in weight. One blessing was that since Kai was our first child, we had nothing with which to compare him. All we had to give us an idea of what should be happening were the guidelines from books and our pediatrician. As each new developmental milestone loomed, we waited, hoping against hope that he would make it, and inevitably being disappointed once again. I felt anxious living in this constant state of not knowing, and at times found myself having dark thoughts about the future. All of this waiting eventually taught us a lasting lesson: there is normal time, and then there is "Kai time."

Memory is a funny thing. It seems to "record" more of the challenging times than the joyous ones. But I have to acknowledge that our first year with Kai did have innumerable sweet moments of joy and delight.

How was our marriage doing during all of this? Primarily, as ordained by nature during the early months of any child, we were both servants to this new being. Our once-soothing bedroom had become a pressure cooker over those early months, where we showed each other our "dark sides." On the intimate sexual level, there was not much of a turn-on, either on my side or Neelama's. At first, I attributed this to the postpartum period, and then later on to our lack of sleep and the challenges with Kai. We talked about it together, but not much came from that other than an honest acknowledgment. I found that it didn't alarm me because, in spite of all this, I still felt close to Neelama—the challenges we were facing had not changed my commitment or feelings towards her. She was my partner and I knew we would make it through this phase. In fact, she was the only one with whom I would have been willing to go through what, at times, felt like a grueling battle.

Neelama had the tougher role to play in this period. A month after Kai's birth, I started to work again: teaching seminars in various cities, leaving for weekend workshops and, three times a year, for ten-day teaching periods. Although I returned home exhausted, I had at least had a break from the churning cauldron of Kai's colic, and could recharge my emotional batteries before returning home ready to relieve her. In fact, on my return, I often felt like a proud hunter, bringing home the prey/dollars, living up to my role as the provider, and creating our financial foundation—on top of being fully engaged with the household and child-rearing when I was home. Looking back at it later, I realized that this was the arena in which some wounding happened—instead of getting acknowledged by Neelama for my contribution, I more often felt her hostility and resentment towards me, because I was the one who could at least go on *leave* from the "battle."

One particularly sensitive issue started to emerge regarding breastfeeding. When Neelama asked me to help Kai transition to a baby bottle, so she could get a break and leave the house, I was resistant. It was not that I didn't want her to have some time alone to recuperate . . . I did want that for her. But I was guided by the belief that the breast was really the only way to nourish a baby. I was stuck in my desire to give Kai *the best* and that had me override the needs of his mother. This is an example where a great "ideal" backfired and caused deep damage to our relationship. Had I not been blinded by what I thought was "right" for Kai, I could have really stepped up and made a sustained effort to try to get our baby boy bottle-trained, which would have allowed Neelama a much-needed reprieve. This was a painful learning experience, to say the least.

Life for all three of us eased up when, after about five and a half months, inexplicably, Kai finally found a more natural sleep pattern and stopped crying to the extreme extent he had during the colicky phase. Hallelujah!

Chapter Seven: The MRI

(Hers): *An Image Shattered*

A month before Kai's first birthday, at the urging of our pediatrician, we finally decided to do an MRI. She felt it might help explain some of the significant delays we were witnessing in Kai's development. I still had my misgivings about the MRI because of the necessity for Kai to go under anesthesia. I had never been under myself, and dreaded the thought of it for my tiny eleven-month-old. Upon realizing that this test could bring us more clarity, I surrendered. Early one April morning, we took Kai to Oakland Children's Hospital and met with the anesthesiologist. She told us to kiss him goodbye and leave immediately so she could administer the anesthetic. Looking down at his tiny body, hooked up to machines and tubes, and already "gone" from the gas, it occurred to me that he might not come back. That is always a possibility, and it hit me over the head like a giant Zen stick. I left the room with my heart ripped open to the reality of death, and the preciousness of each moment we are given with those we love.

In the waiting room, it became painfully clear to me just how often I had taken the fragile moments of life for granted. I was always racing to get on to the next thing, the next moment, a *better moment*—and in that urgency, had so rarely been able to *be* in the moment that was right in front of me. Witnessing Kai in this fragile state had reminded me that we are all that fragile, that death really can come at any moment, that we have no control over when our time is up, when it's over, when our ability to taste, touch, hear, smell, see, and experience life will be gone forever. "It will go like the blink of an eye," my Bubbie once said. And that realization had catapulted me into the now, which was a moment both precious and excruciating. My body was both vibrating with life and aching with grief as I realized just how deeply this little guy had burrowed his way into my very being. Despite all of my doubts, challenges, and the varying degrees of resistance to motherhood that I continued to face, an immense love had been born. A love that was fiercely sure of itself, and even more sure of the unbreakable bond that had formed with this boy, this soul . . . my son.

Something sealed for me then and there: my connection with Kai, and the journey to which our three souls had committed, was solidified in that instant, leaving me with a deep peace. I shared this feeling with Michael as we sat in the waiting room holding hands, our bodies merged side-by-side on hard plastic chairs. We held on tight to each other, our teary eyes meeting with the recognition that something significant had taken place. When the MRI was over, we were brought to the recovery room just in time to see Kai waking up, his face still droopy from the anesthetic. Standing there, holding his finger, I had a profound realization: I was merely one of his "hosts" in this world, here to support this ancient soul on its journey, wherever that might lead.

A week later, we went back to meet the neurologist, a middle-aged woman with an Australian accent, to go over the findings of the MRI. In a tiny sterile room, she showed us the black and white x-ray that confirmed that Kai had microcephaly: his brain was significantly smaller than normal, and his corpus callosum (the bridge between the right and left hemispheres of the brain) was only halfway developed. This "bridge," just like the brain itself, develops during the first three months in the womb. If it doesn't grow there, it doesn't grow at all. Unfortunately, Kai's had grown only halfway. Hearing this, my body actually softened with relief, as if the data finally confirmed something I'd known all along. But this peace was fleeting, interrupted by the mind's immediate onslaught of questions: *What caused this? Why did this happen? What does it mean? Will he walk, talk, feed himself, and function normally? What are we supposed to do to help him?* As it turned out, there were no simple answers to these questions. Even with all the advanced technology, nobody could predict what any of this really meant for Kai. There was a highly technical term for this uncertainty: the neurologist called it a "wait and see" prognosis.

Wait and see? I looked despairingly into her eyes, pleading for her to say more. There was nothing. This was all she could say?

Weren't these people specialists, for God's sake? Wait and see? How were we supposed to live with that? My heart skipped a beat as worst-case scenarios played before my eyes. "What do we do now?" I asked. She gave us the name of an agency to contact for more assistance. Ten minutes later, she opened her door to indicate our appointment had come to an end. As we walked out, I realized that we were completely on our own now, heading into an alien landscape.

On our way back to the car, I saw a child being wheeled into the hospital by his parents. He seemed to be unable to move. I watched the love and care with which his parents touched his tiny body, bent over to kiss his cheek, and spoke softly into his ear, attending to him with a devotion that gave me goose bumps. Watching his father lift him out of the wheelchair and into his arms, I realized that there were no guarantees in life—this was the child those parents had been given, the deck they had been dealt. They had responded to their situation, at least from what I could see, with unfathomable grace. My mind's onslaught of worries stopped dead in its tracks, to be replaced with a profound trust that we would get through this, just as these other parents would, and so many others before us had. On the car ride home, breastfeeding Kai in the back seat, my heart felt a little bit wider. Having made room for both sides of the equation, the fear and the faith co-existed, and I felt we could handle whatever came our way.

Entering his second year of life, Kai was significantly delayed, and still showed no signs of walking or talking. The bond I had experienced in the MRI experience continued to be strong, but I still very much struggled with the daily grind of motherhood. By this time, sleep exhaustion had taken its toll on me, and I felt severely depleted and even a little depressed. On the days I was alone, it felt as if the minutes dragged on like years. My life revolved around taking care of Kai, and hard as it was to admit, I felt unbelievably lonely at times. The biggest challenge was that Kai's developmental progress was so slow, that in many ways it felt like we were still caring for a newborn. The crying, waking up all night, and constant demand for attention were that of a baby, not a fifteen-month-old. While I watched parenting get easier, and sleep begin to normalize for many other mothers, it seemed to be dragging on so much longer for us. One night two of our housemates watched Kai while we went out for dinner, a much-needed reprieve. When we got home, they were exasperated and sweating buckets. One of the women was a mother herself, and I'll never forget her saying, "My God, it's only been a few hours but I feel like he's just sucked me dry!" That tiny sentence affirmed what I'd been going through, and allowed me for a moment to feel OK about just how hard this all really was.

It seemed to be in the everyday things of life that I began to recognize just how difficult a role this was for me. One day, dragging my tired body down the aisles of a grocery store in search of yogurt, Kai became agitated and started to cry. Trying to read the yogurt labels, while bouncing up and down to keep him calm, just wasn't working. He became even more upset, and suddenly belted out his world-famous SCREAM. I quickly unhooked the Baby Bjorn and started race-walking up and down the aisles, turning Kai around and pressing his little head into my chest in an attempt to soothe him. He cried, and I paced, and after what felt like an eternity, he began to settle down. I returned to the yogurt aisle, soaking wet with desperation, grabbing the first yogurt containers in sight, and headed straight to the checkout line. Back in the car, Kai continued to cry while I sat in the front seat, covering my ears to try and block him out, just for a moment. This was the metaphor for my life: I could not get away. Kai's demands to be soothed seemed constant, and I remembered my own mom, and the way she'd pulled her hair, and I felt like I was nearing that same sense of desperation. For the past year I'd felt as if my needs didn't matter—that I had to push a part of myself down in order to attend to Kai. Sitting in the car, that part of me, the one that lived in a pit of resentment at the bottom of my soul, began to scream out in protest. Out of the corner of one ear, I heard Kai continuing to cry, and I finally joined him, breaking down in the middle of the parking lot, with the tears continuing to blur my vision the whole way home.

I realized I'd reached the end of my "stay-at-home mom career," and knew I needed regular help. One day, while Kai was napping,

Michael and I retreated to our master bathroom— where we'd often go to talk, so as not to disturb the little guy, but still have privacy from our housemates. Sitting next to each other on the wide ledge of our tub, I proposed putting Kai into daycare. Michael looked as if I'd kicked him in the mouth. He believed there was one right way to do this: Kai should stay at home with his parents for the first two years. That would be the best for our son's emotional and psychological development.

I was enraged. What about *my* emotional and psychological development? I was breaking down, and couldn't understand why my own husband couldn't see that I had nothing left to give. I was hollow, as if someone had taken hold of the marrow and sucked it out of my bones.

At the same time, I felt paralyzed about going into action without Michael's approval. His point of view meant so much to my fragile sense of self. On one occasion, when I shared how challenged I was, he had said, "You're a woman; you're a mother; you're supposed to be able to do this!"

"You jerk," I replied, "How can you say that? This is so damn hard on me; this has nothing to do with me being a woman or not. I need help!" But underneath my defense, I knew a part of me agreed with him. I couldn't help feeling as if something was fundamentally wrong with me. Where was my huge, limitless heart? I was plagued by my own guilt and felt so ashamed that I couldn't do the "stay-at-home mom" thing, and even worse—that I didn't *want to*. My own self-judgment, combined with the fear that Michael was right, led me to continue staying home full time. The voice inside of me continued to cry out for help. Unfortunately, I didn't listen to her until it was too late.

That was the situation externally, but I knew from the inner work I'd done, that life's outer circumstances were merely triggers for something going on internally. As I reflected, I found myself confronted with a harsh reality. My Judeo-Christian upbringing had taught me that being a giving person was the *right* way to be. Growing up in my house, the worst thing you could be called was selfish. I quickly discovered that the more caring I was, the more attention and praise I received—in all environments, but especially at home. This idea followed me into adulthood and had solidified even more in the last fifteen years of my life. I'd built up quite a persona as a spiritual seeker and teacher who was full of love for God and for people. In my job as a workshop facilitator, I was told time and again how patient and unconditionally loving I was. Prior to becoming a mom, I had secretly believed I was one of *the* most giving people I knew. And then Kai entered my life and smashed that image into a million pieces, showing me the blatant and difficult truth: I had a heart that by its very nature was limited. Over and over, the edges of my personality were revealed, and in the mirror of my life, I saw the conditions of my heart—the places where my love stopped, and the strong will of my ego that insisted its needs be met first, before those of everyone else, even my own son. That unconditionally selfless, loving, devoted person? I couldn't find her. All I found was the part of my ego that was tired of serving, let alone serving without *being seen* for serving. And there's plenty of *that* kind of serving in motherhood.

I looked around at this great image I'd spent a lifetime building—now just tiny pieces shattered on the ground—and knew I'd never be able to put it back together again. I was left with a profound feeling of emptiness. I had no sense of who I was anymore, and felt more lost than I'd ever felt in my life. I wondered whether this was the quick path to enlightenment, or if it was just what happened when your life was taken over by someone else . . . or if they were one and the same.

(His: Under the Spell: "I Know What's Best")

The day of Kai's MRI had finally arrived. I had initially resisted the procedure, in spite of my own rational mind, because a part of me just didn't want to accept that there might be something seriously different about our boy. It was only when the gap between the norm and Kai's development became undeniably clear, that I relented and agreed to the test. I had an unforgettable moment when I saw Kai lying strangely still in his little bed, after the anesthetic took effect. Seeing him lifeless, I felt as if I'd been hit in the stomach. When I left his room, I broke into tears. An overwhelming sense of heaviness descended on my shoulders. I sat down in the waiting room, holding my head between my hands and just wept and wept. The prospect of losing Kai showed me how much I had bonded with him and the place he had taken up in my heart. Neelama reached out to me and we cried in each other's arms, holding on tight and praying together. While we waited to see him again, we fully committed ourselves to do whatever we could to provide him with the support he needed, regardless of the outcome of the MRI. When we walked back into the room after an hour and a half, it was as a single and solid unit, ready to take on whatever was needed for our boy. There he sat, a tiny body in a huge bed, looking like an old man—very wise, very deep. As we picked him up into our arms, our little family unit deepened to a new level.

A week later, we returned to hear the results of Kai's MRI. As often happens in hospitals, we spent at least ten times longer in the waiting room than in the actual meeting with the doctor. Finally, after what felt like forever, we were brought into one of the small consulting rooms—only to find ourselves waiting an even longer stretch. None of that mattered when the neurologist finally came in and told us his findings, and indicated that only time would tell how they would impact Kai and us. I was surprised at my reaction. To my amazement, hearing this news didn't bowl me over. I didn't freak out, as another part of me expected. Instead, I felt calm inside, which was more surprising than the news delivered. My guess is that, seeing Kai go under anesthesia, with the prospect of losing him, had prepared me, in a miraculous way, to hear this news with perspective and commitment. Yes, our child had a brain abnormality . . . *and* we would deal with it, whatever it took.

A postscript: This is the letter "Kai" wrote to the family after the MRI:

TO you all, FROM Kai

To be honest, I actually don't feel my "corpus callosum" . . . I only know it is supposed to connect the two hemispheres of my brain. When I cry, I feel my left brain; when I laugh I feel my right brain; when Daddy kisses me I feel my left brain; when Mommy kisses me, my right brain . . . and so on.

Dad has a theory that I "meditated" too much in my previous lifetimes, and so it left half of my corpus callosum "empty."

Mom's theory is some new age thing about us being on a spiritual journey together.
And me? I am just ME . . ."

To get more feedback on the results of Kai's MRI, we took him to the University of California, in San Francisco, for an examination by a specialist. The whole environment was very impressive—beautiful high tech buildings and gleaming state-of-the-art equipment. The sheer power of the medical institution oozed palpably from the surroundings. The doctor entered, wearing a white coat of authority, flanked by two assistants. He observed Kai exploring the examination room for about five minutes, and then executed a few simple tests, touching different parts of Kai's body. He asked some basic questions and then watched him walk with our assistance down the corridor.

When I asked the doctor questions regarding the missing part of our son's corpus callosum, and what functions that affected, he said that he didn't really know. As a research doctor, the focus of his work seemed to be all about trying to understand the theoretical complexity of the condition. It was Neelama who asked him the *big* question: Would Kai ever be able to talk . . . like us? In response to this, and in a flat and matter-of-fact monotone, he informed us that Kai would never speak more than two-word phrases, would need support all his life, and would never be able live independently. He concluded by recommending that we begin creating a fund for our child, for the time when we would be gone. There was a long and awkward pause in the room, and then I asked, "Doctor, is this your assumption?"

Looking a little surprised, he replied, "Yes, that is based on my observation." Then he looked at his watch and departed, leaving Neelama and I in a complete state of shock.

It wasn't long before I began to feel anger arising in me for the professor's dropping a bomb on us in such a blunt way. When we returned home that night, still shocked and upset, I wrote him an email, which I have kept to this day:

Dear Dr. Sherman,

I've just put my son to bed, and as I lay beside him while he fell asleep, some thoughts came to me in the way of feedback regarding our visit with you today. From what we heard, you answered my wife's question with complete certainty: that our son will never speak or function normally, and will need care for his entire life. As Kai's parents, that was a huge shock to our systems. When I asked whether this prognosis was an assumption, you responded by saying: "Yes, this is based on my observation."

What I am asking you to do is to reflect on the power that you hold as a doctor, and an expert in your field. In Germany, where I am from, there is a saying: ein arzt ist ein Gott in weiss—"a doctor is a God in white." In the eyes of many patients, you hold the position of an incredibly powerful and omniscient authority figure. So whatever you say will have a tremendous impact. You know, of course, about the idea of "self-fulfilling prophesy"—your words have the capacity to remove all hope and to limit new opportunities that parents might explore for a special needs child. You also know, I'm sure, that life is a mystery—nobody really knows for sure what will happen in the future. There is certainty; then there is probability; and then there are always exceptions. That is the whole mystery of life. My suggestion is simply that you start your conversations with patients from that perspective, emphasizing at the outset that your prognoses are based solely on your experience and observations up to that time, and that there may be other possibilities in the future that can't be ruled out. And, I would also suggest offering patients a few different scenarios, rather than jumping to the worst-case scenario. If parents leave your office, as we did, in a depressed and hopeless state, this is the mindset they will be in with their child. I honor your calling to be in research with the goal of alleviating human suffering, and my words are meant as suggestions to that end.

Very sincerely, Michael Schiesser, Kai's Papa

The next day I received a reply:

Dear Mr. Schiesser,

Thank for your input and suggestions. I agree, and I apologize for coming across as too direct. All the best to you (and Kai).

I too, of course, was susceptible to the same high-handed attitude as the doctor I criticized. Working in the field of human development, I was aware of some psychological studies that emphasized the importance of a stable, loving, and nurturing home environment—and this was what I wanted to create for our son. I expected Neelama to understand and agree with me about what I believed to be best: for the first two years, if possible, a child should be with his parents and not in a daycare center. I did not just believe this; I felt it deeply—the best thing we could do for Kai was to ensure that he was breastfed for as long as he wanted and cared for, firstly by his mom and secondly by his dad. And as my life was dedicated to providing for Neelama and Kai first, and being home with them second, I worked my butt off so that this ideal could be fulfilled—that Neelama could stay home with Kai. But, far from feeling appreciated for my contribution, I often felt as if I were under attack. The hardest times for me where when a very stressed Neelama got bitchy with both of us, and in some instances down to the level where I felt she hated me and Kai for having "ruined her life."

I remember one shouting match in particular, where we argued long and loud about whether or not to put Kai in daycare. The best thing for him, the only feasible option, in my mind at the time, was for Kai to be with us, his parents, not in some one-size-fits-all daycare center. The more hysterical Neelama became in the arguments, the more righteous I became in my convictions. I adamantly insisted that I wouldn't do this to our son, although in that argument I more likely used the term "my" son. So here I was again, fighting for my strongly held convictions, just as I had fought for bringing him into the world in the first place, digging in with my idea of what I felt was best: a loving, nourishing, and stable holding environment—a cocoon for our child.

Later, I became aware of a few influences that had impacted me during this time. First, seeing how my mother had stayed home with us, and how all mothers in my little village had done the same, had imprinted in me the idea that *this is how it should be done*. Second, experiencing how my parents had sacrificed for all three boys, made me feel that now it was our turn to make those same sacrifices for our boy. In addition, my work and observations in the field of human development had supported the earlier belief that the ideal way to raise a child was at home for the first two years. I was internally driven to make this ideal a reality at all costs. And I assumed Neelama had signed up for the same thing. Looking back, this helps me understand how I missed the warning signals as to the severity of Neelama's suffering. I just didn't *get* that she was living every day in a pressure cooker. I failed to realize that I had chosen to support my son at the expense of his mother. This proved to be a huge mistake.

Chapter Eight:
It Ain't Easy

(Hers: The Meltdown)

Throughout the next year of Kai's life, I continued to vacillate between moments of surrender to motherhood and moments where I resisted what still felt like a unilateral takeover of my life. Another huge challenge emerged once Kai weaned himself off breastfeeding. He showed little to no interest in solid food, and this stressed me out to no end. There was something so deeply unnerving about our tiny infant not eating; it felt almost as if a biological survival mechanism kicked in, and I would be overcome with fear when we couldn't get him to eat. I spent hours each day pacing up and down the kitchen, holding him in one arm with a tiny spoon in the other, trying to trick him into eating small mouthfuls of yogurt. When this didn't work, and despair gripped me, thankfully my housemate Maria would take Kai from me, holding him to her chest and speaking sweet Italian phrases to him as she patiently attempted to feed him yogurt through a tiny eye dropper, squeezing it into his mouth bit by bit, as he protested and attempted to spit out every drop. And then there'd be the gagging and choking sounds, as if he'd gotten food down the wrong pipe. We realized later that this was due to his brain condition, but at the time I was beside myself with worry. Mealtime often took an hour, just to get through a half a bowl of yogurt, and I still thank God for Maria, who was nothing short of a saint to me in those moments. She and I were a tag team over the next six months, trying every desperate trick up our sleeves to get any amount of calories into his tiny body. Slowly but eventually he began to eat, mostly yogurt, and over time other foods, but not without a serious toll on our nervous systems.

Throughout that year, I became increasingly jealous of Michael and his trips away. Sometimes I fantasized about him being in the various cities where our seminars took place. Every fantasy contained images of him sleeping peacefully through the night. Truth be told, I wanted to be on the road, teaching, doing what I loved to do . . . not to mention getting a normal night's sleep. I missed my visits to the communities where we worked, and longed to go out to a restaurant where I could eat a meal leisurely and have an adult conversation . . . without interruption. In those months, my bitchiness grew and our marriage really began to suffer.

When Michael was home, he seemed to be so busy trying to juggle everything: our business, his clients, computer work, and Kai. It often seemed to me like he was running around with his head cut off . . . even if, as he said, it was "for us." Our fighting matches often occurred when he would arrive home, yet still continue to be busy working. I would storm down the steps into his office screaming, "I am exhausted; I cannot do this anymore. I'm sick and tired of carrying all of this alone at home every time you go away. You don't support me—even when you're here, you're not really here. Where the hell are you?"

He would look up from his desk, over a mountain of paperwork, and shout back, "I am so sick of your nagging; you are becoming a bitch (it was true.) You don't see everything I am doing to provide for us. Why can't you show any appreciation?"

I would storm out of his office, back upstairs, with neither of us feeling really heard or understood by the other. Intellectually, I knew he had to work to support us, yet I felt trapped in a life I had not at all wanted. I remembered a crucial moment, when Kai was just the size of an almond inside of me, confessing to Michael that I was not the full-time mommy type. As we sat on our bed, I told him I could only go forward with the pregnancy if he would agree to be an equal parenting partner: 50/50. He had agreed. Yet, here we were, and I felt like that agreement had somehow evaporated, and my freedom along with it. I felt imprisoned, both by the outer situation and by the bitter resentment growing inside of me.

I had zero desire for sex, or even attraction, to the man who was my husband; it seemed my feminine juices had dried up. With Faisal out of town, we began to see a therapist twice a month for couple's sessions. Unfortunately, we never managed to get beyond the bickering layers of our clashing personalities to the real issues. There were still times when we cuddled and held each other, but the old passionate energy never arose. So we scheduled "date nights," where we'd consciously attempt to get the sexual energy moving, but our bodies wouldn't cooperate. Either Michael would not get turned on, or I would turn frigid when our bodies touched . . . neither of which was a good sign.

One night, after Kai went to bed, my good friend and housemate, Jen, agreed to mediate a conversation between us about my need for help. We all met in the living room after Kai fell asleep. Michael and I sat across from each other as Jen tried to help us create a structure, or a parenting schedule, for the days when Michael was home. He always resisted committing to a regular schedule with Kai, and after the daycare debacle, this was a renewed attempt to bring some sanity into my life. During the meeting, Michael got upset at me for trying to control him and, as he put it, "box him in." He stormed out of the meeting, and I sat there on the couch, sweating with rage . . . for that was exactly how *I* felt: *boxed in*, as if I'd been locked in a closet and was kicking and screaming to get out.

Later that night, Jen and I went out to have a margarita, which for me turned into three. In the middle of the Mexican restaurant, with mariachi music wafting through a room full of happy people enjoying a night out, I shared with her that I was nearing the edge of my endurance with the stay-at-home parenting situation, but even more so with Michael. In strict confidence, I confessed that I was giving our marriage another year. I had never said that out loud before, perhaps not even to myself, but the statement pointed towards a real problem. Jen was the only one who ever heard those words, and looking back, that was a costly mistake. The comment indicated that a serious dent had occurred for me in our marriage, and this was something I should have discussed with Michael. He was my husband and deserved to know just how far gone I was. Yet I withheld this information, burying it deep inside where it would fester and eventually work against us. I learned a valuable lesson from that: tell the truth about what is going on, especially when the relationship is challenged.

One night, Jen, Britta and Maria cornered me in the living room. They spoke with force: "Neelama, we are really worried about you. You and Michael are fighting, and this situation you're in is so overwhelming. You need to get help." "Do I?" I asked, somewhat sarcastically, "Michael seems to think I should just be able to handle this. I wonder sometimes what is wrong with me. Is this normal?" Britta and Maria, the two mothers of the trio, frantically shook their heads, indicating their answer. "Absolutely not! Yeah, OK, maybe in the first few months every mother goes through this, but Kai is about to turn two and *NO*, this is way outside the scope of normal." Britta chimed in, "Kai has special needs, his demands are much more intense than a regular child, and it is so apparent to us that you are burning out. You've got to get help if you're going to make it through this!" I slumped into the floor and could only nod in agreement, knowing they were right, but having no clue how on earth to make this work, especially since Michael was so vehemently opposed.

Shortly thereafter came the meltdown. It happened in May, on Kai's second birthday. Michael had been out of town on one of his ten-day trips to Canada, and I was starting to break apart inside. I needed to go to the party store for the little get-together I'd planned for Kai and some kids from his special needs playgroup. Fortunately, Maria had the wisdom to recognize my state and offered to look after Kai, encouraging me to take some time for myself and go to the party store alone.

I was standing in a narrow aisle in that store, staring at the plethora of party favors, when the ground started to tremble. In California this was not so unusual, but this was not that familiar shake I'd felt so many times before; this was *me*. It wasn't the earth quaking, but my very own legs, releasing uncontrollably beneath me. I recognized what was happening, and abandoned my cart to seek refuge in the car. I had experienced panic attacks before, both in high school and in my senior year of college, usually during periods of intense stress. I had not had a panic attack in over a decade, yet there I was on Kai's second birthday, in my car outside of Party City, going through one of the most intense panic attacks of my life. My whole body trembled, my heart was racing, and I was sure I was going to die. Sheer terror coursed through my body, making my legs shake uncontrollably. My hands went numb, my body felt ice-cold, and a weight started to press itself into my chest. When it felt like I was going to suffocate, I gasped for breaths and began to speak out loud, reassuring myself that I wasn't really going to die. *Neelama, you are okay. Even though this feels real, it isn't going to last. You are absolutely not going to die right now. God would not have you die on your child's second birthday. Don't be ridiculous. This is just a panic attack . . . you've gone through this before and you know it won't last forever.* I repeated this until my body started to calm down until, and after about twenty minutes, the attack passed. But I was shaken to my core. Suddenly there was an immense clarity: enough was enough; my body had spoken; I was done—I could not handle one more day as a full-time mommy. Without a single word to Michael, I enrolled Kai in a home daycare a few days later. I sent Michael an email, letting him know what I had done, so he could digest it before flying back home.

The following week I went to pick up Michael upon his arrival. As I drove to the bus stop in San Rafael, my body tightened in anticipation of our meeting. I watched as he came towards me, noticing the visible disappointment in his eyes. We sat in the car for what seemed like an eternity, a wall of tension between us. Looking out at the parking lot where the bus had dropped him off, I listened to his frustrations and all the reasons why he disagreed with me on the daycare issue, and was surprised when nothing in me flinched. Something fundamental had shifted in me since the earthquake at the party store. I was done having conversations about this; I was done being paralyzed by my own guilt; two years had gone by and there would be no more compromise. Just as I put the key in the ignition to start up the car, he put up one last fight. I turned off the car and looked him in his eyes, telling him he could choose: daycare or divorce. He chose daycare.

This was the beginning of June 2006. Looking back, I realize I had waited one year too long to get the help I needed with Kai. Two of the most difficult years of my life had passed and I felt like a dying flower—in desperate need of water and sunshine.

Later that June, when Michael and I heard from a dear friend about a program in India that was designed for healing and transformation, we took this as a sign. We were both in need of healing, as well as a break from the stress of our daily life. In the past, we had participated in programs such as this to help us on our journey of personal growth, and I hoped that this program could help us with the extreme challenges we'd been facing. The best thing about the program was that it was free. You were simply asked to leave a donation at the ashram upon leaving. With the frequent flier miles we had accumulated through our work, the trip would cost virtually nothing. It was a no-brainer. The moment my mother agreed to help us with Kai, we booked our flights for later that summer.

In June, we decided to make a major change in our living situation. Some good friends of ours had purchased a home in Petaluma, just north of us, and in their backyard was a little cottage for rent. Michael and I thought that perhaps living on our own, as a family, would be a nice change for us. The cottage was small, but charming. It had lovely hardwood floors, and windows in every room, which brought plenty of light inside. There was a backyard that we would share with the owners, and a sweet little rosebush by the front steps. It did need a new coat of paint, and once we decided to move in, I spent hours ruminating over which color to choose, bringing sample after sample home from the paint store, and finally settling on a pale salmon. By mid-July, we had moved out of our communal house and brought everything we owned there, trying to imagine how we would squeeze all our things into the compact space. It was tiny, but it would be our own. Michael and I had lived communally for so long that I hoped the change of scenery would do us good. At the same time, it frightened me, and I wondered if I'd feel even more isolated in this new environment. But I knew something had to shift in our marriage; things had been rocky for far too long. Perhaps this would help; perhaps India would help—Lord knows we needed something.

Just before our India trip, Michael and I were having one of our late night talks while Kai slept. At the end of the conversation, I looked at Michael and said, "This trip is either going to make us or break us." That much I knew: our relationship was fragile. We (or at least I) were teetering on the edge of a very steep cliff.

(His: Peter Pan Grows Up)

Even with the many challenges that had presented themselves since Kai's birth, I still felt good overall about being a parent. Somehow, becoming a father had finally allowed me to leave the Peter Pan in me behind. Peter Pan wanted to be a boy forever, and this archetype is an aspect in every male psyche. My own Peter Pan had resisted growing up because he feared the freedom-limiting responsibilities of being an adult. Being a father had revealed to me that my lifelong spiritual quest had also provided a plausible and great-looking cover story that allowed Peter Pan to do what he wanted, when he wanted, and how he wanted. My decision to marry Neelama had started the maturing process, but it was fatherhood that catapulted me into fully becoming an adult. I realized that, in a sense, Neelama and Kai had made me a man. As a bachelor, with no dependents, most of my thought processes had naturally centered on "me." My son's entry into my life had transformed that immediately, and surprisingly smoothly, into "what about Kai?" That which the "boy-man" in me had feared would be a loss of freedom, proved to be almost the opposite. I had expanded, and opened to parts of myself never before accessible. Most of the time I didn't really miss going out with friends, partying, or doing whatever I wanted. I actually enjoyed the domestication that was happening to me, and plunged enthusiastically into the traditional male role of provider that had once seemed so scary. My guess is that this positive reaction to *vaterschaft*—fatherhood, had something to do with my taking it on relatively late in life. I had enjoyed a lot of playtime during the years when most men my age were raising children and working on their careers. I had explored inner psychological and spiritual realms in some of the most beautiful spots on the planet. So the boy-man, my Peter Pan, had enjoyed more than his fill of naval-gazing introspection and world travel.

Kai's diagnosis was the true beginning of our journey into the world of "special needs." He continued to fall below the curve in all areas of development. We couldn't help but compare our boy to so-called normal infants, and this became a source of pain and worry for us. Comparing was inevitable, though—it's what the human mind does. Having come up with the expression "Kai time" was one way we learned to accept and deal with his slower rate of progress. And in his own time, with lots of long and arduous occupational and physical therapy, and the use of all kinds of special needs contraptions, Kai eventually did sit up, and even stand. The developmental steps *did* happen in sequence, but in Kai time—much later than other children his age, and only with countless hours of work. Nowadays, many parents end up as soccer moms and dads; in our case we were a "therapy" mom and dad, bundling our boy into the car for the next "session."

In my experience as a parent of a special needs child, I lived, and continue to live, in two separate worlds. The first was at home, surrounded by close friends, where I could actually forget that something was different with Kai. He was my only child, and I became used to his condition and the challenges it presented. The other world was out in public, particularly around other children his age, where I had to confront the reality of Kai being so different. Often, another parent at the playground, watching the kids playing together, would ask me how old my son was—with what I assumed to be curiosity, pity or even judgment. Internally, I would wince at these questions, my ego bruised by being seen as the parent of a developmentally delayed child. I confess that I even found myself lying about his age more than once. Because Kai was always, and is to this day, behind in his developmental curve, having to admit publicly exactly *how* far behind he was in his capabilities was often a humiliating experience, and still is to some degree.

I have thought a lot about why I was impacted this way, and realize that my ego, my sense of "I" regarded my son as an extension of itself. In that sense, Kai was an inseparable part of *me*. In having to publicly acknowledge, over and over again, that Kai was behind or disabled, a part of me felt ashamed, as if I too were behind, deficient, or not as good as others. From the big picture it seemed to me that God or Life used this situation with Kai to have me become aware of aspects of myself that I would not otherwise have recognized. My journey was to learn to be compassionate towards those aspects of myself of which I sometimes felt ashamed.

As Kai grew, there was an increasing opportunity for play because, for him, *everything* was, and still is, play. One of our sweetest games was one I called *love attack*, where I pinned Kai on the bed and tickled him with kisses on his belly that had him go into a state of blissfulness, expressing itself in the sweetest giggles imaginable. As with all young kids, his joyousness brought out in me my own dormant joy, craziness and playfulness.

During Kai's second year, the gap between Neelama and me widened. Neelama was clearly distressed, but being caught up in my own world, I just couldn't get the extent of her struggle. At times, one of Neelama's girlfriends would try to make me aware of it or shake me up, but I felt they were biased to her side, so I deflected their comments. I held such an ideal of how I wanted it to be for Kai, that I ignored reality, dismissing Neelama's calls for help, and hoping and assuming things would get better.

When I received Neelama's email after her meltdown, informing me that she had put Kai into daycare, I felt angry and disrespected. I was thousands of miles away in Canada, and felt powerless over the situation. Despite the tension between us, I was fully committed to our marriage, and to Neelama, with whom I wanted to face all these considerable challenges.

The Universe sent me another "warning signal" in the spring of 2006, through a conversation with my oldest friend, Franz, who had come for a visit. After being with us several days, he pulled me aside for a private conversation by the pool. As we sat with our legs dangling in the water, he looked at me with serious eyes and concern in his voice, saying, "I'm worried that you and Neelama are in real trouble as a couple. You are fighting a lot and don't cherish each other enough. It feels very imbalanced to me. She needs to feel more loved."

"I know," I said, kicking the water with my feet, "We've been trying. Faisal is gone for a few months, so we found a therapist, but nothing seems to be working. And as you can see, having been here with us these past few days, our situation isn't easy! I'm worried too."

My trusted friend's parting words to me were, "Be very careful. You've got to work on this." As we left the pool and climbed the stairs back up to the house, I was pensive and felt heavy inside.

I took his advice to heart, and began to look more deeply at our relationship. What could we do to get through this period of fights, differences of opinion on how to support Kai, and the stress his special needs puts on us? And what had happened to the intimacy and sexual passion we once had with each other?

On this last question, I found myself looking back to the beginning of our relationship when we enjoyed very hot periods of passion, and our bodies yearned to make love to each other. Inevitably, as the relationship matured over time, our loving connection shifted from fiery sex to gentler cuddling, holding, and merging, punctuated from time to time with a re-emergence of the old physical passion. Having Kai had changed things even further. We were still hugging and holding each other, and cuddling in bed, but I felt that our sex drives had lessened considerably. In fact, I felt Neelama didn't really want sex at all.

I wanted to work on this problem with our therapist. As a guy, I felt a bit insecure talking about this subject, and feared being blamed. Somehow, the energy I felt from Neelama was that I wasn't *into her* sexually. At the same time, I understood that in this particular dance between a man and a woman, the energies of both are needed for the chemistry to happen. It seemed clear to me that we were stuck somehow on an ego level, and one night I shared with Neelama: "Look, our egos are fighting with each other about everything. It's on the personality level that we're stuck. We need something else to get through this, the spiritual level is missing from our lives." Our deepest bond had always been through what I called the vertical, the Divine, and that had been missing for quite a while.

We were just two starving and tired egos hacking it out with each other. I wanted us to bring this higher level back into our relationship.

Through fate, grace or synchronicity, our old friend, Amrit, called a few days later and told us about a three-week program he had taken at an ashram in India. A deeply spiritual guy to begin with, he told us that this experience had completely rocked his world, and connected him to the source within and without: God. This was the sign I needed. Hadn't I just talked to Neelama about this? She and I had our deepest connections in the realm of Spirit. It was in that dimension where we could let go of our ego differences and turn towards something greater: our shared love for truth and for God.

I desperately hoped this program would help us attain that connection again. We both had complete faith in the recommendation of our friend, and decided to go. Both of us got very excited with the prospect of a break from the roller coaster of the last two years. In addition to our personal reasons, there were also many professional benefits to be gained from our attending the program. From prior experiences, we knew that our own personal development directly impacted our work with clients, and that the teachings and techniques we would receive could be applied in our own workshops and trainings, rippling out to support many more people than just ourselves. This was an investment in ourselves, in our careers, and in the students whom we would guide.

I felt really good about this opportunity, and we worked out a plan that would ensure Kai was cared for while we were away. I would go first; Neelama and I would overlap for one week; and then she would stay on to complete her portion. During our time of overlap together, Kai's beloved grandmother, Oma (Neelama's mom), would take care of our prince. To top it all off, the program was offered in a country which both Neelama and I had learned to love over several previous visits . . . Mother India. We couldn't have been happier at the prospect of this trip!

In June, just weeks before I was to leave for India, and as if to prove that fate can work both ways, I was in a freak accident. I was playing soccer beside our pool. Running along the edge of the pool to stop the ball from rolling into the water, I slammed the left side of my chest violently into the edge of the pool. It knocked the breath out of me. Being a tough guy, I pushed the pain in my ribs aside, expecting it would subside sooner or later. But it had been a brutal fall, the full consequences of which only became clear a week later. While teaching a weekend workshop in Washington, D.C., my voice became weaker and weaker and by Sunday night, I could only whisper. My voice was gone. Ten years earlier, something similar had happened while teaching a workshop. I had lost my voice from overuse, which caused the left vocal cord to be temporarily paralyzed. I thought my voice would return now, just as it had then. July came, and I still had no projecting power whatsoever in my voice, and could only speak quietly. I made my living through my voice, so this was serious.

I ended up at the University of San Francisco, where they discovered that both my vocal cords were paralyzed, and an opening of only about 35% capacity was allowing air to stream in and out of my larynx. It was a complicated injury, likely caused by an injured nerve that was prevented from stimulating the vocal cords. The doctors felt it was best to wait for the vocal cords to recover. But by the time the departure date came around for India, nothing had improved. I had to decide: do I go with a severely restricted voice, or not? I decided to go, and as a "whispering pilgrim," took off for India with great hopes and expectations, and in dire need of divine intervention.

Chapter Nine:
In the Master's Garden

(Hers: God and Man)

It had been almost four years since I'd last visited Mother India, and I arrived with a suitcase full of exhaustion. I found my driver in a sea of a million wide-eyed men outside the airport, and happily sank into the heaven that was air conditioning in the back of his taxi. We drove the nearly two hours to the ashram in silence, as I took in the sights and sounds passing by, as if watching a surreal movie. I was full of mixed emotions. On the one hand, saying goodbye to Kai had ripped my heart in two. I'd never left him for more than a night, and as I boarded the plane that would take me halfway around the world, it struck me that I might never see him again. I winced as the pain of that thought pierced my heart, causing it to bleed in grief-stricken tears. I quickly wiped them away, banishing that idea from my mind. On the other hand, I was desperate for a break and the thought of having three uninterrupted weeks of sleep made my whole body sing. There was some guilt, as a part of me wondered what kind of mother leaves her child to go all the way to India . . . and actually *looks forward* to it? Apparently me. Yet I had to admit that, as painful as it was to leave him, it felt equally good to have my body, my time, and my bed *all* to myself. Yes it was selfish, but my need for rest outweighed the guilt I was feeling. I went around and around in these thoughts until my taxi driver, for some unknown reason, decided to lower his windows and welcome in the outside air. Suddenly, I was back in the *now* of that cab ride, smelling a mixture of scents that cannot be described unless one has the curious good fortune of driving through an Indian town with the windows down.

I arrived at the campus in the middle of the night, and knocked on Michael's door like an excited little girl. He opened it while rubbing his face, eye-mask in hand, his eyes mere slits, telling me I'd woken him from a deep slumber. We shared a long warm hug and suddenly he was awake, leading me by the hand up the stairs to the roof. We sat against the concrete ledge, staring up at the black starry sky, our skins caressed by the balmy air. Michael and I had a shared love for Indian rooftops, particularly on warm nights such as this. He related the story of his journey over the past two weeks, while I listened intently, an air of comfortable familiarity surrounding us. How many conversations had we had over the years, just like this? How many times had we cuddled up next to each other, sharing about the deeper dimensions of life? That night, our warm affection turned into gentle hugs, and then into warm kisses, which got even warmer . . . and to my surprise, sparks erupted between us and we culminated my arrival, and our first night alone in over two years, with some very sweet lovemaking. Before drifting off to sleep that night, I felt hopeful for the first time in a long time.

The next morning, my mood dampened somewhat when I found out that Michael had withheld a small but essential piece of information: it was technically against the rules to have sex here. This was an Indian ashram, after all, and celibacy was part and parcel of the guidelines, along with eating a vegetarian diet and not pointing your bare feet towards the altar. We never made love again during our stay, but in those seven days that Michael and I shared, we were showered by many other blessings, as if God itself was sprinkling down upon us.

The first week felt, for the most part, like a trip into bliss. I *slept* which, for me, was the most sacred of acts. I opted out of the morning meditations in favor of a sleep I had not known for years: deep, long, luxurious, and most of all, *uninterrupted.* Just those precious hours made the trip worth its weight in gold.

One of the highlights of the trip happened the day after my arrival. Michael informed me that I'd be joining his group to meet the founder of the ashram. In India, to meet an enlightened being is considered a great benediction. Our small group was led into a tiny room where we were introduced to one of the most ordinary, yet *extra*ordinary, people I had ever encountered. During our meeting, he blessed a picture of Kai as he looked at us and said, with unwavering certainty, that Kai would be just fine. Upon hearing those words, tears from the past two years streamed down my face, carrying with them the accumulated despair from all those countless and sleepless nights without end, the fear and hopelessness about Kai's future, and the grief I'd been carrying around since my life, as I knew it, had ended just twenty-seven months ago. In those tears was everything my heart had been lugging around, now poured out at the feet of this wise and holy man, whose words, "He will be okay," had managed to lift a burden the size of Nebraska from my heavy heart.

Equally profound, was what happened after our meeting. Our group exited the hall and was ushered outside into the garden, where we spent the next few hours in a state that I had read about but never experienced until that moment. It is widely believed that awakened beings have the power to transmit their state of consciousness to those in their presence, and I truly felt that is what happened to the thirteen of us. We emerged from that room changed—our eyes opened to the magnificence of life all around. Our bodies clung together, as we embraced in a communion that arose from having seen God in all things. We were back in Eden, transported beyond our everyday worries into the arms of a force that held us with unconditional love. It was magical, intoxicating, and one of the most precious moments of my life.

A few days later, Michael's group left the ashram, and I shook with grief as he got into his taxi. We'd had such a wonderful week together, and I was filled with tears at the prospect of what was waiting back home. His departure evoked an even deeper sense of loneliness and separation—the void that lived all the way down at the bottom of my heart. It felt like the existential separation from Source itself. When Michael's taxi pulled away, I went into the little bamboo temple, lay down on a mat, and cried for what seemed like an hour.

During the second week of my program, my sleeping bliss continued, but the process itself became deeper, as we were all asked to confront our lives and look at how we had hurt others. I knew I'd come all the way to India for healing, and so I prayed for the courage to face anything that was not healed in my relationship with Kai, especially in those early months when I fought the pregnancy like a caged animal. The process was unique in that it worked solely with prayer. Depending on the theme of the day, we were asked to pray for something specific (in my case, to feel the pain I had caused my son). After that intense prayer, we were to breathe deeply and relax, as if in meditation, and wait for the inner experience to begin. My prayers were answered, and yet not in the way I'd hoped for. I was suddenly ushered into a visceral experience of Kai's pain, as if I was transported into his body and was directly experiencing what he had experienced, what it was like for him throughout the pregnancy . . . and in those first two years of his life. It was as if I was experiencing what it was like to be actually *be* him. The pain ripped through me, taking me up and down, in and out. There was no factual "proof" for what was going on, but inside myself I knew, with every fiber of my being, that I was experiencing what he had experienced—his very confusion, shock, and suffering—and it hurt like hell.

In the past, I would have run away from such pain, either by justifying myself or blaming something or someone for what had occurred. The beauty of this process was that, through grace, we were invited to take responsibility for the pain we had caused by just being willing to feel it, without any excuses. This was a huge gift. Many spiritual traditions speak of a "Life Review" after we die, which sounds like we are taken through a similar process of feeling the hurt we have caused others. It is said that, by feeling and acknowledging the pain we have caused another, reconciliation happens immediately. And that's what this process felt like to me. After the visceral experience of Kai's suffering had moved through me, a huge weight was lifted—I felt cleansed, healed, and liberated.

Something else was to happen on that trip that was even more pivotal. Towards the end of my second week, I experienced a major shift in consciousness. It occurred after a talk I had with Prem, the monk who was our guide for the process. At the time, I was sitting with him on one of the benches that lined the pretty walkways of the campus. He was dressed in his usual white garb, his hair newly cut, barely an inch off his head. I was frustrated about my lack of progress in achieving mental silence. He listened patiently to my complaints and self-judgments: *What was wrong with me? Why couldn't I stop my mind from rambling? When would I be enlightened already?*

At the end of my rambling, he chuckled and commented, "You spiritual types will probably be the *last* to get enlightened."

I felt totally offended, and as if I'd been hit by a truck. I arrogantly believed we spiritual types would be the *first* to get enlightened. "Whaaat?" I said, showing my annoyance.

Prem's eyes softened and his smile turned tender as he explained, "What I mean is, you spiritual people are always looking for the big bang when it comes to enlightenment. You expect some fantastic explosion and then, "boom," that's it . . . you have arrived! Actually, the process is much more subtle and way more ordinary. You've experienced it many times already, yet all of your concepts about what it *should* be get in the way. In looking for the bells and whistles, you miss it. It's really quite ordinary . . . yet *extra*ordinary."

With that, he stood up and walked away. I was left with the rug pulled out from under me. As I sat alone on the bench, I realized he was absolutely right—I was full of my own spiritual ideas about this thing called enlightenment. Could those ideas be clouding my perception? I imagined so. I spent the rest of the day contemplating what had been revealed to me.

The next morning, I awoke up to find myself completely separated from my thinking mind in a way I had never before experienced. I'd read so many books, studied with so many teachers, and knew so much *about* enlightenment by that time in my life. Heck, I even taught about this stuff for a living. But I'd never had my consciousness altered in such a profound way—I was watching my thoughts, but from the sidelines. And from that vantage point, I neither believed in nor argued with the thoughts. They were there, but I knew *they* weren't *me*. *Me* seemed to be this person sitting on the sidelines, watching the thoughts go by as I would watch traffic, knowing clearly that the cars I observed weaving in and out had nothing to do with me. The longer I stayed on the sidelines, the more I felt filled with an immense peace. It was a peace that included everything: good thoughts; bad thoughts; happy feelings; sad feelings; silence; noise . . . *everything*. I lived in that space for a few days and was expecting that to be *it*—the final frontier. I came, I received, and I figured I'd arrive home relatively enlightened . . . my life's goal accomplished. But God works so differently and surprisingly at times.

It was August 25th, and I still remember sitting in the makeshift room they had converted into a tiny kitchen for us Westerners. I'd just got my lunch from the buffet of rice, dahl, and chapatti. As I sat down to eat the fragrantly steaming food, one of the most gorgeous men I'd ever seen in my life walked through the door. I recognized him from the public Darshan just a few days before, where he'd caught my eye. You'd have to be dead to miss him—over six feet tall, long black hair, relentlessly handsome, and with an air of confidence that only made things worse. I started to tremble, and within seconds, I pushed my plate away, all feelings of hunger extinguished. I was transported to the emotional age of a teenager . . . and as fast as it had arrived, my high and mighty enlightened state went right down the toilet. I asked one of the women in the kitchen if she knew his name . . . she smiled, and delivered it to me like I'd won the lottery: "Alessandro." I came back from my lunch abuzz with thoughts about this man: *God, was he gorgeous . . . those eyes . . . they pierced right through me! Who was he?* I pulled out my journal and wrote, *"Thank you God, for the physical beauty that arrived today in the form of Alessandro. May I enjoy it without being "tripped up."*

That last part didn't work out so well—I became *increasingly* tripped up by this man throughout my remaining days at the ashram. Everywhere I went on the grounds of our campus, there he was— walking down the narrow pathways, sitting on one of the benches underneath the trees, meditating in the temple hut. Every time I turned around, he was there, appearing not to notice me, which only increased my interest. Most days, he was eating in our little kitchen by the time I arrived for my meals. I tried to ignore him, focusing on my food, but it was utterly hopeless—I couldn't eat. By the second meal, he'd caught on and looked directly at me with a gaze that demanded reply.

Awkwardly, I began, "Hi, I'm Neelama. Did you just arrive here?" I knew he hadn't but didn't know what else to say.

"Ciao. I am Alessandro. No, I've been here almost a month."

As we made small talk, my entire body felt lit up by his presence and all that it evoked in me. Throughout our conversations over the next few days, I discovered that he was a long-time practitioner of yoga (like me!). He loved music, and had a song collection (as big as mine!). He was a graphic designer, an artist, and a fellow spiritual seeker who loved India (just as much as I did!). And when he looked at me with those damn eyes, it set my body on fire in a way that nobody else ever had. Within just a few days, I'd constructed an image of who he was and what he meant to me. What had begun as a string of thoughts, had now turned into a full-blown obsession. I debated whether or not to expose to him the intense attraction I felt. I tried to shove it down and hoped, through my silence, that I could will it away. Yet it grew with ferocity, and thirty hours before my departure, it could no longer be contained. On our way to meditation class that night, before my mind could catch up with my mouth, I heard myself blurting out, "It's better that I'm leaving tomorrow because, if not, I will surely fall in love with you." I exhaled. There, it was out. Now I could relax.

But before I could take the next inhale, he replied with equal intensity, "I know . . . I feel exactly the same way."

I temporarily blacked out at that moment, dizzy from hearing this reply, drunk on those few words that came out of what could only be described as the world's most perfect mouth. Inside I was jumping up and down, shouting, *"Oh my God, oh my GOD . . . He likes me too!"* I was ecstatic, shaking, high on life, and totally taken over by this brief exchange . . . but shit, it was time to meditate!

What followed was one of the longest meditations of my life. To be honest, not an ounce of meditating occurred. There's a term used in some meditation circles to describe what happened to me during that session: "mind-fucking"—describing the relentless chatter of the mind, that just doesn't let up, no matter how much the meditator wills it to. I did about ten years' worth of "mind fucking" during those sixty eternal minutes. After the class, Alessandro and I walked back towards the dorms together and found a bench to sit on. The floodgates opened, and we talked with the urgency of new loves that did not have time on their side. We told each other everything, as much as we could in those few hours, about our lives, our pasts, our relationships, our histories. I went into detail about Kai, about Michael, about how much I'd struggled over the past two years . . . and how the passion had finally drained out of me and my marriage. I explained how, in just these few short days with him, I'd come to feel a sense of love and aliveness enter my body and heart, lighting me up in a way I'd never experienced. We both admitted that that neither of us had felt anything like this before, making our connection all the more magical, electrical, exhilarating. We talked late into the night, neither of us wanting to say goodbye, but the promise of one more day together got us through. As I walked back to my room, the thought occurred to me: *Hey, wait a minute . . . you're married!* Somehow that reality had temporarily gone out the window during the past few days. Logic had returned, trying to make me see clearly. But I was too far gone for logic, too far fallen for rationale, too enraptured for mature wisdom. There was a fire blazing inside of me that nothing, not even the ring on my finger, could extinguish.

After our long talk the night before, I awoke the next morning feeling deeply connected to Alessandro. Somehow I felt seen, appreciated, cherished, and loved by this man whom I barely knew. All that had transpired with Michael, particularly over the last couple of years, had eroded our ability to truly see and acknowledge each other. I was like a dried up flower, and Alessandro was pouring his colossal sunshine and rain down on me. Suddenly I was blooming again, and it was a beautiful and addictive feeling, as if something that had been dead was being loved back into existence. He was my Romeo, and I was his Juliet. And with that certainty, came a tsunami-like urge for me to *do* something about this, because time was running out.

A few hours before my taxi came, we said our final goodbye. It was dark outside, and we felt safe in the refuge of the night sky to exchange a hug. At an Indian ashram, this kind of personal contact is something that's frowned upon, especially between an unmarried couple—not to mention when one of the two was *already married* to someone else. The promise we finally made to each other as we said our goodbyes that night, was to do nothing—to simply return home and not go into action. In a way, this was all we *could* do—with Alessandro living in Italy, and I in California with a two-year-old toddler and a husband. What could we do, really? We committed ourselves to praying for Grace to intervene and do whatever was best for our situation. And then there was that goodbye kiss—brief, but on the lips—which ignited something in me that could not be ignored.

(His: With God, All Things Are Possible)

Since my first life-changing trip to India in 1980, I had returned four times. My spiritual quest for enlightenment and God had taken me to various ashrams and spiritual schools, and I had always benefited greatly from the rich spiritual soil of Mother India. What made the trip I was now undertaking different from the others, was my need for healing—to repair my troubled marriage with Neelama, recover from the relentless stress of having a special needs child, and restore my own body. The intensity of the previous two years had taken their toll, and the paralysis of my injured vocal cords had not only reduced the volume of my voice, but had created a shortness of breath which prevented me from running or engaging in any other challenging physical movement. I felt like a battered boxer, beaten up by life, and in dire need of rejuvenation.

What literally gave me a sense of having *arrived* in India, and still does to this day, is the unique smell of its airports. Here it was once again, an odor of a specific Indian cleaning product, with a faint trace of ammonia, which brought a smile to my face . . . I was back! A taxi had been pre-arranged for me, and was waiting outside to carry me to the ashram, about two hours north of the airport. As we drove through the landscape in the still-dark early morning hours, I rolled down my window to enjoy the remnants of the night's enveloping humidity, breathe in the potpourri of fragrances, and revel in the exotic sights. No other place in the world impacted my senses in the way this land did. As the taxi took shortcuts through the town, another favorite aroma wiggled its way through my olfactory system—smoldering fires. Where else in the world were small open fires used—on sidewalks, in front of driveways, and in backyards— to dispose of garbage, and when combined with wood chips and cow dung, to give night guards the solace of light, warmth, and hot chapatti cooked over the fire in the early morning hours? I had always been a "nose guy," and had derived great pleasure from this sense organ, but no smells in the west could compare to the aromatic range and pungency of the nasal impressions of India.

Arriving at the ashram at five in the morning, I was pleasantly surprised by the accommodations assigned to me. I had my own room which, to my delight, was air conditioned, *and* even more amazingly, equipped with its own bathroom. Yeah! There was a small veranda off my room that looked across the garden to the house of the founder of the ashram, less than 120 feet away. The two-story dorm in which I was to reside was surrounded by graceful palm trees, lush gardens, and manicured lawns—all weeded and cared for by the devoted hands of Indian women in their colorful saris. I literally lived in the Master's Garden!

The next morning, I joined the other eleven participants in the group that had been organized by Amrit, a well-known spiritual teacher and author in the transformational field. The group was made up of therapists, medical professionals, actors, and leaders in the field of personal development from the United States and Australia. After a late breakfast, we were asked to wait in the garden for our guide, one of the monks residing in the ashram. Some two hours later, a white-robed Indian man, barely thirty years old, showed up, apologized for the long wait, introduced himself as Prem, and explained that he would be our guide for the next three weeks. He asked us to reconvene in the afternoon for our first meeting. We were told we could rest until then, which proved to be the first indication of the pace of this program. In my many years of workshops and courses, I had never participated in anything as laid-back as this. Our group was to have just two meetings a day with our guide, morning and afternoon, and after each of his brief teachings, we would receive an energetic transmission by a monk or nun. Immediately afterwards, we were encouraged to withdraw to our rooms, lie down, and if possible, to deeply relax and remain completely still. Falling asleep was not considered a problem.

In the days to come, many members of our group began reporting powerful experiences during the energetic transmissions and in the relaxation periods that followed. Just by receiving the energy transferred through the hands of these monks and nuns, followed by lying down and seemingly doing nothing, many people came in touch with long forgotten memories, had spiritual visions, experienced profound healings, and entered into states of joy, peace, and love.

Over time, this process of non-doing worked for everyone in the group—everyone, that is, but me. I had been in situations like this before in various programs, where people around me seemed to have profound shifts and made "progress," when nothing at all was happening for me. Here it was again, and one of the major "inner torturer" voices of my psyche, Mr. Comparison, had taken a center-stage position in my thought processes. The "success stories" of the others just intensified the pressure I felt to experience a breakthrough of my own. My thinking mind went into overdrive and, try as I might, there was nothing I could do to stop it. Any thought of *not* having an expectation just added another expectation. I felt stuck.

In planning and anticipating this trip, I had longed for a time where I would not be required to do anything, where I could just relax, lie down, and rest in peace and quiet. Over the previous two years, my nervous system had become highly strung, and so any possibility of deep relaxation here in India was foiled by restless tossing and turning in my bed. Even though I desperately wanted to rest, to give up, to let go, I inevitably remained alert, tense, driven, and unable to surrender. As a result, I wandered around the campus day and night, and so it was I who observed that Prem was always on his phone. My admiration for him began to increase profoundly as the days went on, as I slowly realized that he was performing seva, the ancient Sanskrit word for service, around the clock. This was a man who dedicated *all* his waking hours to selflessly helping others.

About ten days into the program, the slow pace of things turned from torture to treasure. Doing nothing, having no pressure to produce anything or to reach any goal at all, was finally realized by me as the true gift that it was. The relentless thoughts of my mind began to slow down, allowing my nervous system to relax. I had arrived . . . within myself. The paradox had finally kicked in: doing nothing *was* working!

I anticipated that Neelama would arrive in a few days from the States, and I looked forward to seeing her with excitement and hope. My tensions were diminishing and I felt an inner softening. I longed for my wife, for a fresh beginning for us. When Neelama knocked at my door at 4:30 in the morning, the reunion was sweet and joyous. To my great surprise, the warm connection actually turned into physical passion, which had been missing between us for some time . . . and it threw me into a dilemma. Although couples were allowed to share a bedroom, this ashram practiced celibacy, as do most Indian ashrams and holy places. Caught up in the passion of the moment, however, I had little trouble deciding to overlook that rule, and didn't mention its existence to Neelama. In fact, I enjoyed every moment of "sinning"—not just the exquisite physical pleasure, but in the realization and relief that we had found our "spark" for each other again. When I told Neelama of the rule the next day, she was more put off about this than I had expected . . . and that was the end of the passionate part of our reunion. Nonetheless, even without physical union, over the following week we held each other closely and shared deeply. I felt we were falling in sync again. "With God, everything is possible"—my mantra for this trip seemed to have worked.

The timing of Neelama's arrival couldn't have been better. On her second day, we members of the "Amrit group" were invited to a private Darshan with the founder of the ashram, an opportunity offered only once during the three-week stay. Darshan, from the Sanskrit language, is the term used for a student's or disciple's personal meeting with the teacher or master. Our small group was ushered into a tiny room where we met the Indian teacher, about sixty years of age, flanked by two of his monks. Amrit, who had interviewed the teacher extensively a few days earlier for a documentary, introduced us one-by-one to the founder of the ashram, who was considered to be fully enlightened. Listening to him interacting with and replying to our fellow seekers was a delight, sometimes mind-blowing, because his perspective was clearly not derived from the everyday realm of human experience. I had been in the presence of quite a few awakened men and women before in India and in the West, but what most surprised me about this teacher were the clarity, precision, and matter-of-factness of his speaking style. His responses to the mostly personal, and sometimes philosophical and existential questions, were always short and very practical. Later, we learned that he had a degree in mathematics and was a scientifically inspired teacher, which came through even in some of his most esoteric answers.

When it was our turn to speak, Neelama and I handed him a picture of our two-year-old prince and told him about his condition and the challenges we were facing. With great tenderness and caring in his voice, he offered a reassurance that brought me such instant and complete relief that tears came to my eyes and flowed down my cheeks, washing away the heavy burden of worry that I had carried since our son's diagnosis.

Later on, I analyzed this interaction with my thinking mind. One part of me asked how I could trust that this Indian teacher would know that our son would be fine. What could he know that I didn't know? But a new part in me felt a strong *knowing* that this being in human form had capacities and insights beyond mere human levels, and I was enveloped in a profound sense of relief, possibility, and hope. Both parts existed side by side in me, and still do. And from the big picture perspective, there is no denying that he was right—all has been fine.

I also shared about my personal plight—the paralyzed vocal cords. He assured me that this would work itself out too, which brought about another wave of relief. In completing our interview, we shared briefly about our transformational work in the West, and asked for his blessing in helping to touch the hearts, minds, and souls of our many students and friends—to support them and ourselves on our inner journeys. With a wide loving smile, he blessed us, and I immediately felt an energetic expansion within me.

Shortly after our blessing, we found ourselves outside in the warm tropical night, surrounded by beautiful gardens and an ecstatic state of bliss, the likes of which neither Neelama nor I had ever experienced before. As I held her close, I felt deeply grateful for her arriving in time for us to share this experience together, and to open our hearts to each other so deeply. Surely we had made it through the dark night, and into the light of our relationship journey.

And my joy didn't stop with Neelama. There was a deep sense of love and connectedness between everyone in the Master's Garden—a connection that extended to the night sky, to all beings on the planet, and to life in its perfection just the way it was, which was exquisite.

After the Darshan experience, something in my heart cracked opened. To my huge surprise, at Day 19 of the program, an inner spaciousness revealed itself. It wasn't in any way an extreme "high," just a calm and peaceful expansion, punctuated with episodes of joy for no apparent reason.

On August 15th, I bade farewell to the dear friends I had made, the guides, the Master's Garden, and Neelama. She cried and cried as the taxi left the garden, and although I was sad, I also felt grateful, and hopeful for us—because it felt like everything was possible with God on our side!

Twenty-four hours later, on the other side of the world, geographically and metaphorically, I delightedly held my precious little boy in my arms, who was desperately anxious to continue his task of trying to walk by himself. Towards the end of my first week back, Neelama and I were able to talk for a few minutes over the phone. Even though there were thousands of miles between us, I could sense a profound shift had occurred in her being. She was open, clear, and a deep stillness emanated from her, which touched me on the other end of the phone line. After the call, I said to a friend, "God, she was in such a great space. I wouldn't be surprised if she comes back enlightened. I have never experienced her this way. You might find me sitting at her feet."

Shortly after that phone call, Kai and I headed off with Kai's grandfather, Opa, to a family gathering at one of the Finger Lakes, Lake Keuka, in upstate New York. Kai was the center of attention, and we all had a ball with him, as well as with each other. Neelama's process had ended the day before, and she was en route home. We were all very excited about her joining us the next day. Kai and I went to bed that night in a state of great excitement and anticipation. His Mommy and my Beloved would come back to us tomorrow.

Chapter Ten:
Cupid and Shiva

(Hers: Colpo di Fulmine)

"Colpo di fulmine. The thunderbolt, as Italians call it. When love strikes someone like lightning, so powerful and intense it can't be denied. It's beautiful and messy, cracking a chest open and spilling the soul out for the world to see. It turns a person inside out, and there's no going back from it. Once the thunderbolt hits, your life is irrevocably changed."

— J.M. Darhower, Sempre

I hadn't even reached home, and was already about to break the promise Alessandro and I had made—to do nothing. After my flight landed in New York, I rented a car to drive north to Elmira, where I was to meet Michael and Kai. During the drive, my mind ricocheted back and forth between Michael and Kai . . . to Alessandro. Try as I might, I could not get Alessandro out of my head. Just minutes away from reuniting with my husband and son, I gave in, pulling over to the side of the country road and rummaging around for my address book. As cars drove by, my mind raced with self-judgments: *You are about to reunite with your husband, the man you are married to, and your child, who you haven't seen in over three weeks, and this is all you can think about?* I quickly banished these thoughts. I couldn't just do nothing about Alessandro, and I needed him to know that. I was crazed; I had to hear his voice one more time before re-entering my old life, which was waiting just a few miles up the road. I wanted some assurance that he was feeling what I was feeling, and that what we had experienced was real. Shaking with fear and excitement, I dialed India, and explained to the ashram's secretary that I was calling for Alessandro. It took a while, and those minutes of silence were a playground for my mind to run wild: *Maybe he doesn't want to speak to me, maybe he has resolved to forget what happened and move on. Maybe he has renewed his commitment to his relationship, and decided it was best to cut me off forever . . . maybe . . . maybe . . . maybe . . .*

"Hello, hello?" he said, his voice bold and soft at the same time. Hearing it was a blessed relief to my mind's fears. "Alessandro, it's Neelama," I said, tentatively.

"Oh Ciao, Nee . . . lah . . . ma," he said in *that way*—that warm, intoxicating way that wrapped itself around my heart and claimed it, even from halfway around the world. I stuttered, awkwardly making small talk, all the while trying to gauge exactly what he was feeling—about me, about us. Was this my own private movie, or was he really my co-star? Hearing his voice brought up a mixture of excitement and fear in me—how terribly I missed this man I had known for mere days, how close I felt to him. And how strangely far away I felt from Kai, Michael, and my mom, who were waiting patiently for me just up the road. I had been through so much with each of them—lifetimes. And yet they were strangers in the face of what I was feeling now. I told Alessandro I was scared to see Michael, confused about what had transpired between us, and full of burning desire to be in his arms again. I let him know how much I missed him, how my whole body ached to be his. He said he felt the same, and that he'd never felt this way about anyone before . . . *ever*. Hearing this made me even more determined to not sit back and let our special connection fade into the past, chalked up as some great memory in the Album of Life. Whatever this was, it felt undeniably fragile, like a baby tree, facing the impossible obstacles of wind, rain, and lack of sunshine. Our tree needed to be staked, protected, and given the right ingredients to ensure it would bloom. This call was my way of fertilizing our little sapling.

Alessandro admitted that, being still at the ashram, he hadn't had to fully confront the reality of his feelings for me in relation to his life back home and his girlfriend. He sympathized with me, and encouraged me to be truthful with Michael, as he intended to be with his girlfriend when he saw her again. More than being honest, there seemed nothing else we could do.

Within minutes of hanging up the phone, I found myself hugging my mom, Kai, and Michael. Kai was able to walk towards me all by himself, and it was such a joy and relief to see that he would indeed be able walk on his own. He had begun taking a few steps before our trip but, in the last three weeks, had come even closer to walking independently. After so much worry, seeing him walk to me lifted a huge burden from my heart. I squeezed him tight, but he wiggled out of it after about two seconds . . . on the move again. It was odd to be there—hugging my familiar family members on the one hand while, on the other, feeling like I was standing next to myself, just watching the scene unfold. It felt as if I had been beamed out of one world, but hadn't yet re-materialized in the other. It was the worst kind of culture shock.

The one-hour car ride to the cottage was unbearably long. I needed to talk to Michael, and the moment couldn't come soon enough. The significance of what had happened with Alessandro felt like a weight on my chest, which was beginning to suffocate me. I wanted to speak all of my feelings out loud. By the time we arrived at the cottage, it was quite late, and the rest of my family had already gone to bed. We ate a quick dinner, and then I went upstairs to read Kai a story and put him to sleep, hoping that Michael and I would get a moment alone.

As soon as Kai was out, I found Michael downstairs on the couch, where I sat down and erupted with the entire story of what had transpired between Alessandro and me. Michael looked stunned, and sat there for quite some time before replying, "What does this mean, what do you feel for him?" I told him that I was extremely attracted to Alessandro, but didn't know what that really meant in terms of Michael and I, or the future. This seemed to relax him a bit, and I could only assume he thought this was merely a passing attraction that would subside with time. His trust pierced my heart, because I did not feel the same way. I was certain that what I felt for Alessandro was way more than a crush that would fade over time. We finally went to bed together, our bodies cuddling up as they'd done for years, but I was thousands of miles away.

I woke up before dawn the next day, thanks to the beautiful thing called jet lag, and took a long walk along the road that paralleled the lake. The steel-blue lake looked like glass, still undisturbed by the boats that would be out soon enough. I gazed out onto the water, wrestling with all that I had known with Michael: our life; our marriage; our connection; our work; our child . . . and all that I felt towards Alessandro: the extreme attraction to someone who saw and cherished me; that sense of being lit up and ignited; and the incredible passion. Waves of guilt washed over me, questioning how I could be so obsessed with this new love and have so little desire for my own husband. Yet this is what I felt, and I couldn't figure out how to make that be any different.

Michael and I had struggled with our sexual relationship even before Kai came along. Sexual passion was way more important to me than to him; he was much less concerned with that element in our relationship. But for me, that was *the* barometer that revealed everything. In the beginning, Michael and I had the fire and attraction of new love, but it quickly subsided and we had always been challenged to bring that initial fire back to life. And yet, with Alessandro it was like—call the fire brigade, the house is a blazing inferno! My mind could not focus on anything else. *How could I continue our communication? What did this all mean? Was he my soul mate? Was that psychic maybe right a few months back?*

Earlier that spring, I had been at a hot springs, one of our getaway places north of Marin, and had a tarot card reading. With just three cards, the reader predicted that my entire life was about to change. She said the cards showed that I would go away to some sort of university and learn something. This something would change my life and ultimately lead to financial abundance . . . and I would meet my soul mate. I was a bit stunned about the soul mate thing, given that I was already married. I told her this and she quickly replied, "That's just what the cards say." I remember that her words left quite an impression on me, particularly because I was in a challenging phase with Michael and Kai at the time. In some way, what those cards revealed seemed to provide the possibility of an escape. I eventually forgot about the reading, pushing it down to the basement, only for it to re-emerge . . . here, now. My mind rationalized: *maybe this prediction explained the strong and urgent pull I felt towards Alessandro. Maybe I married the wrong man. Maybe Alessandro was my soul mate, and that is why God brought us together . . . in one of the most spiritual places on the planet.* Yes, soul mate . . . otherwise, I couldn't explain the intensity of the feelings I was experiencing.

I tried to act normally around my family, not wanting them to notice anything awkward. We swam with Kai in the lake, took a ride in the boat, and had a nice dinner. Nobody suspected anything was amiss, and yet my heart ached whenever I met Michael's heavy gaze. On my second morning home, I woke up very early and took the car to secretly drive the ten miles into town where I could access the Internet. In that little café, I composed my first of many emails to Alessandro: *"My relationship with my husband is beautiful in many ways; we've been through a lot together and there's a deep honesty and intimacy between us. But there has also been something missing. Being with you has made me see what that missing piece was, and I realize it's something very important to me. I don't know if I can get beyond this with Michael, nor what this might mean for our marriage. My whole life is with him—I don't even know what there is without this life. It seems like a huge death to think of this changing. And yet, on some level, it seems that my whole entire world has changed, and everything is falling down around me . . . "*

I couldn't get back to the Internet café for a few days, and it was becoming even harder to look Michael in the eye. He had asked me not to communicate with Alessandro, and I'd agreed. I didn't tell him of my email, or my plans to find out if Alessandro had replied. I had never before lied to my husband, beyond an occasional little white lie, but this was a really big huge lie, and I couldn't believe that I, this great spiritual person, could be so out of integrity. But there I was . . . lying, sneaking around, doing just those things I had judged in others. It was as if I was overcome by a force bigger than myself—the train had left the station, was going at top speed, and nothing was able to slow it down.

I was physically back home, but hadn't arrived *back* into my marriage. Michael confronted me, and I finally admitted that I had gone against his request and had been in communication with Alessandro. I had lied to him. He was visibly disturbed that I'd broken our trust, and asked me again to cut all contact with Alessandro. As much as he pleaded, and as much as I may have known somewhere inside of me that this was the right thing to do, I couldn't agree to it. There was a flame in me that just could not be extinguished.

A week later, back in Elmira, I received a powerful message from Alessandro confessing his love for me. It felt as if I was holding the pot of gold at the end of the rainbow, and I wasn't going to let it slip through my hands. This was the confirmation I needed to move forward. I already felt like he was THE ONE: my Romeo, the man who would love me without condition, provide for my every need, and the man with whom that passionate fire would burn for evermore. I'd dreamed about this ONE, just like millions of other women. This was the ONE that every little girl is promised at the end of the fairy tales, the one that women swoon over in Hollywood movies, the one that every woman secretly hopes will swoop in and complete her. It seems that we are driven to search far and wide for this ONE, sometimes even ignoring husbands and children, friends and family for it. I was no different. I was so blind as I fell . . . and fell and fell and fell, far past the point of no return. Within just a few days, on an evening walk with Michael, I told him our marriage was over.

(His: The Knife in the Heart)

Kai and I waited with shared excitement at the Elmira Airport in upstate New York. He couldn't wait to have his Mama back, and nor could I. My heart was filled with anticipation of starting a fresh chapter in the relationship with my beloved wife. Kai, whose hands were being held by Oma when Neelama walked into the car rental lobby, actually took his first real walking steps towards her—a very sweet moment in their joyful reunion. I was fine with there being time for just a short hug for me, because Kai was in heaven sitting on Mama's lap all the way back to the cottage. It took longer than usual for Kai to settle down to sleep that night, but I finally found a moment to connect with Neelama. As I pulled her close to hug and kiss, she pulled back, and then uttered her shocking words, "I met another man!"

Time stood still, and a sharp pain stabbed me in the heart like a knife. My legs buckled, and I started to tremble. I was stunned and speechless. "What happened?" I finally asked weakly.

"I met a man," she repeated.

We were upstairs in the cottage, just outside our bedroom, and I still can smell the musk of the place as I recall that moment. Shock came over me, throwing me into a state of confusion and a sense of being lost. She talked some more, but I don't remember the details, not even where she or I slept that night.

Fortunately, somehow, every dark night comes to an end; we humans make it through, and with a new morning often comes new hope. That hope was short-lived, however, as Neelama proceeded to give me more information the next morning: that he was Italian; that they had connected; and that meeting him had revealed to her that our marriage was not working. The latter apparently had nothing to do with him; it had just become clear to her through their meeting. The following days, surrounded by Neelama's extended family, were more or less a living hell. We tried to keep up the image of the "happy family." We agreed not to expose them to what was going on between us. When we were alone together, my expressed emotions of feeling utterly confused, deeply angered, and plain shit-scared were met by guarded eyes and an icy tone, which clearly revealed to me that it was all over.

There was no Internet at the lake cottage, so Neelama took a car to get into town to check her emails after her long absence. As she prepared to leave the cottage, a sleeping snake of jealousy stirred inside me and I rushed outside towards the car, begging her not to connect with the guy in India. "Wait . . . give it some time, don't rush into anything," I pleaded. "Please. Let's work on this." She nodded, agreeing that she would not connect with him, but a few days later I came across her laptop lying unattended. Possessed by fear and worry, I took the computer to a neighbor who had an Internet connection and logged on. Yes, I knew it . . . they had exchanged emails. His name was Alessandro, and he had written that he loved her. From that moment on, I hated that name. Neelama had lied to me about not having contacted him. Fear and jealousy grew, along with some admission of guilt. Yes, I had been a jerk to her quite a few times during the last two years, and knew I had hurt her. I had messed up. And yet she would actually leave me? I just had not anticipated that one. Another voice came in: *Try to love her through all this. Give her space. She will come to her senses.* At some point, I suggested to her that we call Faisal, who was teaching in Europe, for help. She stated flatly that she didn't want help.

On our last day at the cottage, the extended family rented a boat and we all went out on the lake together. It was overcast, and a rather cold wind was blowing across the water. As usual, Neelama was unprepared for the rough weather. As she sat across from me, I saw her trembling, pressing Kai tightly against her body for warmth. I moved over and put my jacket around them both, holding them in my arms. Her entire body stiffened and I felt her as frigid as the wind. I backed off, upset, feeling rejected, and shocked that all my attempts to reach her were shut down. Waves of hopelessness washed over my body, and I struggled to choke back the tears. Coming from just a few feet away were the sounds of laughter, the clinking of beer bottles and cigar smoke in the air . . . Neelama's family members were celebrating their joyous reunion, while all I wanted to do was sink down to the bottom of the lake.

The following day we drove back to the home of Neelama's mother, Marilyn, who, on learning what was going on with her daughter, was very worried about such a sudden development. At the urging of both her mom and I, Neelama agreed to have a phone session with Paula, her therapist in California. *Maybe she can at least slow her down, to give us a chance,* I hoped.

Marilyn and I waited in the kitchen during Neelama's phone session. I felt as if there was a roaring inferno raging inside me that couldn't be extinguished, until she finally came out. When she walked into the kitchen, she responded to our exasperated looks by saying, "It was good to talk to her." That told me nothing.

"What did she say?" I asked, in a mixture of hope and despair. Neelama's mom, who'd been doing dishes, turned off the water and leaned her head towards us, with the same sense of urgency.

"Paula shared with me that she went through something similar when she left her husband years ago," Neelama replied. It was clear to me that she felt confirmed in her decision to leave our marriage, rather than work to save it. I was stunned and furious. "What?" I ranted, "How can *she,* as a therapist, bring her own issues into a session? This is unbelievable! Your mind will use this now to have your point of view confirmed. Can't you see this?" No she didn't. The whole intent of the call had backfired.

That night, as Kai peacefully snuggled up with his Oma, Neelama and I went for a walk. Under the night sky, she delivered the biggest blow of my life: our marriage, for her, was over. She was done. The air was warm and humid, but I could no longer feel it on my skin. An icy cold shock slammed through my body, paralyzing my voice and blocking my ears. I cannot recall further details of that moment; all I know is I had never *ever* felt anything like this before.

In the days that followed, the world as I knew it came crumbling down around me. With Neelama, I had always felt we could make it through our stuff. We had said *yes* to each other and spoken our vows. We had tremendous communication skills, teachers to guide us, and our shared connection to Source. I had believed that no matter what came up, we could find a way to handle it. That was the inner frame in which I had held the picture of our marriage. This was as real for me as gravity, and to have it overthrown threw me upside down, into chaos.

In the days that followed, *I've got to do something* was the recurring thought that occupied my mind. Whenever Neelama flatly reiterated her line of "I am done," I would either use my rational approach of, "Please, we have a life together, Kai, and Inner Journey," or my emotional pleas of, "You can't just walk away; I deserve another try; Please stop it with this guy and give us a chance! For the sake of Kai, slow down!" No matter what I tried, nothing seemed to have any impact.

Later in that week at Oma's house, Neelama informed me that she wouldn't be moving into the Petaluma cottage that we had rented before our India trip. Hearing that she wouldn't be coming with me set off another time bomb in my system, obliterating all the secret hope I'd carried that the intimacy of our little family in that charming cottage would bring her back to her senses. This only deepened my shock, seemingly shattering any chance I might have of recovering our relationship. I lived continually in the feeling that the floor was about to drop out from under my feet.

A few days later, I left upstate New York for Ottawa, Canada, where I was scheduled to teach two workshops to a group of my students there. Neelama and Kai would head back to California, and in a way, our parting felt like an emotional reprieve. I needed to get away from everything, and to my great surprise, found myself functioning fully as a teacher. It was at night, lying in my bedroom looking into the blackness, that the uncertainty of the situation hit me like a ton of bricks. Streams of worrying thoughts chased each other around endlessly in my mind, and I began to realize the extent to which the prospect of our separation was impacting me. I recall two things in particular from this trip. The first was a teaching that came to my mind from a prior mentor, who had said, "Even if you are in the deepest personal turmoil, keep giving. It will help you pull through." This proved to be true for me. Being focused on "giving" to my students shifted me from self-absorption and brought temporary relief from my own struggle.

The second was the gift of awareness—the capacity to stand back and objectively observe oneself. There is an old adage that to be a true teacher, one has to practice what one teaches. Since the first shock of Neelama's revelations, the aware part of me had been hijacked by the onslaught of deep emotions, and was "missing in action." Helping others to be present had reawakened that dormant capacity in me, as well. During this trip, I had an opportunity to pause, to look within, and to inquire as to why the threat of separation created such an immense upheaval. I discovered that the situation with Neelama had caused me to emotionally regress back to the age of three, the time of my younger brother's birth. The special bonding and intimacy that had developed between my mom and I came to an abrupt end with the arrival of baby Guenter. And, as any newborn needs and deserves, it was *he* who became the center of my mama's attention. Nevertheless, the little boy, Michael, experienced this shift of her attention as heartbreaking loss. I felt suddenly replaced and abandoned, yet could not process those emotions, and so they were stored in my unconscious.

Fast-forward forty-seven years, where a scenario unfolds in which "mama" Neelama withdraws all her love and attention from Michael, and replaces him in her affection and attention with the younger Alessandro—it was a perfect set-up. It was helpful to realize that this wound was already in me way before Neelama came into my life. She triggered its re-activation, but was not the original cause.

By now, I knew that Neelama and Kai were back in California, and I imagined they were staying in the little cottage. It was painful to remember that we had consciously decided to rent this place to give our little family unit a chance to bond more deeply. That dream of our happy family was dying, and this was about to become the most challenging chapter of reality I would ever live through.

Chapter Eleven: Heaven and Hell

(Hers): *Amore and Colpa*

I stood in the living room of the tiny cottage that was supposed to be our home. Our furniture was in place, but along the walls were uneven piles of cardboard boxes, many of which would never be unpacked. It was the middle of September, and Michael was still in Canada. Kai and I had just arrived back in California the night before. He was with the babysitter and it was my first chance to be alone in weeks.

As I stared at the pale salmon paint on the walls, it felt so surreal. I'd picked out that color just eight weeks ago, with both excitement and trepidation. It all seemed so important then, choosing the *right* color to put on those walls—the walls which were supposed to encircle us as a family, holding and preserving our memories for years to come. All of that seemed like another life to me now. As I walked through the little rooms in the cottage, I knew our dream would never become a reality. This little house would never become my home. There would be no family dinners at the little round table we had put in the corner, no movie nights on the new couch we had bought, no Christmas or Thanksgiving holiday celebrations, no pancake breakfasts in the sunlit kitchen. Grief struck my heart like a thunderbolt, and tears welled up at the loss of something that would never "come to be." I lowered myself slowly onto the bed, and was pressed down by a heaviness that took hold of my entire body— a feeling I could only identify as "guilt." It landed itself in my heart like a ton of bricks, carrying with it the weight of tremendous responsibility. I was killing our dream; I was destroying our family unit; I was making Kai yet another child of divorced parents; and most of all, I was breaking Michael's heart. I felt smothered under such a huge burden, and had to do something.

I jumped up, out of bed and my own skin, and dove headfirst into the car, racing to the nearest Target store, where I pushed the red cart and my guilt through the aisles looking for something . . . *anything* . . . to lift this unbearable weight. The cart was quickly filled with new sheets, towels, pillows, a bathmat, a cool-looking microwave, and anything else I could find. I told myself all these things were really for Michael, to fill the lonely empty cottage he'd be coming back to. Returning home with a carload of red and white plastic bags, I got to work immediately, cleaning and sprucing up the place, doing all I could in my external world to make things look nice . . . all the while feeling horrible in my internal world.

Back in the kitchen, I opened a large white box from my mom, which had arrived a few days earlier. In her excitement at us having our first "home," she had mailed a care package full of dishes, glasses, and a new set of silverware. Sitting on the black and white tiled floor, I unpacked each of those items, so carefully wrapped with her sweet love and well wishes. They were wet with tears by the time I finished, and I had to dry each one before putting them into the cupboards of their new home. *Their* home. Oh how my leaving would disappoint my mom, and sadden so many others who carried that same love and hope for our little family.

When Michael returned from Canada, he requested that we have a couple's session with our friend, Amrit, who was shocked to hear the news about us. During the session, a mountain of stuff came out, which was very cathartic and somewhat healing. Afterwards, Amrit made a suggestion about Michael and I doing more "work on our marriage." Those words struck me like a sword, and I admitted to them both that I didn't want to work on our marriage. I wanted to leave our marriage and be with Alessandro. I cringe at how this sounds now, but at the time, I thought nothing of it. It is simply what I felt.

I moved back into the communal house in Novato that we'd left just before India, and rented a room for me, and a much smaller one for Kai. Most days, Alessandro and I continued to be in contact, and the distance between us only made the fire rage beyond containment. By that time, he had returned to Italy and had ended his relationship also. We both felt "free" and began making plans to meet again.

Just a few days after the couple's session with Amrit, I announced to Michael that I would be going to Italy for ten days. It felt so empowering to simply state that I would be going away, versus having to ask for permission. As much guilt as I felt for what I was doing, there was an equal sense of power, as if I was taking back the reigns of my independence—or so I believed at the time. I had very little money, having rarely worked over the previous two years, but all reason was flung out the window by my crazed need to see Alessandro again. Thus began the impulsive habit of charging romantic getaways on my credit card, hoping I could pay them off one day.

Two weeks later, I found myself at the International Terminal of San Francisco Airport, waiting for my flight, and suddenly overcome by a sense of urgency to make a phone call. By now, almost everyone in my family knew what had happened, yet somehow, standing near the duty free shop, staring at the perfume billboards and the rush of people whizzing to and from business trips and vacations, I felt strangely obligated to call my eighty-three-year-old grandmother. We were not in touch on a regular basis—I called her only a few times a year. Yet somehow, in my mind's strange logic, I felt it was the right thing to do—to alert her, before I boarded that plane, that I had separated from my husband. Somehow that would make it okay to go gallivanting off to Italy. I nervously dialed her number, and covered one ear so I could hear her amidst the buzz of the airport. I bent over to block out the world, in hopes of having an incredibly private conversation in one of the most public places on earth. The phone rang and my breath quickened, and all too soon she picked up.

"Hello?" she said in a faint voice.

"Grandma, It's Julie." She still knew me by my birth name, which I hadn't used in four years, since taking on the spiritual name of Neelama. I found her habit endearing, and had never asked her, nor anyone else who still called me "Julie," to do otherwise.

"How are you, dear, is everything *okay*?" she asked, with the strain of worry in her voice.

I blurted out my confession quickly, like ripping off a Band-Aid, "Well Gram, actually no. A few weeks ago I decided to leave Michael. As you know, it's been a very rough two years for us since Kai was born. I'm just not in love with him anymore, Gram, and we've been fighting so much recently. I love him, but not as a husband, if that makes sense. So I decided it was time to separate." My voice trailed off, leaving out any mention of Alessandro. I couldn't bear to tell her—not here, not now, and not in the middle of an airport with a mountain of shame in my heart.

"Oh, I'm so sorry to hear that, dear. Yes, I know you have had a very challenging time. But you are a strong and smart woman, and I trust you are doing the right thing." She said this with no hint of judgment in her voice. My body immediately relaxed; it was, for my psyche, the next best thing to an absolution.

"Oh Gram, thank you. It was not an easy decision, but one I felt I needed to make."

She asked about the details—how it would work with Kai and where I would live—and by the time I had hung up the phone fifteen minutes later, I felt relieved. It was done. Now everybody knew, and even Grandma was okay with it. *I am forgiven*, I thought—or so I wished, I hoped, I so badly wanted to be.

In my zeal to make this trip happen, I had forgotten to choose a seat. This can be a brutal mistake on an international flight, and I faced the consequences of that now—sandwiched between two huge men. Ironically, this was exactly how I felt on the inside: jammed between two conflicting feelings—on the one side, an exuberance that I hadn't experienced since my teenage years, and on the other side, a grief that felt like somebody had died. It was difficult to find space, both in my seat and within myself. I felt an anxiety enter me somewhere over the Atlantic, when it suddenly dawned on me that I didn't really *know* Alessandro. My heart raced as my mind continued on its thought-binge. Apart from our few days together in India, and the phone calls and texts we'd shared since coming home, I knew surprisingly *little* about someone for whom I'd left my husband, someone whom I'd been calling my "soul mate," not to mention someone with whom I'd be spending a week in a tiny remote town in the mountains of Northern Italy. It was in that moment that I realized just how much I'd put on the line for something so unknown.

There was also the ongoing heaviness regarding Michael. Whenever I imagined him and Kai at home alone in that little cottage—eating alone, playing alone, being alone—my heart would lodge itself into my throat and explode with pain. I wouldn't surrender to that feeling, I couldn't—it was just too unbearable. This avoidance only strengthened the undercurrent of guilt, which was always with me, a constant companion buried just beneath the joy bubbles I felt on the surface.

When the plane landed, I was momentarily overcome with panic. Thoughts raced in my head: *What if we end up not liking each other? What if there's really no chemistry? What are we actually going to do together? (Yes, I know . . . of course . . . but other than **that**, what will we do?) What would we talk about? Do we actually have anything in common?* This went on for a few minutes, and before I knew it, I was being shuffled off the plane, surrounded by Italians clutching their cell phones and talking with a racecar speed that left me dizzy. I made my way to the bathroom, and wasn't so pleased with what I saw in the mirror. After the long journey, and so many sleepless nights leading up to this moment, I looked terribly worn. And one thing I remembered about Alessandro, apart from all the other details, was that he did *not* look worn. He was the complete opposite of worn. And now here I am—*Hello new boyfriend!*—looking tired and drained. There was little I could do about that now, so I put on some moisturizer, fixed my hair, and hoped for the best.

The thing I hate most about the International Arrivals section of major airports is walking out through *that door*—all those people waiting, watching, and staring. It made me uneasy even on a normal day. But this day was anything but normal: I'd staked my whole marriage, my secure life, and my entire future on this day. That damn door—what was on the other side? What was on the other side of the life I had just deconstructed? Time sped up, and I found myself going through the door, accompanied by the marching band that had taken up residency in my chest. I looked around, and through all the staring, I couldn't find Alessandro anywhere. My heart skipped a beat. *Where is he?* I tried to play it cool, but my insides were shaking. Minutes ago, I had been so afraid to see him, and now I was panic-stricken at the thought that he hadn't come. *Maybe he'd changed his mind; maybe he'd realized how crazy and sudden all this really was;, maybe he'd had a change of heart and decided to try again with his ex-girlfriend. Maybe, maybe, maybe . . .*

As my mind continued spinning in this whirlwind, I looked up and saw Alessandro at the end of the hallway. He came towards me with a smile so immense it banished every doubt. Sporting dark blue jeans and sneakers, he looked so different than in the all-white clothes I had last seen him wearing in India. He was even *better* than I remembered—taller, darker, and more handsome. Those big hands reached down, lifted my chin, and engaged me in a tsunami-like kiss that erased everything in its wake.

Our time together was a total honeymoon, complete with many delirious passages of first times that all new loves go through. We stayed in a little cabin in the mountains, in a tiny, picturesque Italian town, and played house for a week that was painfully short. It was October, but the weather was warm, and we sat for hours on the ledge of a huge window that opened up to the sun, looking down on the emerald valley below us. On that ledge, we spent hours talking about how we had surely been *brought* together, how we *had* to be soul mates, and how we would create our new life. All the boxes required for a perfect relationship were ticked off. Romance and passion? Strong! Fights? None! Sees me as the most special woman on the planet and loves me just the way I am? Of course! Thus began our relationship.

(His: When Things Fall Apart)

When things fall apart and we're on the verge of we know not what, the test of each of us is to stay on that brink and not concretize. The spiritual journey is not about heaven and finally getting to a place that's really swell. — Pema Chodron

It was just after midnight when I turned onto Sixth Avenue in Petaluma, on my way home from the airport. There were seven or eight cross streets before our little cottage, each marked with a stop sign. With each stop, I became more and more annoyed. My frustration with my life situation was somehow further provoked by these series of stops, and when the last stop sign appeared before me, something came over me and I pushed down on the gas pedal, driving right through an intersection at, maybe, fifteen miles per hour. A hundred yards down the road, I pulled my car over to park in front of our landlords' garden. I felt some form of relief, having finally done *something* "my way" instead of somebody else's way. I enjoyed this feeling for no more than ten seconds—a siren wailed behind me, flashing lights appeared in my mirror out of nowhere, and a police car stopped right behind me. *Oh Scheisse!*

My whole body contracted, and if life could have mirrored my inner state in my physical body, it would have been a four-year-old boy who handed his driver's license and proof of insurance to the visibly irate cop, and *he* would have been about ten feet tall. The officer was absolutely furious—that someone, in front of his very eyes, could drive through a stop sign at full speed. "Don't move," he yelled at me loudly, shining a strong flashlight directly into my eyes, before returning to his car. Five minutes later, blue-flashing lights broke the darkness once again, and yet another police car pulled up. Now two flashlights were shining down on me, and I was asked to get out of my vehicle. Very naturally, these policemen assumed I was drunk. In my defense, I tried to explain the circumstances in my life that had so frustrated me, and led to my driving infraction. But clearly, in their minds, they had a serious offender in front of them.

Being confronted by two huge and angry policemen was not a comfortable experience. Worried that I might provoke them even further, I decided it was best to just shut up and let them do their thing. They asked me to breathe into a breathalyzer, touch the tip of my nose, and then walk along a straight line. In the end, since I passed with flying colors, all they could do was give me a much-deserved traffic ticket for not obeying a stop sign.

Recovering from the shock of my adventure in rebelliousness, I stood on the little porch, staring at the door to the tiny white house that had so quickly turned from "our new home" into a symbol of separation. As I entered, icy hands of loneliness gripped my heart. I switched on the light, and to my surprise, found the cabin neatly arranged—I could see Neelama's feminine touch in every room. Tears welled up and gently rolled down my cheek, as my mind tried to interpret this surprise: *Does she care? Does she still love me? Did she make this so beautiful to give us a chance after all?* Then the more likely realization came to me: *No, she feels guilty and just wants to create a cozy home for Kai. This doesn't change anything*! As this was to be the case for many nights to come, I had a very restless sleep.

I woke up early, and went over to Susan and Jerome's house, just thirty feet from my cottage. They had participated in an Inner Journey workshop with us a few years before, had become our friends, and were now my landlords. As I stepped through their backdoor into the kitchen, the smell of freshly-brewed coffee filled my nostrils, evoking a sense of "home." Susan was sitting at their black kitchen table having breakfast. "Come in, Michael. Welcome back. How are you?" she said, with a compassion that soothed my aching heart. Her warmth enveloped me, and I sat down, gratefully accepting her invitation to join her for breakfast by serving myself a re-heated croissant.

"How is it to be here?" she asked gently, knowing the delicateness of the situation. Too raw to try to hide anything, I allowed my tears to well up, and shared my mixed feelings of being grateful for Neelama's home-making efforts, while still struggling to accept the sharply painful reality that she had chosen not to make it her home too. Susan listened quietly and caringly, giving me all her attention—one of the greatest gifts we humans can give to each other, and one that I needed and appreciated like never before.

During my trip to Canada, it had become clear to me that I was facing a pattern: Neelama was now the *third* woman to leave me for another man. In the midst of the inner turmoil of confusion, blame, and fear, I was graced with a clarity, whereby I knew and felt that it was time for me to face the inner demon of my fear of abandonment that had now been reactivated. And I also understood, being in the "helping profession" myself, that I couldn't do it alone.

I looked around for help. With Faisal still in Europe, I reached out to our friend, Amrit, who had brought us to India. By chance, he had returned from his trip and happened to be in our neck of the woods. Quite shocked about the turn of events between Neelama and me, he said he was willing to offer us a couple's session. I was grateful that Neelama actually agreed to participate in it. Sitting together, in the living room of the cottage that was supposed to have become our new home, I tried not to do anything that might threaten the withering possibility that we could repair the relationship and move forward together. Many previously withheld issues came to the surface, and at some point I looked at Neelama and said, "I know I have made mistakes, was not there for you enough, and was sometimes controlling and an ass. But you know me, I am committed to look at "my stuff," and own it, and take action on it. I knew we were in trouble, and that's why I pushed for us to go to India in the first place. I want to be with you. I am committed to do whatever it takes to heal our relationship."

Amrit's invitation to brainstorm possibilities for continuing our marriage sparked hope in me: *Maybe, if we work together on this, we could still make it happen . . . just maybe.* After a long pause, Neelama looked up and said simply, "I don't *want* to work on this relationship." It landed like a cannonball on the deck of our already sinking "relation-ship" and left a huge gaping hole. First stunned, then shaken, I felt no hope left. As I looked into Neelama's eyes, shame and rejection burned in me with an intense heat, and then a shock wave of deep fear passed through me. *She is really leaving. Oh my God!*

After this session, the reality sank in even deeper, and I turned to my friends to create a support network. At its base were Susan and Jerome, who became my first line of support. In the following nine months I spent many hours in their kitchen, while they listened to me recount my story and express my feelings, sometimes feeding me and sometimes just holding me. I knew how lucky I was to have this loving couple right next door. I soon realized that it was necessary to dive even deeper into my inner abyss, and called on my dear friend, Howard, whose presence and wisdom allowed the profound inward journey that was yet to unfold.

Howard and I had met seven years before, and had started out in a student-teacher relationship. He was a highly successful D.C. business professional, who became a participant in our Inner Journey seminar. He had fallen in love with the work, adopted me as his teacher, and soon decided to embark on the process to be trained as an Inner Journey facilitator, in order to teach the program himself. During the training period, which lasted about two years, our relationship had progressed to a deep friendship, and a partnership in the running of the Inner Journey business. When I reached out to Howard for support, he responded immediately, with an incredible commitment to support me day and night if that were needed. I knew, from my work with people, that the worst of a client's turmoil had often subsided by the time they arrived for a session. When I most needed the non-judgmental presence of a loving human being, was when I was right in the middle of the "inner muck," and that could not be planned or scheduled. Most of my female friends were also close friends with Neelama, and I expected they might naturally see things more from her perspective. So, when Howard was not available, I felt I needed to turn to my other male friends, to create an emotional "emergency network" for myself.

A few days after the failed *relationship rescue attempt* with Amrit, Neelama dropped another bomb. She told me she would be flying to Italy for ten days at the end of September, to visit Alessandro. So far, we had managed the caretaking of Kai in alternating weeks. Now she wanted me to extend my week with him by a few days so that she could have more time in Italy. Difficult as it was, I put up no resistance, probably in the vain hope that, through not fighting her, I might gain some points for the future—my hidden hope for reconciliation was still alive against all odds.

Just before Neelama was to catch the bus to San Francisco Airport for her flight to Italy, the three of us had a picnic together in a little park in downtown Petaluma. We actually had a very sweet time—my little family together again—and I felt how very precious this was to me. After Neelama headed out to the airport, the pain hit me doubly hard. She was off to be with her lover, while I was enabling her to go by staying at home to care for our boy. Her trip to

Italy, the land of romance, now threw me into a whirlwind of jealousy like never before in my life. My mind started doing what all minds do in a fit of jealousy: fantasizing. Those fantasies were mostly about what I imagined she might be doing in the land of *amore*—hot, passionate sex in a myriad of exotic ways. This was always followed by spurts of heart-breaking pain and bursts of hot anger.

It amazed me to see the extent to which jealousy was a kind of mental self-mutilation. Even knowing that it would cause me more hurt to imagine my wife having sex with another guy, the thinking mind still went there . . . over and over again. The "mind machine" gave me breaks only when it calculated the time difference in Rome and knew that they were very likely sleeping. It was the jealousy and pain that birthed the support system I created, starting with daily check-in calls with Howard, whenever I found myself overwhelmed by the obsessive imagining of the "lovebirds in Italia." In the following month, usually when Kai was asleep or in pre-school, after having shared with a friend one of the ongoing and intense emotional episodes I was experiencing, I would close my eyes and try to focus on what was happening for me, besides my never-ending obsessive thoughts—the sensations in my physical body.

During the first six months of my separation from Neelama, this became my journey, with the help of my friends and teachers: to face the pain in the core of my body that my thinking mind tried so hard to avoid. Describing this painful period might give the impression that I was constantly crying and wailing on the couch. But no, I *had* to function and *did* function. Besides my devoted friends, I had another "savior" in the form of a two-year-old toddler, who was just learning to walk and was very dependent on his "Papa" to take care of him—my beautiful son, Kai.

Chapter Twelve:
The Rose

(Hers: Creation and Destruction)

Ten days after I arrived in Italy, I bid a heart-wrenching goodbye to Alessandro, and got on the plane to go back home. Michael had sent an email telling me he wanted to pick me up, and was waiting to greet me at the airport in San Francisco. Standing outside the door from the baggage claim area, he looked exhausted, and clung to a single rose as if it were his last hope. He seemed broken—cracked in two by life, by love, by me. There was no denying the depth of his grief, and seeing it only excavated the guilt I'd been trying so hard to bury. My insides ached knowing that I was the cause of this pain. He handed me the rose, and I felt its meaning in my hands—the weight of so many desires, none of which I would fulfill. I would not return his affections; I would not do more work on the relationship; I would not stop seeing Alessandro; and I would not give our marriage a second chance. My arm went limp, and the flower with it, revealing what I already knew: I had forsaken my old world, and entered another. Alessandro was my hope now. With him there would be no disappointments, I told myself, just a never-ending expansion of the love and passion we so clearly shared.

Michael put my bags in the car, and we drove the familiar road north towards San Francisco. We talked mostly about Kai and our work, but I was a thousand miles away . . . sitting on that ledge with Alessandro, dreaming our dreams in the warm sun, starting our new life together. That's where I wanted to be, not in the car with all this pain. I had to force myself to keep returning to the car, to Michael, and to the forlorn flower at my feet. It was grueling to feel Michael's desperation and know there was nothing I would do to fix it.

Doing nothing was not my usual response to people's pain—it actually went against the grain of my entire personality. From a young age, I learned to find my value and worth from pleasing others. I wanted to be seen as the one who cared, the one who was always there for people. What looked, on the outside, like helping was really just an illusion, an age-old compensation mechanism to make me feel that I mattered, that I was needed, and that people loved me. I always felt I had to be *doing* something to earn people's love—and that something was always some version of making them happy. To *not* follow this instinct with my own husband challenged my entire identity as a "good person." My ego tried to compensate for this threat, telling me that I deserved to be happy, that I was a withering flower who had been deprived far too long, and that it was *my time* to have love and passion again. This helped on a mental level, but did nothing for the guilt that ate away at my insides.

We made small talk all the way to the Golden Gate Bridge. As we crossed the huge red structure, which glowed as the sun sank into the bay, we both became quiet. Driving north on Highway 101, we passed the familiar towns of Marin County, which held so many memories for us. We finally reached Novato, and as we pulled into my driveway, I looked down to find my ring finger staring back at me in its nakedness. I had removed my rose gold wedding band before the trip. Michael had not wanted me to take it off, but I couldn't bear going to Italy wearing it, *feeling* married. The ring was all alone inside my jewelry box, just a few steps away. I knew for certain that, after this trip, I wouldn't be putting it on again. Even if we weren't legally divorced, in my heart, my marriage to Michael was over.

We went inside, and Kai came barreling into my arms, reminding me that I was a mother. Michael said his goodbyes to us, and Kai and I got ready for bed. The little "Boo" was so happy to have me back, and clung to me with a joy and innocence that eased some of the pain from the car ride home. He knew nothing of wedding rings, or roses, or the death of a marriage. Part of me longed to be that innocent again. As Kai lay beside me in bed, using my arm as his favorite pillow, with his tiny body pressed against mine, I wept and prayed that we could all get through this separation with as much grace and love as possible.

A few days later, Michael and I sat on the front steps of his cottage talking about how we were going to maintain our business together through this difficult time. It was the middle of October, but it still felt like late summer in the air. I looked around at the dry earth, burned golden from summer's fiery sun. The heat was a blessed relief on my skin, bringing some warmth to a raw and sensitive conversation. Since the birth of Kai, Michael had become the primary provider, and I had been mostly at home. It had been almost two-and-a-half years now, and I was beyond ready to return to work. Our separation was the catalyst to put that in motion. We needed to begin the arduous task of creating a parenting schedule that would allow each of us to work enough so that we could support ourselves. We decided to alternate caring for Kai every week, which gave us each two weekends a month to teach. It was an equal sharing of the responsibility, and the part of me that had always wanted our co-parenting to be 50/50 finally felt vindicated. Michael picked up on my emotion, "Finally you've got what you always wanted," he said, "You resent us, and now you've got us out of your life."

For me, it wasn't that simple. Yes, I had moments of feeling resentment towards Michael, and even Kai, although I had a hard time admitting that. The past couple of years had taken a heavy toll on me. I was exhausted from the daily "job" of mothering. I wished it were different, I longed for it *not* to feel like work, for it to be joyful, for it to be how I assumed it was for other mothers. But a lot of the time it just wasn't, and a part of me did resent that. I didn't know what to do with this feeling.

We muddled through the rest of the conversation, stumbling and bumping into each other, and came to an agreement that it was best to do as little work together as possible . . . with one exception. We had spent the last eighteen months creating a brand new workshop, called The Immersion, with four colleagues who were also dear friends. The workshop was scheduled to take place at the end of the month, and there was no turning back now. It would last nine days, and Michael and I would have to find a way to facilitate together, while keeping our personal issues away from the participants. Our co-facilitators had offered to support us during the workshop as we navigated through this difficult terrain.

The next step was to let our communities know what had transpired. Over the previous seven years, we had created Inner Journey communities in three cities across the United States and one in Canada. These were groups of people that loved our work and hosted us on a regular basis to facilitate various workshops. Structures had been created for people to gather and be supported in-between the courses we offered. We had many dear friends in these cities, mini-families so to speak, and hundreds of others who had been in our workshops and knew us personally. In our roles as facilitators and teachers, many of them held us in high regard, and some of them quite naturally projected authority figures or their version of idealized parents onto us. We knew that our separation would cause ripples for quite a few of our students. It was important that the news come from us. As the afternoon sun gave its farewell, we sat at the little kitchen table in Michael's cottage and composed a heartfelt email in the midst of our storm.

Writing this email was one of our best moments in the early months of our separation. It gave us a bigger perspective on things, a view which we had lost so many times along the way. Pain will do that—the hurts of the heart take us over more often than not, as Michael and I knew all too well. He fluctuated from anger and blame to deep love and compassion, and everything in between. I vacillated from guilt and shame to justifying myself for leaving him. Sometimes he pulled the "guilt card" on me, telling me how damaging this separation was for Kai, although I was quick to react, saying Kai was fine and showing no signs of distress. At that time, I wouldn't let myself begin to consider that, in addition to all the pain I was causing Michael, I was also hurting my own son. So I defended myself, insisting that Michael was projecting all of his issues onto Kai. In the end, I came to see that the truth was somewhere in the middle of his attack and my defense.

During those months, I felt so split apart inside. Half of me was living this new life of building something together with Alessandro, the other half was going through the death of my life with Michael and our family unit. Creation and destruction were living side-by-side in my tiny heart, and some days it felt like it would explode.

Alessandro and I were starving for more contact, and decided to meet in New York City. Something about that city seemed exciting and romantic. It was almost a halfway point between us in distance, and it would be relatively easy for me to steal away for a few days. I could use my frequent flier miles, and had found us an inexpensive place to stay. It would work. We planned this reunion to immediately follow the nine-day workshop in a few weeks time. For me, it couldn't come soon enough.

The date for The Immersion workshop arrived, and I was anxious about how it would unfold. Michael and I had been living apart for six weeks at that point, and the thought of spending nine days together again terrified me. At the same time, the space we were about to enter was sacred for us both. It was in guiding others to connect with their deepest selves and their Divine Source, where we felt the most at home and fulfilled. Over the years, in the space of these workshops that we were blessed to call our livelihood, we had experienced our most profound connections as a couple. Where Michael and I met the most deeply was in our love and devotion for God, which was the specific theme of this nine-day workshop. We were called upon to be our best selves in those days, and were asked by the circumstances to set our own issues aside many times in order to "be there" for others. It was a bittersweet experience, feeling our deep love and connection solidified on the spiritual level, and at the same time, feeling our marriage and family unit being deconstructed on the human plane.

Within hours of finishing The Immersion, I was on a red-eye flight to New York. I had brought my favorite pillow with me in hopes that I could sleep on the plane, but it was doubtful I would be able to calm down enough to rest. Since Italy, I'd counted down the days to this moment—boarding the next plane that would take me to my love. The butterflies in my stomach had flown the coop, spreading out to occupy my whole body. I vibrated with an excitement that made it difficult to do anything, let alone sleep. But I squeezed my pillow into that space between my seat and the window and closed my eyes anyway, letting the buzz in my body give way to thoughts of what it would be like to see Alessandro again. Somewhere after the bumps over the Rockies, I must have dozed off, because the next thing I was aware of was bright light streaming in through the window as we approached JFK. The sun was blazing in full glory as the plane touched down, and I felt such joy knowing, that in a matter of minutes, I would be in Alessandro's arms. His plane had landed before mine, and I knew from his text message that he'd be waiting at my gate.

I couldn't get off the plane fast enough, and walked excitedly towards my prince, who stood there ready to receive me. Seeing him always produced such a rush of warm, tingling energy in my body.

He looked relaxed and totally self-assured, standing there in jeans, a crisp white shirt, and those sexy black boots. *How did he manage to look so good after a night flight from Europe?* His long black hair was pulled back in a ponytail that looked like it had been washed and styled moments ago. Seeing him, I was reminded that he was . . . perfect. And those eyes, those dreamy eyes . . . they found mine and claimed me as their own. Our bodies met and he swallowed me up with a giant embrace that felt eternal. I could hear the airport buzz around us, but I didn't care—let people come and go, brushing by us as they shouted on their cell phones. All that mattered was this embrace, his strong arms and big hands, and that soft chest into which I wanted to burrow myself forever.

Like excited teenagers, we jumped into a taxi and headed for our hotel, where we spent a whirlwind five days together. Our bodies were never separate, even while eating mountains of pizza. We stayed in bed to our hearts' content, getting reacquainted with each other. Our chemistry still proved to be fantastic, and once again, I felt sexually reawakened after the desert I'd been in over the past couple of years. When we did feel like eating, there was a restaurant right next door to our hotel that was a typical New York diner. The diner phenomenon didn't exist in Italy, and Alessandro was like a kid discovering candy for the first time. We sat across from each other in the neon blue booth, and I watched him fall in love with American food. He was in sheer delight over the notion of an all-day breakfast, and in awe at the discovery of pancakes, French toast, and waffles, all of which he gobbled down to replenish the calories we had burned that morning. We sat there for hours in our little booth, just talking and listening to the sound of each other's voices.

In the afternoons we took long walks in the warm sun—New York in the fall is stunning—and we roamed through Central Park, gushing at the vibrancy of the leaves. Being in this state of new love, it didn't really matter *what* we did, as everything was coated in a sense of bliss. Drenched with this feeling that somebody loved me so intensely, I felt wrapped up in a blanket of contentment. This put me in an altered state—on a high unlike anything I'd ever experienced. We talked incessantly about the new life we wanted to build together, fantasizing about all that we would create. We were completely drunk on love.

Those days, like everything else, came and went—it was suddenly time to say the dreaded goodbye. As we rode the subway back to the airport, everything began to look gloomy, and our bodies started to slump over in response to the ominous ending that lay at the end of those tracks. Curled up next to each other on the cold, hard seats, I grabbed hold of Alessandro in defiance, protesting the reality that, in just a few minutes, we would have to say farewell. My body ached and tears fell from my eyes as I imagined the pain. Through my choked voice, I vowed to him that we would meet as soon as possible. We needed a ray of hope, and suddenly, the idea to meet over Christmas was born as the perfect antidote to our sadness. Alessandro offered to fly me to Italy. There were a multitude of obstacles to making that happen, the first and foremost being Kai and Michael, but the thought of it pacified me anyway, and I released my grip on his arm. When we arrived at the airport, we lingered as long as we could, sitting on the marble floor for a tearful goodbye, holding on to the hope that we would be together again in December.

The flight home was grim, and once I got there, I found things there were in bad shape. Michael, in a conversation with my mom, had lost his temper and gone on a rampage about what a terrible person I was. I felt betrayed and attacked. Then there were the nasty emails he sent me, which began arriving with ever-greater frequency and intensity. Those email messages became the battleground for our separation. I guess some couples scream at each other in the kitchen, or on the phone. For us, the battle took place largely through email. He would send over a big cannonball, and I would fire back. Who knew that one could wage a war with black letters typed on a white screen.

At the bottom of all our fighting was the same basic issue: Michael was deeply wounded by the way I had left—flinging him aside and running off to begin my new life with Alessandro, without ever giving our marriage a second chance. This was the knife in his heart. I didn't understand the depth of his pain at that time, especially since it was often not his hurt that got communicated to me, but rather his "beast"—the part of the personality that, when we are deeply hurt, just wants to hurt back. According to Michael, I didn't take responsibility for the severity of the pain my choices were causing our family.

Looking back now, it's easy to understand that Michael's attacks came precisely because he was in so much pain. Yet at the time, I felt attacked, and pulled out my own sword in defense. What was I defending exactly? My self image. His onslaught of judgments threatened my image of the good and caring person I had strived so hard to become. I couldn't bear to be seen as selfish and uncaring, nor to see myself in this way. And thus began my rationalization campaign—an obsessive attempt to justify my actions. My replies to his emails became line-by-line comebacks to every accusation he threw my way. I tried desperately to redeem myself in his eyes, and ultimately in my own. The mind has a funny way of constructing everything to fit its story, and my mind found a way, over and over again, to prove my innocence: I was doing the appropriate thing by starting my new life with Alessandro, and I had done nothing wrong by leaving our marriage and pulling our family unit apart.

I found anyone around me who would corroborate this story, and had long conversations with friends, leading them to agree with me about how terrible my marriage was and how *of course, this was just bound to happen.* It was as if the part of me that felt so guilty was running around to get others on its team. I felt this team backing me up as I imagined approaching Michael, saying, *See, see? I was so unhappy, everybody saw it!* In my fantasies, he would finally see the light and admit it: *Yes, you are right, you are not to blame; this is all my fault.* Those would be the words that would release me from the shame I felt inside. This never happened, and it wasn't until much later that I realized that it had all been my ego's trick to bypass my own sense of guilt and responsibility, as well as a feeble attempt to maintain my "good person" image. Those tactics were temporary, like a Band-Aid that provided some surface comfort . . . until the next angry email arrived in my inbox.

One of the mistakes I made when I returned from New York, was springing my ray-of-hope Christmas idea on Michael, asking him to change our parenting schedule for the holidays. Michael deeply resented the idea that he had to adhere to *any* kind of schedule with Kai. Every discussion about the schedule was heavy and charged. And so, when I launched into the Christmas conversation, he exploded. Looking back at that, I can't believe how insensitive this was of me. It was way too soon, just a few months after our breakup, for me to think of spending that Christmas in Italy. Christmas was Michael's favorite holiday, and it was unthinkable to him, at that time that I would not be with Kai at such a special time. For me, Kai was still way too young to understand Christmas, but I would have been happy to delay my trip until after Christmas just to placate Michael. Yet it was too late for that—too much damage had been done, and the die was cast. We debated long and hard for a couple of months about the Christmas trip, and Alessandro was burdened with every detail of that debate. One day I was going to Italy, the next day I was not; one day I suggested Alessandro should just come here, the next day Michael said *no way in hell* to that idea. On and on this went until, by the time it was settled that I would go to Italy for two weeks over Christmas, Michael and I were two weary and wounded soldiers walking off a bloody battlefield, barely able to look at each other.

Our email fights exhausted me. So after those weeks of our heated online battle, I asked that we cut all communication for two months. I was in dire need of a break from the constant back-and-forth.

Daily life with Kai had normalized into an every-other-week rotation between us which, to be honest, was one of the greatest benefits of the separation for me. It felt, and still feels, taboo to admit that, but for the first time since Kai's birth, I was finally getting the break I so badly needed, some semblance of a routine, and the return of my work-life and independence. This did, I believe, make me a better mother. The resentment I held towards Michael, and even towards Kai, had lifted and I could more fully enjoy my time with my son. During the week, we spent quite a bit of time driving to and from daily therapy appointments, as well as to daycare and his special needs playgroup. I set up a little table in his bedroom, where we practiced the exercises given to us by Kai's speech therapist to strengthen the muscles in his tongue and mouth. Kai's speech was still severely delayed, and he was diagnosed with Speech Apraxia: a condition that causes a breakdown between the brain and the tongue, making it extremely difficult to talk. Every night we practiced these exercises, in hopes of increasing his ability to make simple sounds . . . sounds that I had taken for granted my entire life.

By two and a half, Kai was able to walk more, and on weekends we started going to the park to feed the ducks and romp around in the playground. I squeezed myself into the tiny slides and stairwells made for little people, helping him climb onto the play structures, as he squealed with glee. With a lot of assistance, Kai got around pretty well and never wanted to leave. As I watched him take ten minutes to climb the stairs that the other kids ran up in seconds, I couldn't help but wonder what the future would bring: *Would Kai ever walk, talk, or function like other kids?* These thoughts only made me anxious, so I tried stuffing them into my pocket—where they would remain until our next outing, when the harsh contrast between Kai and other children would stare me in the face again. But I could also feel the gifts of Kai's condition, especially recently, when life had become easier for me. The biggest gift was witnessing the immense joy and innocence he seemed to exude. For him, life had but one purpose: PLAY! I laughed when I realized how much time and money I'd spent on my own therapy and spiritual endeavors in search of Life's great meaning. Could it really be that easy? Kai certainly had so much to teach this student called Mommy.

(His: Encounters with the Shadow)

Unfortunately there can be no doubt that man is, on the whole, less good than he imagines himself or wants to be. Everyone carries a shadow, and the less it is embodied in the individual's conscious life, the blacker and denser it is. If it is made conscious, one always has a chance to correct it. But if it is repressed and isolated from consciousness, it never gets corrected.

— Carl Jung

Desperation leads a man do foolish looking things. Those were such painful days and nights, knowing Neelama was in the arms of her Italian lover boy. And still, I volunteered to pick her up upon her return. There I stood, next to my little Mazda van in the pick-up lane outside the San Francisco Airport, holding one single red rose in my hand. My body shivered from the cold Pacific wind and in fearful anticipation. When Neelama exited the baggage claim area, the first thing I did was hand her the rose—empty of words, but full of my yearnings and hopes and apologies. As might be expected, Neelama was a bit taken aback—visibly stunned and not so subtly unresponsive to this act of desperate gallantry. The ride home was painful and awkward to say the least.

While it was, in a sense, hard to keep it all together, needing to function for Kai became a huge gift essential to my healing. Kai needed to be dressed, fed, entertained, and his diaper changed regularly—a routine which could be relied upon to bring me back quickly from any difficult emotional state I might fall into, to the reality of the moment, especially on occasions when Kai emitted a powerful odor indicating he needed a clean-up.

In my new role as an every-other-week single dad, I joined the ranks of millions of other parents who serve as full-time chauffeurs. In our case, the driving was to various therapies, as well as back and forth to childcare. Special needs children typically have special financial needs too, and it was essential for me to function, and to carry my end of the increased financial burden. I had to keep my business going—to continue working with clients, creating courses . . . and marketing them, often the toughest task. To offer one's skills to others as one falls apart is a herculean task. Although I frequently fell into the ditch of self-pity, ultimately I had no choice but to climb back up on the road—I just had to keep going.

When I picked up Kai for "my week," the alignment of my universe changed and I became, like every loving parent of a toddler, a servant to my child's every need. I functioned quite okay until, often suddenly, some interaction with Neelama would throw me for a loop. Either I'd get an email from her, or a phone call, or some face-to-face verbal exchange was needed when I picked up Kai, or a friend would tell me something about her and Alessandro. And then *BAM*, waves of emotion would arise and flood my body, cloud my mind, and send me into overdrive. I was still experiencing regression. The outer incidents evoked inner ones that literally took me over. Although I might drive home from one of Kai's appointment like an adult, emotionally I had become that three-year-old who had lost Mom's attention. The same deep feeling set in: *I was abandoned and no longer loved.* The real-life event with Neelama had again brought up the repressed emotions from my past. This happens often within intimate relationships because childhood was, for most of us, where a lot of the wounding happened in the first place: our first intimacy with our parents.

When I explain this principle to my students, it is often hard for them to grasp at first: that present-day situations trigger the dormant feelings of our past. It can feel so real to us that it's the current situation that's making us upset or angry. Yet it became very clear to *me* when I was on my couch in the living room, with Howard on the phone holding space, that this was not the case. After the initial waves of anger at Neelama or a particular situation subsided, I could feel that I had regressed into the emotional feeling world of a three or four-year-old, crying helplessly and hopelessly, sometimes even curled up in a fetal position with my body shaking in fear. From the outside, this might look like a hidden form of masochism, yet from my experience with clients, I knew that ultimately there was no way around it but to face the unfelt feelings directly. And I was now ready to fully commit to doing that. In prior relationship sagas of being left for someone else, I had never fully gone to the bottom of the pain and hurt—I hadn't dealt with the source. The experience at the ashram in India had created a lasting determination to face myself. The image the teachers had used to describe this aspect of the spiritual journey, was to be willing to "put one's head into the tiger's mouth," the tiger representing the unfelt pain of our past. The determination I'd found in India proved never to have wavered—I wanted to stop running, and I did stop running.

The fact that Neelama left me for another man added another dimension: I was also really hurt in my male pride. Accentuated by the age difference between Alessandro and myself, it felt as if a younger bull had come along and taken my mate. She preferred *him* over me, the older bull in the pasture. When I knew she was with him, I felt as if the mask of my male identity had been pierced by a sword. Self-doubting thoughts about my sexual prowess would snake their way through the dark and winding tunnels of my mind. Having worked with many men over the previous fifteen years, I knew how sensitive and insecure the male psyche could be, however machismo its outward appearance. Now I was experiencing that same uncertainty myself—an inner wobbliness, arising from my own self-doubt. *He must be a better lover than I. Maybe he has a "bigger one." Maybe he can satisfy her better . . .* and so on.

Beyond potency doubts, an overall self-doubt permeated my thoughts, ultimately leading to inner questions of self-worth. *Something must be wrong with me. Otherwise, why is she with him?* When that thought train wasn't interrupted by a session with Faisal, or work with Howard on the phone, or a clearing conversation with a friend, it led to low energy, and at times depression took hold. In those moments, I didn't want to do anything—I withdrew, or stayed in bed. I assume most people have experienced something like this at some point in their life, but for me, this was the first time I had remained in that state for any length of time. Neelama and I both had to explain many times, and to many different people in our circles, what had happened, what was happening, and where things would go from there. For me it was all too easy to slide into the storyline of the victim, the "poor me," the man who was betrayed by his disloyal wife, the man whose wife had an affair and was leaving him behind, breaking the family apart. Even if I didn't consciously intend to make Neelama look bad (*that* happened later), I know that, unconsciously, it felt good for my wounded self to be seen as the victim and she as the perpetrator. And in my bleeding heart, I felt truly helpless, and not in control of the situation. I desperately wanted to save the marriage and our family while, as she had so clearly stated, she was *done*. Another huge piece of the puzzle was revealed sometime in October, when Neelama stopped in to drop Kai off at my little cottage. After Kai fell asleep, she stayed for a while and we talked about how our process was unfolding. Sitting opposite me on the couch, I recall her saying that she had felt pushed and persuaded by Faisal and me to have Kai, and now realized that something big had happened to her as a result. She admitted that, while not knowing it at the time, something in her had shut down sexually towards me, never to open again. Hearing this, I experienced first relief, and then anger. In the previous two years she had accused me many times of being the culprit in our sexual difficulties—something was wrong with *me*. And now she had become in touch with the real truth. A big wave of sadness overcame me and, when Neelama left shortly afterwards, I curled up on my couch again, with tears streaming like rivers down my face, my mind going into overdrive: *How could this have happened? All I did was fight for the life of our child!* And then more defensive thoughts came in: *Faisal didn't push her; that's not true; she came to the decision to have Kai by herself. No, I didn't want the abortion, and was fighting that, but I didn't force her to have the baby. How could I have? In the end it was her decision. And now she tells me that this is when she started to shut down towards me? That I set this in motion with wanting our child? Perhaps my uttering the desperate threat "if you have an abortion, our marriage will be over" had much more of an impact than I'd ever intended.*

Sharing this experience later on with my friend, Doug, he stated the blunt truth: "You got your way; you won the battle. You got your boy; and you lost his mother." His simple naming of the bare facts hurt, and yet I couldn't deny the truth of it. I realized that, from the first moment of Kai's existence, I had chosen the well-being of the child over Neelama's. The old proverb, "the road to hell is paved with good intentions" had manifested itself in my life.

Because we had furnished the cottage together, but Neelama had never moved in, she needed to pick up the things she had left there. Not wanting to be home when she arrived, I called Amrit, who lived in the foothills of the High Sierra, and invited myself up for a visit. Generously, he and his wife hosted me for a few days in their home. My friends were incredibly caring, and held space for me whenever the waves of the separation process arose. Clare in particular, Amrit's wife, gave me a great deal of motherly attention and nourishment. On the last day with them, I decided to take refuge in Mother Nature, and drove up to the High Sierra. It was a gorgeous fall morning, with a wide clear-blue sky above, and Donner Lake below. I hiked up to about nine thousand feet through a grove of alpine pines, crippled in their growth by the relentless winds and the sparse nourishment of the soil. I stopped when waves of self-pity overtook me as I identified with those struggling trees that, in my anthropomorphizing mind, suffered just like me, from undernourishment and life-crippling battles. My preoccupation with thoughts of myself as the poor victim was pierced by a sudden cool fall breeze that had me put on a jacket and ushered me out of my suffering daydream into the present moment. From that moment on, I consciously made an effort to stay present with the spectacular surrounding beauty of the snow-dusted mountains and the glittering lake below. Donner Lake was named in remembrance of a tragedy during the mid-1800s western migration, in which the Donner Party of eighty-four pioneers set out for California in a wagon train, only to become trapped by heavy snow in this rugged terrain, with more than half of the group dying from starvation over the winter, and others resorting to cannibalism to survive. That sure helped put my personal woes in perspective!

As I came down from the mountains, I felt blessed by Mother Nature, who had delivered her healing balm, connected me with my physical senses, and reminded me to stay with what *is*, rather than the obsessive imaginings my mind wanted to whine about. Internally refreshed, I left my friends the next morning for the four-hour drive back home to Petaluma. Past Sacramento on I-80, close to Vallejo, it hit me that a different house was awaiting me: Neelama's furniture, books, clothing, and all the little personal touches with which she had made the cottage a home would be gone. Highway 37, connecting I-80 with I-101, would never be the same for me again. I grabbed my cell and called my friend, Doug, for emergency support. He spent the next hour on the phone with me, as this became my

"Highway of Wailing and Grieving." It's hard to understand why I never thought to stop the car, or that Doug didn't insist on it. I had never cried that intensely and for that long . . . in a car . . . while *driving*. There must have been a very alert and gracious guardian angel patrolling that piece of road along the North Shore of the Bay of San Francisco.

It was late afternoon when I arrived home. When I opened the door of the cottage, it felt empty. On entering, my feet hit the cold wooden floor, and I realized that Neelama had taken away her white rug, among many other things. Some of the pictures had also been taken away, leaving holes in the wall, just like the holes in my heart. The huge plant in our living room, which we had purchased together to serve as our first Christmas tree at Upper Road, was gone. I opened the closet and saw that all her clothes were removed. As I looked around, it struck me that there was no more Neelama in the cottage, and the full realization set in: *she has moved out . . . it's really over!*

All I could do was lie back down on my wailing couch and let the tears run themselves dry. Another layer of hope had died, leaving behind a bleak inner desert—devoid of life. It was a long time before I finally fell asleep and found a few hours of peace.

The end of October had another challenge waiting for both Neelama and myself: six of us had previously co-created a spiritual program on the theme of Spirit, God, and the Divine, which we were scheduled to facilitate together. My first thought was to demand that Neelama be excluded. Fortunately, after deep reflection, prayer, and meditation, an inner message came to me that that this would not be in the best interests of the participants. However, the nine days of this intensive immersion program was the most challenging workshop event of my life. It was heaven . . . and hell. One of the deepest connections, maybe even *the* deepest, between Neelama and me had been our shared love and passion for God.

The workshop began, and it felt so great to teach upfront, sitting next to Neelama again. It felt good to "kind of" have her back in the familiar routine of facilitating, planning, creating, and being together on a team. A few times we even hugged and held each other, which elicited a ray or two of hope. But hell was waiting at the end of every day, when I found myself alone in a single bed, knowing she was sleeping only a few rooms away. One night, my desperation took over and I found myself knocking on the door to her room. She invited me inside and I lay down on her bed, separated only by the covers. As I admitted the hell I was going through, she held me while I wept like a child. We lay there for about ten minutes, before she gently ended the embrace, indicating it was time for me to go back to my own bed.

By the end of the course, I felt badly depleted on all levels, but a two-and-a-half-year-old was waiting for me back home with his smile, hugs and needs. I had to kick in and function for Kai.

During Neelama's New York honeymoon trip with Alessandro, I was graced with an amazing experience of expansion. It happened in the parking lot of the Whole Foods grocery store. I was walking towards the entrance, when my cell phone rang. Out of the blue, right there on the pavement, Prem, my guide from India, had finally responded to my desperate pleas for help. I shared an abbreviated version of what was going on for me, and he responded with supporting words of guidance. I have no recollection of what he actually said, but a lot more must have been transmitted than just words on that call. By the time I hung up and walked into Whole Foods, everything was different for me. My chest seemed to have cracked wide open, and I was present, *really present*, with the piles of stacked apples and pears, the subtle hint of spicy cinnamon in the air, the vivid colors, and the amazing spectrum and abundance of produce. I felt deeply connected with the people around me—not just with one or two people; I felt love for *everyone* I encountered. It was nothing like the fever of romantic love for *the* one, or the warm affection between friends. This was another feeling entirely—a glowing sense of fully appreciating, caring, and loving *everyone*. I remember exchanging pleasantries with an elderly man in front of the bakery, conversing with a plump woman in the fresh produce aisle, joking with a teenage boy in front of the dairy section, and chatting with a gorgeous woman waiting in the checkout line next to me . . . and for all of them, I felt the *same* love. A warm, caring vibration in the middle of my chest seemed to emanate, ripple, and flow towards everyone around me. Twenty-five years earlier, one of my earliest mentors, Jeru, told me that "real love" is like a light bulb—it shines for everyone . . . not just for one special person, one's family members, close friends or countrymen, but for every being on the planet. That was exactly the love I felt in the unlikely surroundings of a grocery store. An unforgettable shopping experience!

One of the key teachings of Buddhism is that "nothing is permanent," as I was to experience a few hours after my shopping excursion. But I have never forgotten the blissful experience of impersonal love that graced me on that day.

A few days later, the extreme roller coaster ride of my emotional journey continued with a huge swing of the pendulum to the opposite side of love. My guess is that, as long there was some faint hope in my unconscious that I might win Neelama back, the negative emotions were not fully allowed to surface. This changed as the late autumn days grew shorter, and with it, my capacity to contain my anger. Now, whenever my thoughts dwelt on the fact that Neelama was "done," and had moved on into a budding new romance, the underbelly of my emotional world would show itself.

The conscious part of me, which understood that the recent challenging events were life's way to have me grow and learn, sat on the sidelines, while "the shadow," as Swiss psychologist Carl Jung called it, took center stage. As December came around, "Mr. Understanding," who had vainly continued his hope that the relationship could be saved, was fired and "Mr. Want to Hurt Back" had come out of the shadows to replace him.

One night, while Kai was sleeping peacefully, his far-from-peaceful dad was pacing back and forth in the living room like a wild animal looking for blood. *I want to hurt you, bitch. I want to cause you pain, and him too, that asshole.* My fuming and fantasizing led to images of me driving to her house and stabbing her tires, then trampling on top of her car, enjoying each new dent in the roof, imagining her coming out in the morning, and then savoring the shock and fear on her face . . . *Yeah!* When the rant was over, my emotions had subsided and I felt cleared.

Through my extensive work with Faisal, I had been blessed with an understanding of this shadow side that lurks within me, and within everyone. I knew the important difference between letting myself go into the inner feelings and imaginings of it, versus really acting it out externally. Faisal described the human psyche as having a series of layers, three of which relate to our shadow side. These were called the Jackal, the Alien, and the Beast. In short, the Jackal layer shows up as agitation, frustration, sarcasm, and hostility, and this layer had leaked into many of my communications with Neelama during the past months. As it became clear that she would not be coming back, a deeper layer began to emerge—the Alien, which manifested itself as a hot and fiery energy that wanted to lash out and hurt Neelama. Its name is reflective of the creature in the movie *Alien* that unexpectedly lunged at its victims from zero to a hundred in a split second. By the beginning of December 2006, the deepest of the three layers had arisen: the Beast. This was the part in me that had plotted to put a knife in the tires of Neelama's car, and had enjoyed planning how that would hurt her. As far as I know, this Beast layer exists in all humans. It's the part that, when deeply hurt, contemplates how best to hurt back. It's the cold-blooded "planner," seeking revenge. It's the part in us that waits, coiled like a snake, for the right moment to strike, to deliver the most deadly blow. On a collective level, the "Beast" manifested in the 9/11 attack on the World Trade Center. The events of the last months had now unearthed that raw and even scary layer in me like never before.

The most important part of this teaching was the notion that *underneath* all of these shadow layers was a core wound. Once my hopes of getting Neelama back had died, and my abandonment was triggered, the Beast arose in order to protect me from experiencing that pain. I had observed this protective mechanism in myself before. Rather than feel the wound directly, I found myself attacking the other person, as I was doing now with Neelama. There is, in fact, no other area of human life that evokes these shadow layers more than an intimate relationship. One of my teachers once said, "Love brings up anything but love." Now I found myself the living proof of that—the cold-hearted Beast in me was leaking out all over the place.

So it was no wonder that, by the middle of December, Neelama had blocked me from her email list. I was forced to communicate with her via a mutual friend, who was given discretionary powers to censor my writings before passing them on. This activated my resentments and infuriated me even more. Feeling cut off from being able to "hurt" her back, the Alien part in me was furious, exploding in hot anger like a volcano spewing out hot molten lava. This part in me felt so deeply that Neelama deserved to feel the same kind of hurt I was enduring. Years before, I had worked with a client who had coined his own word for this aspect of the personality, "The Hit Man," and now I got to experience from within what he meant.

Fortunately, throughout all this, there was still a sane and aware part of me alive, nurtured by daily meditation, prayer, and ongoing support from Howard and Faisal. The line remained clear between fantasy and acting-out physically; the need for lashing out verbally was eventually sated; and the worst of the anger and resentment finally subsided. Through the crisis period, however, I came to understand why there is so much domestic violence between couples when going through a separation. *Love brings up anything but love* was a phenomenon I was personally experiencing.

Chapter Thirteen: Joy and Pain

(Hers: Romeo is Mortal)

Right before my Christmas trip to Italy, Alessandro dropped a bomb on me: he had committed to leading a weekend workshop in France, and an evening class in Milano, while I was visiting, which meant our trip would need to be structured around both of those events, resulting in less time for us to be together. I had a huge reaction to this. One of the pains I'd felt in my relationship with Michael was that I felt he often put work or something else above me. I never felt like I was his priority, and Alessandro's change of plans pushed that very same button—*I wasn't important; I didn't matter.*

Intellectually, I knew that one of the gifts of the masculine energy was to have a sense of purpose. It was clear that Alessandro was following his purpose, yet I took it personally with my emotional need to be number one on his list. I think this is a common challenge that shows up in relationships. In most relationships, there is interplay of the two core energies of life: what the Chinese call "yin and yang." It is the polarity of these two energies that creates the spark—the attraction. The partner who embodies more of the yang principle, Alessandro in this case, often places the need for purpose over the need for relationship. For the partner who embodies more of the yin principle, the need for relationship usually dominates. The challenge is that we unconsciously expect that the other has the same priority of needs that we do. When our partner doesn't match our expectations, we take it personally, not understanding that there's a deeper dynamic involved that is actually impersonal. This common misunderstanding was part of what fueled my intense reaction.

Looking back, I can see that my reaction also stemmed from circumstances in my childhood, mostly regarding my dad, who moved away when I was very young. As an adult, I can understand why he made that decision, and how that decision had nothing to do with his love for me. Yet, as a child, I couldn't comprehend, in my little head, why my dad would live so far away if he loved me. *Was something wrong with me? Was I not important, not good enough? Did I not matter?* And even though I knew with certainty that my Dad loved me dearly, that little girl inside still reared her insecure head from time to time, particularly in these kinds of instances. Suddenly, Alessandro, my Romeo, the one who cherished me above all else, became imperfect. Up to that moment, I really believed that, with him, I would never have to feel unimportant again. A crack began to form in the rose-colored glasses through which I'd been looking at him.

This crack deepened on that Christmas trip to Italy, as I experienced a side of him that came as a complete shock to me. I learned, fairly quickly, that passion in one domain meant . . . well, passion everywhere! It seemed our passion had begun to spread from the bedroom into other parts of our relationship. This resulted in heated arguments between two egos that desperately wanted to be right, and shared a similar kind of stubborn pride. The first argument took place just days into the trip. I had attended the meditation workshop that Alessandro and his friend, Luca, were teaching in France. During this workshop, one of the participants went into trauma and began to disassociate from her body. I recognized the signs immediately, having seen it many times before in my own workshops, and went over to offer her support. This helped the participant to return to present moment consciousness. I spoke with her afterwards, as I had been trained, to explain what had happened and to make sure she was okay, but the episode was never addressed formally in the workshop setting.

Later that night, while Alessandro, Luca and I were having pizza, I wanted to talk to them about what had happened. I knew they were relatively new to teaching workshops, and I thought my experience in dealing with such an episode could be helpful to them. I remembered that, in the beginning of my own career as a facilitator, I knew nothing about dissociation or how to deal with it, and had been thankful to Michael for teaching me what to do in these situations. So, with this intent, I began, "Did you know that the woman I spent time with was disassociating during the process today?"

"What do you mean?" Luca asked.

I began to explain the basics of what I knew from the work I'd done when suddenly, midway through what I thought was extremely helpful information, Alessandro abruptly cut me off. "Nee-lah-maah," he said with condescending eyes and an accusatory tone that made my whole body tight and inflamed, "How do you know what was going on with her? You have no idea what process she was in. That is between her and the Divine. You should not interfere."

My body went rigid, and the pizza literally fell out of my hand. I was so frozen that I could not respond. But just underneath the frigid shock, I was infuriated. Had we been alone, I would have burst out, "*How dare you speak to me like that! Who do you think I am . . . some beginner in this?*" I was boiling inside, and screamed at him over and over in my head, but nothing came out of my mouth; it wouldn't, it couldn't, not with Luca there eating his pizza, oblivious to what had just transpired. I simply got up from the table and left the meal, going into our bedroom where I paced back and forth like a caged animal.

Later that night, when Alessandro came to bed, there was a cold and heavy presence in the room between us. We bickered for a few minutes, mostly him blaming me for being judgmental, and me blaming him for being so arrogant. We went back and forth and got nowhere. Neither of us was willing, or perhaps able, to understand the other's point of view. Nor could either of us admit we were wrong. In retrospect, I think that this relatively benign situation somehow evoked a deep wound in each of us. In my case, I felt completely "not seen" in my capacity as a teacher. I'd been facilitating for seven years, and yet he treated me as if I knew nothing. And I think my behavior brought up something deep for him too. This must have been the case—the hurt went so deep that we both immediately went into defense mode and our armor took us over. It seems that our armor manifested similarly in each of us: stubborn pride. Unfortunately, this standoff was to become one of our deepest and most painful patterns. All of my partners had pointed this trait out to me—my stubborn pride. And yet I had never been on the receiving end of this personality trait in another . . . until now. This gave me my first bitter taste of the harm pride can do. The ego, cloaked in it's stubbornness, will always do what it can to remain in the right: it will choose being right over being connected; it will choose its point of view over getting how it really feels for the other; it will choose its version of truth over the higher road of love. I felt the immense cost of this as I lay in bed, feeling torn apart inside.

I had fought so hard to come on this trip, moved mountains with Michael and Kai to make it a reality, and now I was in a bed with the man I loved . . . feeling so separate, but unable to surrender. *He hurt me,* I thought, *he needs to apologize first.* I was too defended to reach out, to make the contact my heart yearned for, and felt trapped within the limitations of my own personality structure. In that moment, I missed Michael terribly. Although Michael had his blind spots and his righteousness, he didn't have *that* kind of pride, and had usually been the one in our relationship who would wave the white flag in moments like this. He somehow managed to overcome his stubbornness and reach across the lines, making sure we at least cleared the air before sleeping. Alessandro, on the other hand, turned out to be more like me . . . so we lay there next to each other, digging our heels deeper into the ground, the dirt between us turning into a fortress of separation. I cried myself to sleep, feeling an immense grief. The image I'd built up—the great relationship, the man who finally "saw" me—was all starting to deconstruct, and with it came a deep sadness. I wept and wept, mourning the loss of something I'd spent my whole life believing was out there, something that every fairy tale and Hollywood movie had promised me, something I was certain I'd found in Alessandro. My face was wet with hopelessness when I finally passed out in the early dawn.

The next morning we made up, which also became part of the pattern: intense separation followed by equally intense lovemaking. Still carrying the agitation from the night before, our bodies exploded in a declaration of passion, after which we merged together—burrowing ourselves into each other's chests, softening the still-tender places with sweet kisses and oozing apologies, declaring how much we cherished one another, laughing that the egos had got the better of us, and promising never to hurt each other again. Then we were fine . . . for a few days.

An even bigger explosion happened towards the end of that trip, in Milano, where we had come for Alessandro to lead a spiritual class. We were in our hotel room getting ready for the evening, and I was feeling a bit snappy and agitated about going. My old wound was activated again—feeling unimportant. At the time I still didn't know that this feeling was the underlying force, so what came out of my mouth instead was something bitchy: "I've arranged my entire life to come all the way to Italy. Why couldn't you have found someone else to lead this class?" My remarks set off a volcanic eruption in Alessandro unlike anything I'd ever experienced with anyone before. Words hurled out of his mouth in a fury of English and Italian, finding their way to my heart like knives. He found my weakest and most insecure spots, and to those he aimed his daggers. Where Michael had criticized my behavior, or my actions, Alessandro's judgments seemed to penetrate deeper—into my very self-worth. I blocked most of it out, but some of the words I do remember being flung at me were: "You stupid, idiotic, selfish bitch. What is wrong with you? I don't want to be around you. I wish you'd never come here." After this eruption of wrath, which ended in an Italian monologue that I was, by that point, relieved *not* to understand, he went into the bathroom, slamming the door behind him.

I stood in the corner of the room, shaking, held up only by the wall behind me. Any remaining notions that Alessandro was "the one" had been eradicated in that instant, and I felt as if the ground had been pulled out from under me. I knew now that the man who I had wholeheartedly believed to be my soul mate was nothing more than any other limited human being—capable of hurting me just like anyone else. My perfect image of Romeo had been shattered, and nothing could restore it ever again.

I felt hopeless about this realization, and was suddenly deeply saddened that the idea I'd built my whole life around, the idea I'd left my marriage for, could have been destroyed so quickly and irrevocably. Desperation spread through my whole body, and I grabbed my phone in an attempt to reach out for support. With trembling fingers, I dialed my mom, praying for her to pick up. It rang and rang, with no answer. As I hung up, I looked out of the hotel window at the busy city below, feeling so afraid and so far away from home.

I dragged myself, bleeding heart and all, to the meditation class in a small room on the outskirts of Milano, with Alessandro. Neither he nor I had uttered a word since the fight. There were about fifty of us in that room, packed closely together in chairs, and, after a brief talk, the lights were dimmed and we were invited to close our eyes and meditate. In the dark and quiet room, I closed my eyes and suddenly remembered to pray. Prayer had always been a powerful vehicle for me, and I'd been blessed in my life with tangible experiences of the Divine Presence, especially when I remembered to turn towards It. During the meditation, I saw more clearly the part of me that was still looking for *that* love in all the wrong places. I was barking up the wrong tree—one that would never bear the fruit my heart craved: the constancy of unconditional love. My pattern, unfortunately, had been to try to get that inner experience of peace and love from the outer world. It never worked, and here again was another powerful reminder. I so badly wanted people, and men in particular, to give me the kind of love that only God was really capable of providing. That had been one of my biggest challenges, and became one of the most important lessons in this life—one that I'm still learning to this day.

With this realization, something suddenly softened in me, and tears of compassion poured out as I thought about all the people looking for that love. I saw Alessandro, Michael, and even Kai—all, in their different ways, searching for that presence—and I realized that, even with my best intentions, I myself was unable to provide *that* kind of love to any of them either. Tears flowed as my heart broke open for us all—limited human beings on our quest for healing, trying in countless ways to get that healing, that wholeness, *from the other*. I, like many others, had inscribed a very famous line from *Jerry Maguire* on my heart. I believed that there was a Tom Cruise out there who would one day speak those magic words: "*You complete me.*" In the middle of a meditation hall in Milano, I wept with the realization that no human being could do that for me. How can one empty bucket fill another? In that moment of connection to God, I remembered the importance of being completed by the love that was already within me. Only then could I hope to share it with my son, my partner, and my loved ones. An immense healing took place that night, as I was internally held and embraced by The One that never leaves. It soothed the tender and vulnerable spots that had been so exposed by the fight with Alessandro just hours ago. It also helped me to release my need for him to complete me . . . that was not his job.

Afterwards, back in our hotel room, we reconciled. My pride had been softened by the healing that took place, which made it possible for me to do what my ego usually resisted doing— apologize. Once I admitted my part, it opened the door for Alessandro to say that he was sorry for flying off the handle.

The next morning, at breakfast, we had a serious talk about how the trip had brought us to a new juncture in our relationship. As we ate, there seemed to be disillusionment present between us, which felt like a heavy weight. Our honeymoon had come to an abrupt end. We had officially fallen off each other's pedestal, and stood face-to-face in our humanness—all our flaws exposed. We did not, as we had naively believed, have some magical love that would ensure happiness forever. We were human, and we would hurt each other, disappoint each other, and cause each other pain. The fantasy was dissolving, and it was uncomfortable to sit there in that truth. I searched my mind, looking for other reasons why this relationship was still special and worth fighting for. We talked for hours, analyzing what had happened and attempting to resurrect some semblance of hope for our love. By the end of our long breakfast, there was an opening created where we both felt our desire to continue the relationship, and even some curiosity about what the next phase would bring.

(His: Single Fatherhood)

Although I had initially fought Neelama's request that I take Kai for two weeks, so she could be in Italy over Christmas, in the end, I relented. Off she went on her Honeymoon Part Three, evoking once again the demon of jealousy within me. The guidance I received from some of my male friends, including my brothers, was very direct: "Go out and get laid. That's the fastest way to get over it." Although the idea was sometimes tempting, I couldn't even think about dating women, given all my parenting and work commitments. In any event, a deeper part of me had decided, this time, not to look for escape routes, including looking for another woman, but to stick it out. I was grateful that my commitment to face my inner feelings remained strong.

I spent a lot of time in congested traffic on our drives down 101 south, with Kai in his little car seat, looking contentedly at his books and playing with his favorite toys. This gave us extra hours of father-son bonding time in the car, on the way to his various therapy appointments. Christine, his physical therapist, had her office on a little peninsula right next to San Quentin prison. The prison holds about two thousand high-security prisoners in the heart of Marin County, right on the Bay of San Francisco. In the Bay Area, for some reason, they liked to assign prime real estate to prisons—both Alcatraz and San Quentin are prominently situated on stunning properties. Often, after I dropped Kai off for his hour with Christine, I would walk a few hundred feet to the edge of the bay, to view San Quentin on my left and the San Rafael Richmond Bridge on my right. San Quentin symbolized for me the imprisonment I felt in my changed circumstances. The bridge represented a possible escape route. The clearer it became to me that it was all over with Neelama, the more a part of me longed to just take off and leave everything behind—to get away from anything related to her. This part of me wanted to escape the pain evoked by the unavoidable weekly contact with my son's mother. Because of my connection to Mother India, my implausible fantasy was to ride the Richmond Bridge all the way to Goa, to live a very simple life, near a warm beach on the Indian

Ocean, licking my wounds, and maybe losing myself in the arms of another woman. But then the hour was over, and a very sweet little toddler would tumble back into my arms, bringing me back to the joys of fatherhood . . . and all the duties that came with that.

As hard as it had been over the previous few months, I had adjusted to being a single father, and had created a prescribed schedule of day-to-day parenting chores, congratulating myself on having pretty well nailed it down. And then one night, Kai suddenly got sick. He began to cry like never before, and because his speech was basically expressed in only two words, Mama and Papa, asking him about what was wrong did not elicit an answer. I walked him around, holding him tightly in my arms, which seemed to provide some temporary relief. But as the evening wore on with no real diminishment of his discomfort and wailing, the more worried and fearful I became. I felt the limits of my parenting abilities, and I instinctively wanted to turn Kai over to his mommy. I guess millennia of female specialization in human child-rearing still lives on in my unconscious. At that time, with Neelama in Italy, the woman who was nearest to me was Susan next door. She became my best hope for possible rescue. I ran over to her house with my screaming boy held to my chest, feeling utterly helpless. With great relief, I placed Kai in Susan's arms. Having raised three children of her own, she was able to cite a number of potential ailments, and proceeded to systematically check for the possibilities of an ear infection, diarrhea, constipation, and a host of other typical childhood complaints. Finally, she came to the conclusion that a tooth was trying to break through his tender gums. She found a child suppository in her medicine cabinet, which she felt might soothe him, stop his crying, and put him to sleep. Miracle of miracles, her gentle care worked like a charm. I wondered whether distress and panic was my unique response in this situation, but was pretty certain that most single fathers (and perhaps some mothers too) also felt they'd reached the limits of their caregiving capacities when faced with the dilemma of a crying child who cannot be calmed. Even now, at the first sign that Kai may be getting sick, I instinctively want to turn him over to Neelama, or any other "mommy."

One of my greatest joys has been, and still is today, simply to lie next to Kai as he sleeps. The innocence, the trust, the sweetness and, yes, the *purity* of a sleeping child touches my heart like nothing else, and I feel awe and gratitude for what it means to be a father, and even more, a human being. Kai had always been a little "merger." The routine he'd developed was to sleep with one arm wrapped around his teddy bear, and then, when I joined later, the other arm wrapped tightly around my body. Sleeping beside my son every other week, merging with him in that way, gave me a healthy dose of the healing warmth of human connection, offsetting the isolation and touch deprivation I was suffering since Neelama had left. Our arrangement of alternating weeks of caring for Kai worked well for Neelama, but I was never completely happy with it. Having him leave at the end of my week felt like a deep loss each and every time. I have heard many divorced parents say they are comfortable with this kind of shared childcare set-up . . . for me, it was brutal. But, I had no choice but to accept the loss of our family threesome.

I had consciously given up on romantic love and, instead, sought solace before an altar I had created. Upon it I had placed sacred icons of Christ, Buddha, Osho, Quan Yin, and a single statue of Mother Mary, Joseph, and baby Jesus together. My teachers in India gazed at me from their pictures: Saint Francis fed his beloved birds; Krishna played his flute; Muslim prayer beads represented the tradition of Islam; and a quote from Rumi's poem, "The Guest House," brought in the wisdom of the Sufis. A single candle with the Star of David completed the collection of icons representing the spiritual traditions and teachings that I called on in prayer and meditation.

I spent many evenings in front of the TV too, looking for distraction through movies, sports, and world news. Yet my deeper nourishment always came through when sitting in prayer before my altar, either in silence in the Buddhist style of meditation, or in sound through chanting various mantras or listening to devotional music. Sometimes I talked to the altar, sometimes I cried, and sometimes I lamented. I loved sharing my life with these divine figures in the tradition that I first heard about from Stevie Wonder in the song "Have a Talk with God." This sacred altar, my beloved Kai, an amazing support network of devoted friends, and my spiritual teacher, Faisal, held me together through this dark night of my soul.

That Christmas, Kai and Papa had the good fortune to join Susan and Jerome and their three children for a five-day holiday at Incline Village, on the shores of Lake Tahoe. The Lourdes were a tight-knit and loving family; they took us into their fold and, held by their love, we had a thoroughly enjoyable holiday respite in one of the most stunning lake areas in the world. I will never forget receiving a call there from my two brothers in Germany, wishing me *Froehliche Weihnachten*, Merry Christmas. It was an astoundingly warm Christmas day, and I was standing on the shore of Lake Tahoe when my cell phone rang. As I spoke with them, I noticed the noon sun sparkling off the snow-capped mountain peaks, and the luminous surface of the lake blinding me when I turned towards it. Feeling deep love and caring from my brothers over the phone evoked the pain of the loss of my own little family unit. Sobs erupted from my throat, much to the concern of my bewildered brothers. I wondered when these emotional takeovers would end.

Chapter 14:
Jewels Along the Way:

(Hers: Revelations)

Shortly after my return from Italy, I received an email from Michael, asking me to spend his birthday with him, since I would be driving over to pick up Kai at his house. He longed for family time, a chance for the three of us to be together, as well as some time for the two of us to connect. He promised not to use this as an emotional dumping session, and so I agreed. On January 1st, I made the drive up to his cottage. As I looked out my car window at the Sonoma landscape, I noticed in myself an unusual calmness about seeing Michael. Something had shifted in me since the meditation evening in Italy, bringing a deeper compassion for the whole situation in which we found ourselves. As I entered the cottage, the little "Boo" ran towards me, jiggling with a joy and innocence that melted me into a puddle. I squeezed him hard, and he managed to endure it for a few seconds. Kai was a real wiggler, so having a sustained hug with him was a rarity. It had been two weeks since we'd been together, and this was a welcomed reunion for us both.

The three of us went on a beautiful nature walk, something Michael loved to do, and it felt like a great gift for us to be together in this way on his birthday. Later, Susan took Kai so that Michael and I could have some time alone. We sat on the couch in the cottage, sharing our respective processes over the past few months, even laughing at times. At the end of our time together, our eyes met in recognition of the authentic connection we had made between us, a connection that had been so deeply buried during the months of our ego battles. I headed home with Kai, driving south on 101, with a bittersweet feeling in my heart. It was strange—Michael still felt like the closest person in the world to me, even after all that had transpired. We shared the deepest soul-to-soul bond that I had ever known. Yet the attraction to him in a romantic way, and a desire to be his wife, had ceased. This both saddened me and gave me hope that perhaps it could be our friendship that would survive this storm. As I glanced at Kai in the back seat, I prayed that it must.

Things between Michael and I continued to ebb and flow, with the occasional inevitable eruption, either in the form of an angry email or a phone call, when the wounds would be reopened, oozing their blood into our lives again. I still carried around tons of guilt. I spent a lot of money to attend a workshop with an expert in forgiveness, in hopes of ridding myself of that weight. Despite all my attempts to forgive myself, I was still left with a gnawing ache for all the pain I'd caused Michael. I began seeing a new therapist, Rachel, that spring, who was connected to our teacher, Faisal, and worked in a similar manner. Talk therapy had done nothing for me— I needed to delve more deeply into the emotions and subconscious forces at play, and Rachel's body-oriented approach really helped with this. We explored my guilt, and she was the first person who really challenged me to take a hard look at the way I had left Michael. When I looked back at how abruptly I had left him, it brought me immense shame. My early Catholic upbringing still had a very deep influence on me, causing a feeling that I had sinned, or gone against God, by breaking my marriage vows. My reaction to that feeling made me more defensive, and my mind shouted out protests, justifying to Rachel why I *had* to do it that way. She listened, but continued to lovingly confront me, and I came to understand that all my justifications were, in some strange way, my ego's attempt to get a pardon from God. I wanted so badly to be "off the hook," to be redeemed. None of my excuses got me any further down that road towards redemption, and Rachel again asked me to simply take responsibility for what I had done, without any rationale. Redemption, in her opinion, would only happen when I admitted my mistake: that I had left our marriage without giving it a second chance, and that ending things in that way had immense repercussions . . . period. That was the real, but extremely hard, work that continued in these sessions for many months to come.

In the course of that work, I realized that leaving men in this abrupt way had become a pattern for me. Michael was the third serious relationship that I'd left suddenly, after falling in love with another man. We explored this, and began to unpack my strongly-held beliefs about love—beliefs dating all the way back to my childhood. Most of us learn about love from the first relationships in our life, with our parents or earliest caregivers. In looking at my own relationships, I realized that my earliest imprint of relating to men came from my father. My dad and I had a very unique relationship. Because he lived in Colorado, we only saw each other a couple of times a year, and so we made the most of those visits. I remembered countless holidays, Christmas in particular, where my dad and I had a whirlwind time together. He always came bearing gifts, and we'd spend our days together doing all the things I loved: going to the toy store; playing games; watching movies; sitting on his lap driving the car. Our time together was like one big, fun and exciting "honeymoon." I actually used that word once, while describing it to Rachel. She pointed out that *honeymoon* was an interesting choice of words to describe a relationship with one's father. We discovered that I, like many little girls, had fallen in love with my dad in early childhood. Sigmund Freud, the great founding father of psychoanalysis, had labeled this the "Oedipal Phase," and viewed it as a natural part of child development. During this phase, my dad became my hero, whom I idolized—the perfect man, who could do no wrong, and who made me the center of his world in those weeks we spent together. Reflecting on this in Rachel's office helped me realize that those early experiences with my dad created a lasting impression on me, and formed a strong, but unrealistic, imprint about love. Based on this relationship, I believed that love *was* this heightened honeymoon-like state, and that if a man loved me, he would me make me the center of his life. Whenever I was feeling that for a man, I'd think, *Oh, maybe he's the one!* When the romanticized feeling eventually faded, as it was bound to do in any long-term relationship, I believed that something was wrong—that love had left and the relationship was dead. And then, when another man came along who induced that high in me again, all my hopes would be transferred onto him.

After so clearly seeing my part in our marriage, I suddenly began to feel that I was the one to blame for its demise. Rachel, however, illuminated an even bigger truth: it always takes two to tango. In most separations or divorces, we spend our time fighting over who is the bad guy, and who is the good guy. Life is not that black and white, especially in relationships, where there are *two* complicated human beings. She reminded me that, although I was the one who left, i.e., walked out the door when I fell for Alessandro, there were many other determining moments that led up to that event, and those were on both of us, not just me. I was not totally responsible for the failure of the marriage—we each had our 50 percent of the pie—but I did need to be a hundred percent accountable for my half. These were deep revelations that initiated an important process inside me—I began to accept more clearly the wrong I had done, but also to release other pieces that were not mine to carry.

The long distance relationship with Alessandro continued—with a little less of the dramatic sparkle that it had in the beginning, but with the attraction between us remaining—and we managed to see each other a couple more times that spring. When he made his first trip to California, I was very worried about how he and Kai would get along. Kai took to him almost immediately. The awesome thing about Kai's brain condition was that it created an openness in him that is rare to find in normal humans. He approached Alessandro the way he approached everyone else—as a potential new best friend who, Kai assumed, was willing to do whatever he wanted. He would drag Alessandro along from this toy to that, making him play. For the most part, Alessandro was up to the challenge. He didn't feel he had a natural "father instinct," but did his best to accommodate Kai. One of Kai's greatest joys was when the six-foot plus Alessandro lifted him way up into the air—he had never been that high up before, and he squealed in glee. The biggest difficulty was that Kai assumed that life revolved around him . . . all of the time. When Alessandro visited, we had our own selfish needs for private time together, and were challenged by the need to sacrifice our romance to make more time for Kai. It was a good test of our budding relationship, and I'd say we passed.

Our passionate fighting continued to be an ongoing pattern for us, but we were better able to process things as they happened, and even learned a lot about each other along the way. In those months, the relationship became less and less rosy, but much more real. As spring ended, Alessandro invited me to attend a new program at the ashram where we had met almost one year ago. It was a new ten-day process, designed to take us further on our journey of personal growth. I desperately wanted to attend, but was financially struggling. Being a single mom, in one of the most expensive places on earth, had taken its toll. When Alessandro offered to help me, I was very grateful. However, I was unable to commit, knowing that the changes to the Kai schedule would need to be negotiated with Michael, which I dreaded. At my next meeting with Michael, I brought this topic up. He was infuriated that I planned to return to India, *our place*, with the man who had destroyed our marriage. As it turned out, Michael himself wanted to return to India to take advantage of this same new offering. He knew, however, that if he prevented me from going, I would have grounds to prevent him too—so, reluctantly, he had to agree with my plan to attend with Alessandro. I hoped and prayed that this trip back to the ashram would bring radical healing to us all.

(His: Rejection, Betrayal and Resurrection)

Back at home, New Year's Day came, and along with it my birthday. Neelama had just returned from Italy, and she came over in the afternoon to congratulate me and to pick up Kai. It was, as we say in German, a *suess-sauer* (bittersweet) moment, because I could feel that underneath all of the pain and shadow layers, there was still love between us. Maybe not the kind of love I wanted, or thought I needed from her, and yet, as we walked up the green hills of Sonoma County, I could feel it, recognizably there and palpable in its presence: *another kind of love.*

In the following months of winter, life seemed to normalize somewhat for me. The daily routine of household duties and my work brought some stability, while the frequency and intensity of my emotional ride subsided . . . although I was definitely not yet off the roller coaster. My most vivid memory of the seven-month period between January and August 2007 was Kai's morning routine. It was cold in our little cabin, and the gas heater in our corridor made this area the warmest in the house. So I put a soft blanket on the floor right next to the heater in the small hallway to do our early morning diaper change and dressing routine. Kai's physical therapist had ordered a special little blue suit for him, made of a sturdy felt material. Every morning, after his diaper change, we were required to bundle him up in this outfit, which was quite a project. It was specifically designed to stimulate Kai's nervous system, and needed to be tightly and methodically wrapped around his small body using a dozen Velcro pieces. It took between ten and twenty minutes to get him into it properly, depending on whether he cooperated or resisted, and looking back, it was quite amazing how patiently he endured this challenging ritual. The kiddo looked like a little Superman in this tight blue suit, over which he wore his normal "Clark Kent" clothes. His doctor had prescribed orthotics for him, made out of hard plastic, in which his feet and lower legs were bound. Our Superboy, in his little blue suit, missing only the *S* emblem on his chest, happily stumbled and slid around on the hardwood floor of the living room in his plastic footwear like an ice skater, bumping into the couch and table legs. It was a sheer delight to observe. Kai brought such a joy into my life, and when he was away, my life often felt cold and miserable. I began to realize that whenever I held Kai, fed him, slept next to him, or transported him around to his many appointments, it was actually *he* who was giving to *me*. Caring for my son gave meaning to my life, and a reason to get up and keep going. His oozing sweetness, and the joyousness that came through his giggles, gave me great comfort as I continued to grieve my separation from Neelama.

It is said that raising a child takes a village. Whether Neelama and I were together or not, caring for a special needs child like Kai did indeed take a village: of special needs caseworkers; various therapists; doctors; government agencies; school officials . . . and on and on. It was also required that both parents be present for many of the meetings or appointments. So, in the midst of the so-called separation process, and despite our resolve to see each other as little as possible, Neelama and I frequently *had* to come together, and function as reliable, reasonable, and responsible parents for Kai. From the longer-term perspective, it was our son who helped us get beyond our small ego-battles, and live for something much bigger: him.

One afternoon, Neelama and I met outside the office of Kai's wonderful speech therapist in San Rafael. As I watched Neelama climb up into my Mazda van, waves of nostalgia flooded through me. She looked so beautiful and radiant, and was really warm towards me, wanting to know how I was doing. Her gentle demeanor and caring voice softened me, my protecting wall came down, and at some point I blurted out, "Neelama, do you have any romantic feelings left for me? Even 5 percent? One percent?" I waited, holding my breath, looking across to the person I thought I had loved the deepest, the person whom I had shared with in the most profound ways, laughed most with, sat in the deepest silence with, exposed myself to most deeply, and had brought our little prince into the world with—the one whom, even with all that had happened, I wanted back.

These uninvited thoughts, which the shadow part of me had not allowed for so long, had finally broken through. I suddenly felt very vulnerable, and could feel my male pride cringing in the corner, utterly embarrassed. Then Neelama spoke, "I'm so sorry, Michael. No, there is zero." This was said in a whisper, showing me that she knew the answer would hurt me. Nonetheless, the message pierced my heart like a long, sharp dagger. Feelings of shame and wounded pride followed—for having exposed myself by even asking the question. *"I told you so!"* a voice screamed inside, *"you got exactly what you deserve for being so stupid as to ask."* My shadow's wall came up again. Rejection—only nine letters, but so painful and humiliating for the tender and sensitive heart. And yet the truth *had* to come out: I still wanted her; she did not want me; and I was devastated inside. We sat in silence, staring at the blue dashboard.

That night, I called my friend, Peter, a member of my still-operating support network, who listened to me as I shared that Neelama had just blown out the last dim flicker of hope. All that remained was a feeling of not being wanted. Peter's presence and love helped me to travel into my physical body, and to feel and name the sensations in which this rejection manifested itself. Presencing the physical sensations as they moved between different areas of the body, in varying densities and intensities, eventually brought me to a state of peace.

The inner processing I underwent with Peter that night did not permanently take away the feeling of rejection. For a long time, I had hoped that one session would do it. One of my early spiritual teachers taught that some deep core issues may need to be faced dozens of times. The first time I heard him say this, I was shocked, and arrogantly dismissive of the idea. Now I understood the wisdom of his teaching and was beginning to wonder exactly how *many* dozens it would take. But the breakthrough I had experienced on the phone with Peter was a wonderful gift. By facing my rejection directly, a transformation had unfolded which led to a sense of wholeness. This confirmed what the great teachers and mystics in all the traditions have promised us: *that which we look for is within.*

The months progressed into spring, a season I always loved in Marin—the rolling green hills reminding me of my Bavarian homeland. In May, the opportunity for a big change in my living situation came my way. The extra miles driving to and from Petaluma, and the numerous times I'd been stuck in traffic, had me longing to return to the heart of Marin County where I'd lived before, and closer to Kai's kindergarten in San Rafael, where most of his therapists had their offices. Also, I was ready to live communally again. My first communal home in San Rafael, on Upper Road, had always come closest to giving me a sense of home. Neelama had originally found this wonderful house from an online advertisement. It was located just at the edge of San Rafael, a mile away from China Camp, which was a wonderful State Park. It stood atop a steep hill, the last house on a dead end street, with a spectacular view of the North Bay and its surrounding swamps and lowlands. We had invited a few friends to form a little community and lived there together for four years.

Monica, who was the last of our original group still living there, had asked me over to facilitate a mediation between herself and her housemates. As I walked onto the deck of 500 Upper Road, I felt I was coming home—the California Oaks all around, the dramatic view of the bay below, even the smell as I opened the door and stepped into the large, open living room. Everything told me, *this is your home*. Little did I know that a miracle was about to happen. By the end of the mediation, it became clear that one roommate had resolved to move out. As unfortunate as that was for him, I couldn't help thinking that life had just presented me a huge gift: with a room now opening up, we decided that Kai and I would move back in.

Kai and I enjoyed our last month of June with the Lourdes, replete with barbecues, ping-pong games, and gardening. I grieved our moving away from them, and would be forever grateful to my dear friends for their unforgettable support and love during the hardest year of my life.

As summer approached, another opportunity came my way. I was still in touch periodically with Prem, and had heard that the ashram offered a new ten-day course every month, which stirred some interest in me. Around the same time, Neelama requested that I take care of Kai towards the end of July, because she wanted to go back for this program as well . . . with Alessandro.

Just hearing Alessandro's name brought up instant anger in my system—hot energy rising up, and a desire to hit him. I didn't want her going back there with him, and pondered whether I should still go to India myself.

On my couch, I did some serious self-inquiry, and came in touch with an inner part, voicing itself furiously, that felt betrayed . . . by God! *After all, didn't the meeting between Alessandro and Neelama happen right there in the Master's Garden? So why did it turn out the way it had? I went there to save my marriage and came back home with it lost forever. How could something like this happen at place that's supposed to be so spiritual?* I gave free rein to this voice, and let the anger, spite, distrust, and disappointment towards God express and release itself. This part of me felt unfairly punished and was enraged. During the next few days, my practice at the altar looked quite different. It turned from mantras of sweet devotion to screams of spewing anger at all the faces of God for what had been done to me.

Shortly thereafter, in a session with Faisal, I discovered that under my feelings of betrayal and anger was a deep pain of feeling abandoned by God. He described this process I was going through as "The Great Betrayal"—a feeling that Christ may have experienced on the cross, even momentarily, when he turned towards the Father and asked, "Why hast thou forsaken me?" Faisal's loving and silent presence allowed me to face that same question, and helped me to experience my own feelings of being forsaken. Somehow, grace intervened, taking me beyond my usual grief of losing Neelama into an even deeper pain: the separation from Source itself. There was a sickening sense in my gut of being ripped apart. I wept ancient tears from my soul, which broke apart in hopelessness and, to my amazement, was miraculously resurrected from within. Leaving Faisal's house, I looked out at the majestic expanse of the bay, feeling grateful that my love for God had returned. That night I got myself a ticket for India, courtesy of American Airlines' "one world" frequent flyer program.

Chapter Fifteen:
The Garden of Forgiveness

(Hers: Liberation from Guilt)

I landed back in India almost exactly one year after my last trip. Alessandro and I had taken a few extra days to spend by the ocean before our workshop. We stayed at a beautiful hotel, an experience I thoroughly enjoyed. Michael was not a huge fan of high-end hotels, nor anything that hinted at luxury for that matter, and one of my pains in our marriage was feeling as if we did everything the cheap way—when we vacationed, we usually camped out and roughed it. I wanted to feel special, pampered, and in my mind I associated this with staying in a nice hotel. Alessandro was of a similar mind, and since this was in the Third World, he could afford to treat us both to this gift.

The hotel was on a gorgeous property full of fruit trees, tall palms, and exquisite little walkways through emerald green grass—something quite rare for India. It bordered the Bay of Bengal, and we took long walks on the white sandy beach, the waves crashing at our feet, sending sprinkles of water and warm breezes our way. The restaurant served up gourmet delicacies, and there was an infinity pool, which seemed to roll lazily into the vast ocean before us. Alessandro and I were having an amazing time, until day four, when we unfortunately found ourselves in another huge fight; it was the first time in our yearlong relationship that I seriously considered leaving him. This fight started over a tiny disagreement, but our pride had got the better of us again, and we spent the rest of the day ignoring each other. I went for a walk on the beach that night, fuming inside, wondering what the point of all this beauty was when I couldn't enjoy it. Staring at the candlelit pathways, and hearing the laughter from couples enjoying another romantic meal under the stars, I felt my stomach boil with anger. After my walk, back in our room, I broke the silence, "I want to get a taxi. I'm going to leave."

"What?" he said, seemingly shocked.

"Yes," I replied, "I can't do this anymore. It's completely ridiculous. I don't want to be here, in this uncomfortable situation, with you. I would rather be alone. I will go by myself to the ashram."

"Nee-lah-mah," he said, clearly annoyed, "You cannot go anywhere now, it's way too late. You have to wait until the morning."

I fought that idea a bit, but ultimately had to agree. It was very late—too late to be taking a taxi in a very remote part of India. But I was determined to get up and leave first thing the next morning.

I slept as far away from Alessandro as I could in the bed, gripped by an intense frustration. We couldn't seem to break our ongoing pattern of becoming two stubborn kids, backs turned to each other, arms folded, in a standoff—waiting for the other to admit they were wrong. It was so infuriating for me to realize that, even after all the growth work we had done, the egos still got the better of us at times. I judged myself: *"You know it's just your defensiveness and pride. Why do you let that part of you win? After all this spiritual work, you still can't let go. What is wrong with you?* But I didn't know. All I knew was that I felt powerless underneath my armor, as if I was trapped in a suit of steel. Just like the Tin Man, I couldn't find my own heart. I felt cold and bitter. *NO way . . . I will not cave in this time!* I went to sleep in that indignant state of mind, and woke up in the same state just six hours later. Lying in bed, I was crushed by the sheer power of my ego, relentless in its determination not to lose this battle. Even though I could see what was happening, and recognized it was my ego at play, I still felt helpless in its grip. I couldn't bring myself to reach out to Alessandro. In my mind, he had become the enemy.

Thank God something different happened that morning. For some reason, in contrast to our previous fights, in that moment I remembered to pray. I asked for help to be released from the ego structure that kept me so trapped. The more I prayed, the more the tears flowed, melting the armor, softening the defenses, and returning me to my heart. And suddenly, miraculously, Alessandro had softened too, rolling over in bed to embrace me with his apology. Grace had intervened. We enjoyed our last day at the resort together as a happy couple again.

The next morning, we made our way to the ashram for the start of the program, and I was quickly thrown into a deep process. There were about one hundred of us gathered in a huge meditation hall with teak walls and no windows. We sat on the bamboo floor, on little metal-framed cloth seats, called backjacks, looking up at a podium where various teachers from the ashram guided us through teachings and exercises. We were asked to be in silence, which turned out to be impossible in a group of one hundred Italians. But I did my best, realizing that I had a good deal of inner work to do in this retreat. I still carried a mountain of guilt about the way I had left Michael, and hoped that these ten days would provide some desperately needed resolution.

We hit the ground running on the very first day, as we delved into the topic of suffering. Having studied Buddhism during and after college, this was not a new subject for me, but now I could hear these teachings differently, having endured a substantial amount of my own suffering. As we explored this theme, I could see that my need to be loved, to be special, and to get recognition had been the cause of immense pain my life. I was dependent on the outer world, and on my mates in particular, to validate me. When I felt special with my partner, then I would feel, *Oh he loves me, I'm worthy, I'm loveable.* When I didn't feel cherished, then my mind would say,

"Well, he must not love me anymore." It was as if I associated love with getting my needs met. I realized in that moment that, even at thirty-six years of age, I had no clue about love. I approached love like a child, selfishly thinking it was all about me. Boy, did I have a lot more growing up to do. This was a huge and painful revelation.

As music played, and the room lights dimmed, we were asked to go beyond the mental understanding of suffering, and open up to the *experience* of it inside ourselves. As memories from my life played before my eyes, I felt the pain of feeling unloved, which felt like an empty hole. It became clear that I had strived my entire life to make myself more loveable: prettier; smarter; funnier; better . . . *anything* to avoid sinking into that dark void. No matter how many times people had affirmed me, it never filled that hole which was waiting for me between every ego high. What made this process a success for me, was the essential ingredient of Grace. We were encouraged to call on our higher self, or higher power, to help us face these difficult feelings. I reached for the hand of God, and felt an inner presence accompany me into the dark void that I'd spent most of my life avoiding. Grace worked quickly, and I found myself in the middle of that void, experiencing an entirely different kind of pain— not of my usual "poor me" variety, which often had complaints or stories attached to the them, but raw and primal feelings that my body released without any mental associations at all. After these feelings cleared, something miraculous happened. It was as if, out of that emptiness, I was filled—but not from the outside, as I had so desperately tried throughout my life. This filling rose up from the inside, and I came in touch with an unbelievable knowing that *I was Love*. I experienced myself as *made of* that very substance, and knew with every fiber of my being that love was my true nature. There was a palpable sense that this love that I was could not be earned, nor taken away. This was only day one of the program, and yet I already felt reborn.

On the fifth day, we learned what was to be the most pivotal teaching of my life. It was called Setting Relationships Right, and was based on the premise that our life IS relationship. We exist in relationship: to ourselves; to our family; to our friends; to our colleagues; to mother nature . . . and on and on it goes. Life could be seen as a bicycle wheel, with our relationships the individual spokes helping the wheel to rotate and stay balanced. When *even one* of those relationship spokes was broken, bent, or destroyed in any way, the wheel of our life wobbled. Our guides asked us to take a good hard look at our relationships, and do an inventory from the perspective of where we had caused pain to others. This approach was revolutionary to me. Up until that moment, I had mostly looked at my relationships from the point of view of how *I* had been hurt. I had been to countless spiritual teachers and therapists, and very few had ever asked me to examine how *I had caused* pain to the people in my life. It was a powerful exploration, and of course Michael was at the top of that to-do list.

After completing our inventory, we were guided to the next level of the process: to be willing to *feel* the pain we'd caused. Grace was essential for this, as it was virtually impossible to know what another person felt, let alone experience it directly. I praying earnestly for Grace, and after some time, suddenly found myself catapulted into Michael's experience of our separation and divorce. Scene after scene of our conflicts played out in my mind's eye, and in each scene I was taken into his emotional experience and could feel it as my own: the intense shock he'd felt when I first told him about Alessandro; the helplessness when I ended our marriage at the drop of a hat; the sheer grief and heartbreak as he slept alone in the tiny cottage, knowing I was off gallivanting in Italy; the loneliness of single parenting; the anger and confusion of having absolutely no say about our separation. My body went limp, as I spread out on the floor and wept. This seemed to go on for hours, scene after scene playing out as I experienced how my insensitivity had caused Michael such immense pain.

In the next stage of this process, we were invited to seek forgiveness for the hurt we had caused, and to forgive the other for the hurt caused to us. I broke down sobbing, as I stood before Michael in my mind's eye, asking him to forgive me. And when I forgave *him*, I suddenly saw the two of us embracing, opening our hearts to the shared pain of our humanity. In that moment, all blame was cast aside—nobody was right or wrong anymore. We were just two limited, broken human beings, who had acted in unconscious ways that hurt each other. This realization created an immediate sense of forgiving and being forgiven. I felt love and compassion flowing between our two hearts, and for the first time in a year, I felt that a powerful healing had taken place.

In the days that followed, I noticed something was missing. The gnawing sense of guilt that had been my most familiar companion was nowhere to be found. I realized then, that the guilt I'd spent a year lugging around had actually been a way for me to avoid feeling Michael's pain. It was much easier to feel bad *about* what I had done, than to really *feel* what I had done. I saw that my guilt had functioned as both a defensive mechanism, and a subtle way of keeping my good self-image alive: *See, I really am a good person. Look at how bad I feel for what I've done . . . that means I've got a conscience.* Having gone through this powerful process, that layer of protection, in the form of guilt, was no longer needed. A huge weight had finally been lifted from my heart, and a feeling of liberation took its place.

Towards the end of that week, Alessandro and I met with one of the monks to seek advice about our own relationship. He recommended that we take some time out, stop the romantic part of the relationship, and continue on as friends. He said that since we had come together in such a sudden and intense way, creating plenty of karma for all involved, it would be best to begin anew—in platonic friendship. This advice came as a shock, and we simply ignored the monk's advice.

At the end of our program, we flew together from Chennai to Germany, where we had to part ways at the Frankfurt Airport, Alessandro heading back to Italy, and I returning home. We hugged and cried, vowing to see each other again as soon as possible.

After landing in San Francisco, I drove straight from the airport to San Rafael to pick up Kai at daycare. Michael was leaving the next day on his own trip to India, and we had decided to wait until he was back before seeing each other.

Soon after Michael's return from India, we met at his house to debrief on our respective experiences. I drove the familiar route to Upper Road, where he was now living once again. As I approached the front door, I stood for a moment on the deck, taking in the sunshine and burnt golden earth around me. It was early September, but still late summer in Marin. As I looked around, I was flooded by memories of countless times we'd sat together on that deck—for meals, parties, designing workshops, even holding a crying baby Kai in the first few months of his life. I was so happy that Michael had found his way back here. I stepped inside and walked over to his bedroom, with its huge sliding glass doors that overlooked the bay. What had transpired in my visualization process in India instantly became a reality when we saw each other. We embraced in tenderness and compassion, crying our hearts out in forgiveness. Those were precious tears, hard earned and worth everything. As I drove away after our reunion, I had my first inklings of hope that we would survive this storm.

(His: In Neelama's Shoes)

It's a long schlep from San Francisco to Hong Kong, then to Singapore, and on again to the southern Indian metropolis of Chennai, once called Madras . . . all courtesy of my frequent flyer miles. I checked into a small Indian hotel after midnight, weary and exhausted. I awoke the next morning both excited and nervous to be embarking on another journey—of an inner kind.

In the afternoon, I made my way to the ashram, and was guided to Block A, a three-story building that could house about 150 visitors. As I looked over the long list of participants to find which room I had been assigned, suddenly my heart started to race wildly—at the sight of one name: Alessandro. *Oh my God, is he still here? In my course?* A flood of anger boiled up inside me, followed by images of me spitting in his face and pouring water over him. All this inner turmoil took me over just by glimpsing a single ten-letter name on the roster. Later, I was to discover that "Alessandro" was a very sweet and friendly elderly man, who had no idea that he had propelled me right into the process before it had even begun. While still in a state of shock, I found my assigned room, A-3, and chose a bed from the twelve available. I lay down just to "be" with the onslaught of negative emotions that had caught me unaware.

My sleep was disrupted that night with disturbing emotions and intense dreams, mostly centered on Neelama and Alessandro, and the "whole enchilada" of sadness, anger, jealousy, and grieving. Strangely, even though I dreamt deeply, some part of me remained aware that all these thoughts and feelings were not part of reality. It was a lucid dream state. In the midst of my dreaming, I heard an inner voice: *See, see, see? All of these are just the thoughts of your mind.* Later, I must have entered deep REM sleep, because the extraordinary state of having watched myself dreaming stopped, as suddenly as if a light switch had been turned off.

The next morning, we were officially welcomed into a meditation hall with sweet-smelling flower garlands, as if to soften the impact of the inner descent that was awaiting us. During that first day, we were to look at our deepest desires and focus on how to manifest the things we wanted in our lives. When we were asked to create a list of the most important things we desired, I wrote "health" on the first line. On the next line I immediately wrote, "I want my family back. I want Neelama back as my wife." Actually seeing this in black and white, I was truly astonished to realize that, despite all the anger, blame, and hurt that filled my thoughts, deep down I just wanted her back.

The following day, our teachers introduced us to a subject which, through the ages, we humans have persistently tried to avoid examining, but have never really been able to get away from: suffering. We were taught about three levels of suffering.

The first level, physical suffering, I knew quite well from my throat condition, my own aging body, and the sleep deprivation we had endured with Kai.

The second level, psychological suffering, is where I had spent the entire last year of my life, so I was all ears when this teaching began. I hung on every word, as our teacher explained that psychological suffering that stemmed from our innate need to love and be loved. When this need was not filled, we suffered. In my present condition, I fully understood this. I realized that, at the root of all my fears and insecurities, anger and rage, jealousy and possessiveness, was simply the deep, aching need to be loved. While our teacher continued to amplify the theory about *the* most powerful human obsession, the need to love and be loved, I was literally experiencing it in my bones.

In the afternoon, the third and final level of human suffering was introduced to us: existential suffering—the deep sense of meaninglessness, dissatisfaction, boredom with life, and the disappointment at having reached the top of the ladder . . . only to realize that "nothing does it anymore." In our day-to-day life, this layer of suffering is usually covered up, showing up mostly when we are in crisis. It is said that existential suffering is the deepest suffering of all—it can be even more painful and devastating to experience than either psychological or physical suffering. I had dipped into this layer myself over the previous year.

It was existential suffering that, some 2,500 years ago, prompted a young prince named Siddhartha Gautama to leave his father's kingdom in Nepal, and embark on a quest for that which would last and never die. Seven years later, utterly exhausted from his spiritual journey, he sat down under a very old and sacred Bodhi tree, in Bodh Gaya, India, preparing to die. Three days later he was graced with enlightenment, and known henceforth as the Buddha, the Awakened One. The theme of suffering was central to his spiritual teachings, and because of that, Buddhism often gets a bad rap, sometimes viewed as a "downer." I am not a Buddhist, yet I've learned that life *does* involve inherent suffering. Buddhism offers a complex understanding of this, as well as a path for dealing with the unavoidable reality of suffering. At the end of that painful topic, most Westerners were about to leave the meditation hall thinking, *My God! What do we do now?* The solution offered by our teacher was simple: "There *is* no solution . . . just become *aware* of this level of suffering, and that alone will make you more peaceful." And with that he left the room. That night, as I fell asleep, something in me was stirred up, and I felt that the pressure cooker of this program was heating up.

The next day's theme hit the nail on the head for me: relationships. From a spiritual perspective, the arena of "relationships" provides a tremendous opportunity for us to transform. Life *occurs* in relationship—that's where we get hurt the most, and where we hurt others the most. I couldn't help but smile inside, feeling that this curriculum was designed especially for me. The process started off with a big shock: we were asked to begin by looking at the hurt *we had caused others*. Admittedly, I had not done a lot of looking in that direction. I had been so consumed with my own pain and grief that a good deal of righteous indignation had taken control of my mind. Thoughts about how I might have hurt Neelama were few and fleeting. It was mostly all about me.

The time had come. I was asked to do nothing but sit and contemplate, calling on my Higher Self or my Inner Divine to *show me* how I had hurt Neelama . . . and for what felt like an interminable amount of time. It was awkward and slow going at first. Then I began to pray earnestly to be *shown* how I had caused her pain. Suddenly, it came trickling in: memories; images; scenes playing themselves out in my mind. I saw how I had been driven by my self-preservation instinct, especially in being tight with money. When Neelama had wanted to hire someone to help babysit Kai, or go on a romantic get-away together, I had balked at the additional expense. I remembered the battles around planning our wedding where, again, we had many fights over the cost. I was shown how my righteousness had hurt her countless times: *No, that's not that way; it's this way. No, it's not twenty-five miles home; it's eighteen miles. I know how to facilitate this situation; this is how it is done; let me show you.* It was very painful to *see* these different parts of myself, and to really *get* how they had hurt Neelama and pushed her away. More insights flooded in regarding our upbringing of Kai. I saw how much I had projected my mother onto her, comparing her parenting style with that of my mom, making her wrong, judging her, scolding her. And then there was the push for having the child in the first place, amidst Neelama's serious reservations.

The light was dimmed and quiet music played in our meditation hall, as all of us, 150 men and women from around the planet, looked sincerely at our lives and how, in particular, we had hurt those closest to us. Our guide spoke to us on the microphone, encouraging us to go one step further, inviting us to call on God to help us to put ourselves in the shoes of the person whom we had hurt the most, "Ask for help to be willing to feel the pain you caused the other. Call on the Divine, Christ, the Buddha, Allah. The human ego does not want to do this, and you cannot do it alone. Pray sincerely to feel the pain you caused—consciously or unconsciously, it doesn't matter how it happened. Pain is pain. Be courageous!"

This guidance really took me completely by surprise. *Thinking* about the hurt I had caused was one thing, but *feeling* that hurt was a whole other matter. Resistance arose immediately inside of me, hesitation, not wanting to be there. With no other options, I decided to give it over to prayer. And I prayed, sincerely and fervently. It wasn't all that long before I began to have a sense of what it felt like to be at the other end of Michael's righteous comments, ego attacks, pushing, controlling, judgments, and rejection. I felt the hurt mostly in my chest, sometimes in my belly. I kept praying to allow even more, and finally the closed floodgates of my tear-ducts burst open and I broke down in sobs. From my chair, I went down to the floor, put my head down on the bamboo mat and cried, and cried, finally feeling the pain and hurt I had caused Neelama.

Those were precious tears, bringing me relief, like rain to a desert. As the process ended, I felt a deep gratitude for the Grace that had descended upon me, allowing me to feel how I had hurt this woman that I claimed I loved so much. Finally exhausted, I stretched out onto the floor, and a deep stillness descended within me. Again, our guide's voice came through the speakers in the room, inviting us to turn towards God, the Divine, Spirit, and ask for forgiveness. Another wave of weeping swept through me as I felt forgiveness happening inside my heart. The process came to a conclusion with our guide inviting us, if it felt right, to tell the person we had hurt: "I am sorry for what I have done." This brought everyone in the room to tears, with a deep emotional release, and I spoke my words out loud and earnestly to the image of Neelama in my mind, "Please forgive me. I am so sorry."

By the time I left our session room on that afternoon of August 19, I felt like I had been through a divine washing machine—soaked, rocked and spun, another cycle of soaked, rocked and spun . . . and then wrung out to dry. There was not a single tear left in my swollen eyes. I felt emotionally cleansed for the first time in a year. I felt truly graced. What a sublime state in which to just walk around, be with people, be with nature . . . and to sleep peacefully like a Bavarian angel!

Two days later, in a meeting with Sudhiro, one of our Indian guides, I told him of all I had gone through in the past year. I was surprised to learn that he remembered Neelama and Alessandro from the previous month's course. He shared with me that he had worked with them at some point, and had invited them to open up to the pain they had caused me. My heart raced as he spoke, and hope shot up in my mind like a rocket on the fourth of July. *Maybe they see now that what they did was wrong, and Neelama will come back to me! Even the guide is on my side. He knows that what they were wrong . . . maybe they've come to their senses.*

The guide continued, looking me straight in the eye, and said, "You think you have gone deep this year, but you haven't. You are still resisting feeling the pain."

If there had not been a strong inner censoring mechanism present in me, I would have definitely grabbed Sudhiro by the shoulders, shook him, and told him: "How dare you say this to me? I have spent *hours* facing the pain, over and *over* again, for days, weeks, months. And now *you* tell *me* I haven't gone deep enough yet? How dare you?"

For the remaining four and a half days of the program, I thought on and off about what Sudhiro had said, but I just couldn't get it. Then on the last day, a female participant shared something over the microphone about her experience. I don't even recall what that was, but as I listened to her, suddenly "the penny dropped." An insight came to me in a flash: *Yes, you did do intense inner work after the breakup with Neelama, and put yourself into the fire of transformation. You didn't run; you faced yourself many times over . . . AND, you did it with the hidden hope that you would be able to GET RID of the pain, the fear, and the hurt. That's what Sudhiro meant—that you didn't go fully into the pain; you went into it to be done with it, which meant you were, in some form, resisting it. And you were not aware of this, until NOW!*

For me, this insight was huge. I had never realized that, underneath all my intense inner work, had been this hidden motivation to get rid of the pain once and for all. From my work with my own clients, I knew that this was natural for everyone. In general, we want to move away from pain and towards pleasure. The revelation for me was that my spiritual quest was not only fueled by pure love and longing for God, it was also driven by my hidden hope to get away from fear and hurt.

Becoming aware of the depth and deviousness of the mind's resistance mechanism brought me a new freedom. One of the core teachings of this program was that, when we become aware of a pattern or behavior, the task was *not* to change it, but just to *recognize* it. This recognition was called awareness, and it was awareness itself that would set us free. Years ago, another spiritual teacher of mine, Osho, had said, "Awareness is the Alpha *and* the Omega," referring to the first and last letters of the Greek alphabet. Awareness as the Alpha, the beginning, had always been obvious to me. I knew that the first step in any process of learning was to become aware—I have to see and understand that I am stuck or blind, before I can do anything about it. What I had never fully understood, until now, was Osho's teaching that awareness as the Omega, the end, was *also* the solution. When one is really aware, present to WHAT IS, solutions will reveal themselves; therefore awareness can be understood as both the beginning *and* the end of the journey.

Back in the West, my community of dear friends at Upper Road welcomed the return of a refreshed and renewed Michael. The reunion with a certain three-year-old was super sweet, and his mom and I arranged to spend some time together to share our experiences from India.

When Neelama visited me at my house, it was the first time since the separation that we truly *met* each other and connected. Both of us had been deeply affected by our "inner journeys" in India. As each of us shared our core experiences, while the other listened intently, it became clear that the "being in each other's shoes" process had been a turning point for both of us. As Neelama recounted how she had experienced the shock I went through when she left, something deep inside me melted, finally feeling understood. Just before we parted, I asked Neelama what building she had stayed in.

"Block A," she said.

"But isn't that building only for male participants?"

"Yes, but the female building was full, so some of us were sent over to Block A."

"Which floor?" I asked

"First floor."

"Hmmm, me too. Which room?'

"A-3", she replied

"No way!" That was my room too! Which bed?"

"Hmm." Neelama thought it over. "The second bed from the far left corner, as you enter the room."

"What?" I was astounded! "That was my bed too! Unbelievable! Out of 150 beds on campus, we ended up sleeping in the same one!" *What synchronicity*, I thought, *this was not just chance.* I took this as a great sign from Life or God. We were through the roughest waters.

While I watched Neelama driving away from Upper Road, I felt for the first time the real possibility of the return of our friendship.

Chapter Sixteen: Rebound

(Hers: Lord Help Us!)

After the healing experience at Upper Road, Michael and I enjoyed a relatively easy six weeks or so. But, at some point that fall, I mentioned that I wanted to move forward with the legal procedure of the divorce, and this threw a great big wrench into our newfound friendship. Our connection suddenly felt very fragile to me, and I questioned whether the healing that had taken place between us would ever find real roots. My hope for a speedy recovery dimmed, as I realized that our separation, like all immense changes in life, was going to be a very long process. I knew from my own life experience, and all the years of teaching workshops, that healing and growth were not linear. It was much easier to teach this than to live it, especially when we were in the midst of another downward spiral. My patience was challenged, as part of me wished Michael and I could just have an easy friendship, and I found myself judging him for taking too long. Although there had been an undeniable shift since India, there was still a lingering pain and resentment that was beginning to show itself again.

Things with Alessandro had also been more challenging since the trip to India. Whatever amount of the "fallen in love" feeling that had been left was now almost completely evaporated, and I found myself in extended periods of disinterest in our long distance relationship. I still associated love with that passionate high we had in the beginning, and the more this feeling faded away, the harder it was to determine what exactly I felt towards him. Appropriately so, Alessandro called me out on this, and asked me repeatedly if I wanted a real relationship or not. It took me a good year to answer that question. We navigated through my periods of disinterest by analyzing the numbness I felt towards him at times, eventually chalking it up to a coping mechanism on my part—a protection against feeling the pain of being apart. We decided it was time for him to come for another visit, and so we made plans for him to fly over at the end of November.

Given all that was happening with Michael, I decided not to tell him about Alessandro's visit. I didn't want to rub salt in the wound, and hoped my omitting this detail would make life easier for him. Unfortunately, this was to backfire one night, around Thanksgiving, when Kai became sick, and Michael, in an exasperated state, brought him over to my house unannounced. Alessandro and I were cuddled in my bed, watching a movie, when suddenly I heard booming footsteps rushing into our house, and a crying Kai. Before I knew it, my bedroom door was flung open and there was Michael, holding our very sick little boy in his arms, his face white with shock at the sight of Alessandro in my bed. He started screaming at Alessandro, and I quickly mounted a defense, telling him he had no right to scream at us, especially in front of Kai. I scooped Kai out of his arms and took him into his little bedroom adjacent to my own. Michael stormed out of the house in a total rage, slamming the heavy front door behind him.

Later that night, lying in bed with Kai, his tiny head curled up in the crook of my neck, I broke down. I felt so badly that this little being had to witness this kind of "Jerry Springer" moment in my bedroom. Replaying the scene in my head, I was shocked. *We aren't those kind of people; we aren't that ignorant; we don't fight in front of our child.* We were . . . we did . . . and who knows what impact that had on Kai. I was deeply ashamed, and gently rubbed Kai's head, asking for forgiveness for all that we'd put him through.

For the next month, Michael and I had virtually no contact. Alessandro returned to Italy at the beginning of December. Christmas was approaching, and my housemates and I were busy preparing for the gathering we would host. I was so looking forward to having a Christmas celebration with our longtime friends, and had also invited Michael and Kai. My hope was that the Christmas spirit might open Michael's heart and get us back to that great place we'd been post-India. After all, he loved this holiday, and this particular year had a wonderful addition: Michael's nephew, Johannes, was in town visiting for the season. Johannes and I had a special bond, as he had spent quite a bit of time with us before and during our marriage, even coming to live temporarily in our home. After our breakup, Johannes had told me he would still like me to be his "Tante," his Aunt. I was deeply moved by this, and we had tried to stay in touch, albeit loosely. I knew that Michael, too, had a deep affection for Johannes, and I prayed that having him around would put Michael in a good mood.

Christmas Eve finally arrived, and when the doorbell rang, I went out to receive them. Kai embraced me with a huge hug and squeals of glee, and Johannes and I were thrilled to meet again. Seeing him brought back so many memories, and it was a bittersweet moment for us both. But, when I went to hug Michael, he stepped back, not wanting to touch, speak to, or even look at me. *Merry F*****g Christmas* was the energy I felt coming from him, and I was really shocked by his coldness. Thus began our evening.

Michael was friendly to everyone else, but there was a steely armor that closed around him whenever I was near. After dinner, we all gathered around our tree to open presents. Towards the end, I handed Michael the present I had bought him, which was a self-help book I secretly hoped would support our healing. He opened it and tossed it back to me with a hint of sarcasm, for everyone to see. My heart sank; I felt terrible inside. We had come so far, healed so much, and sitting there, in the middle of Christmas, the holiday that was the very symbol of love, it felt as if we had made no progress at all.

I found myself increasingly distressed, and as the night progressed, I drank more Prosecco to dull the pain and block out the awkwardness factor. One at a time, I pulled friends into my bedroom secretly, to say, "What the heck? What is going on with him? Why did he come here? He's being cold as ice. This is so messed up." Each of them listened compassionately, and some even nodded in vehement agreement. Then one of my male friends finally said, "Neelama he's just still in *so* much pain." My head could get that, but it didn't take away the anger I was feeling. I felt resentful that Michael was ruining my Christmas. *If he didn't want to be around me, he should have stayed home. He could have dropped Kai off and done his own thing.* On and on my mind went with its judgments.

Later that night, my girlfriend and I drove into San Francisco for Midnight Mass at Grace Cathedral. We arrived with throngs of others yearning to bring a deeper sense of the sacred into their Christmas Eve. I was embraced by the warmth of this beautiful Gothic cathedral, dimly lit with candles and fragrant with the scent of frankincense, all of which transported me beyond my anger and pain into something much bigger than myself. As I knelt down, the Christmas choir of angels filled the room, reminding me that there was something greater in charge of my life. I wept at my inability to control the situation with Michael, and prayed to God to help us, to heal us, and to intervene quickly for us, and for Kai.

My heart began to soften, and I felt held up by an immense presence whose simple message was: *All will be well.* My challenge, as always, was to trust this presence. Just before the communion ritual, the Episcopalian minister came on the microphone, encouraging everyone to receive the Eucharist that night. All I remember were her words: *Everyone is welcome at this table . . . all are welcome to partake of this gift . . . it's meant for every single one of you.* My heart melted at that invitation. One of the challenges in my early Catholic upbringing occurred when I realized at some point that everyone was *not* welcome at the table. There were rules—conditions I'd never been able to wrap my head around. Hearing those welcoming words pierced something in my heart. I hadn't identified myself as Christian for some time, yet I felt, on a deep level, that this is what Christ himself would have said: *Come on up everybody; join in, this bread and wine is meant for each and every one of you; you are all sons and daughters of the Great Parents.* After I received the communion, I returned to my seat, feeling the most beautiful presence loving me unconditionally. No matter what my circumstances were in the external world, no matter who was angry at me, or whom I had disappointed, or what limits I had in giving and receiving love, internally I felt embraced and at peace on that holy night.

Driving back home over the bridge, with the city of San Francisco twinkling behind us, things looked vastly different than they had just hours ago. I felt that the spirit of Christmas had entered my bones, and along with it, a sense of relief that, although I couldn't control this process Michael and I were in, I no longer needed to try.

Months passed, and Michael and I had more moments of opening and healing, followed by contractions in varying degrees. I learned to live with the spiral that was our process, and worked hard to manage my own reactions as best I could.

Things continued to be up and down with Alessandro too, and we decided that the only way to see if our relationship had the bones to sustain itself was for him to come and stay with me for an extended period of time. We both felt we needed to test how it would be to live together for a few months, for him to be in America, and also for him to live with Kai and me in a much more significant way. Our relationship was about to be put on trial, and although excited, I feared the impending verdict.

(His: Two Steps Forward, One Step Back)

The process in India had finally brought me an acceptance of the unhappy events over the past year, and the reality of my changed life in the present. The healing that had taken place between Neelama and me during our tearful reconciliation at Upper Road after India had brought great relief.

Kai, of course, was the most important beneficiary of this new and improved dynamic between his parents. Looking back, I think Neelama and I did our best to keep Kai out of our battles most of the time, but the reality was that our personal moods and energies towards each other still impacted him. Kai, like all small children, was very open; he picked up our states of well-being, as well as the tensions we were facing. It seemed now that the healing between us was helping our son settle into deeper and longer sleep patterns.

For myself, yet another shift was occurring—I was starting to notice attractive women again. My sexual drive had completely shut down after the shock of the separation, but to my relief, was reawakening. I found myself calling up Donatella, an ex-girlfriend in San Diego. I'd recently heard that she, too, was recovering from being left—by her hot-blooded boyfriend. We both had many good memories of our times together, and we now shared our respective breakup experiences on the phone. Because of the closeness of our past relationship, it was easy to renew our friendship, and we planned for me to visit her. We spent a few days cuddling together as we used to, both of us enjoying and drinking in the healing nourishment of warm and caring physical contact . . . for me, nothing could have felt better than to merely sleep beside her.

Back at home, during one of our "Kai hand-over" meetings, Neelama suddenly spoke the "D" word, saying, "Michael, I want closure on the married chapter of our relationship; I want a legal divorce." I didn't react with much outward emotion in that moment, but her announcement landed on me like a bomb, setting in motion another round of withdrawal behaviors. I began to avoid contact with her after that. Although I didn't want to admit it to the world, or even to myself, this came from an extremely painful part of my psyche that was hidden away—the part of me that still dreamed of a "miracle."

One evening, just before Thanksgiving, Kai suddenly became increasingly restless, and none of the usual tools in my belt were of any use—nothing would calm him down and get him to sleep. Then I noticed that his temperature had risen. He was definitely sick, and I didn't know what to do. I soon came to the end of my rope, and decided to call Neelama . . . but got no answer. Feeling ever more desperate about the crying boy next to me, I finally jumped in my car and drove the eight miles north to our old home at Anton Way in Novato, where Neelama was now living. Seeing her old Audi parked out front, I was greatly relieved. Clutching our wailing boy to my chest, I ran straight to her bedroom and barged in.

As the door swung open, the first thing I saw was Neelama and a man in bed, and upon seeing us, jumping up. *Alessandro!* We'd never come face to face before, but I knew it was him. With that recognition, a volcano shot up through my body to my head, and I was overcome with an intense molten fury. As I moved towards him, I saw the man who was the cause of the demise of my marriage, the breakup of our family, and the loss of my happiness. A shout broke from my vocal chords, "You f***ing a**hole! I want to kick your ass!" The "Alien" part of my psyche wanted revenge. It had awakened from its slumber, was fixin' for a fight with my rival, and wanted to hurt BACK.

Fortunately, for both of us, new cries of discomfort from my sick three-year-old jolted me back to reality and demanded priority in that moment. I turned to Neelama, and with the speed of a machine gun, fired off a list of Kai's symptoms and the remedies I had tried, delivered our boy into the arms of his mother, and without another glance at Alessandro, left the room in a storm of fury.

I was sleepless for what remained of that night. I had come abruptly face-to-face with the startling realization that, although I had acknowledged my own contribution to the breakup, and had begun the forgiveness process around Neelama, my inner work had not extended to Alessandro. I could sense that underneath my "Alien" anger was a deep hurt. I felt violated by him for engaging with Neelama, even though she was still married to me at the time. And I resented that he had never reached out to me to acknowledge and take responsibility for that. The deepest pain was about having lost her to him forever. My subconscious was reacting just as Faisal had taught us it inevitably does——it felt so much better to attack than to just stay with and feel the pain of the underlying wound. Neelama was aware of the seething anger I had towards Alessandro, and this was undoubtedly the reason she had decided not to mention his visit. From an objective point of view, I could see that it really was none of my business, but at the subjective level, it felt like an intrusion into my reality that was very personal and painful. In the following weeks, I found myself in a "contracted phase." After the heart expansion I had experienced over the summer, my surprise encounter with Alessandro had now caused a total regression.

With the wound of abandonment opened up and bleeding again, my state of emotional contraction peaked over the Christmas period. My nephew, Johannes, who was visiting from Germany, was pleasantly surprised that the three of us were to drive over to celebrate Christmas Eve, the highlight of the season back in our homeland, with Neelama. To my own surprise, I too was in a lighthearted holiday mood as we drove over. However, as Neelama greeted us at the door, I suddenly felt my warmth drain away in a single moment, replaced with an icy transfusion coursing through my veins and freezing my heart. Her cheery and welcoming mood irked me. With the "D" word still fresh in my mind, and the memory of seeing Alessandro in her bed just a few weeks before, I was faced with the painful reality that she had turned the page . . . and I still could not. Even her Christmas present, a self-help book, was seen by me not as a gift but as a criticism—she wanted me to be in a different place than I was. I tossed it back at her in disdain, and remained cold and steely towards her for the rest of the evening.

Chapter Sixteen: Rebound

This kind of energy might have completely ruined the get-together for everyone, had it not been for the entertaining distraction of a three-year-old who, fortunately, worked his magic on us all.

From the moment he arrived, Kai was in seventh heaven. As the only toddler present, he was the center of everyone's attention, delivering a particularly crowd-pleasing performance during the gift-giving exchange. It was immensely amusing for all of us to witness Kai's unbridled joy and excitement in tearing off Christmas wrappings with wild abandon, which seemed to be a great deal more interesting to him than the gifts inside. It was a bittersweet evening for me. Before I fell asleep that night, I was struck with the thought that I could truly enjoy the spirit of Christmas through Kai while, at the same time, be holding a grudge against his mother. Two lines from *Faust*, by Germany's most famous poet, Johann Wolfgang von Goethe, came to mind:

Zwei Seelen, ach, in meiner Brust untergebracht
Two souls, alas, are housed within my breast
Und jeder wird für die Beherrschung es Ringen.
And each will wrestle for the mastery there.

For the next few weeks, the "Beast" layer in me was running the show when it came to my interactions with Neelama. This part of me was determined to make her feel rejected, and was out to punish her.

The aware part of me was shocked by my dismissive and cold shoulder treatment towards her, but was powerless to change it. The shadow had re-emerged in full force, just when I thought I had conquered that difficult passage of my separation journey.

Neelama suggested we see a therapist together which, in classical male tradition, I resisted for a while, just as so many of my clients' husbands had resisted *my* suggestions that they participate in a couple's session with me. The male aspect of my ego structure prides itself on solving problems on its own, so going to someone for help, particularly in my own field of expertise, felt like a sign of weakness and defeat. But a more rational part of me, along with some pressure from Neelama, gained momentum, and by the time March rolled around, we'd had our first couple's session with Rachel.

My behavior on that day can only be compared to that of a stubborn and uncooperative four-year-old. I had clearly regressed, dug my heels in, and left my adult self in the car. "I will *not* divorce you. *You* can't make me. No way." Then, as a kind of protest, I threatened, "I'll go back to Germany. I've had enough of you; *you* can take care of Kai on your own." There was a good deal more of this acting out that I don't remember, but the cat was out of the bag—I just didn't want to let Neelama go. To enter divorce proceedings with her seemed like the last nail in the coffin of our relationship, and I simply couldn't bear that thought. During most of the couple's session, my professional persona as "the *great* teacher and facilitator of others" was totally eclipsed by a willful inner child, saying *no* to a woman who, on some level, represented his mommy. It was just too scary to even *consider* being without her. So he did what any four-year-old might do . . . he threw a tantrum.

Over the next few months, our interactions were teetering precariously between reasonably well functioning and painfully struggling. Yet the commitment to our own personal healing work, and especially our shared love for Kai, ultimately broke the gridlock—we knew we had to find a cooperative resolution for his sake . . . and we did. Time is a powerful healer too, it is said, and so I eventually came to accept the inevitability of a divorce.

Chapter Seventeen:
Endings and Beginnings

(Hers: Spring Has Sprung)

Alessandro arrived just as the Magnolias were in bloom, and the hills of Marin had turned that undeniable shade of green, pronouncing to the world that spring had finally claimed them. I had been in a whirlwind of activity getting the house ready for Alessandro's stay, overloaded with Kai and being unusually busy at work—all of which contributed to my late arrival at the San Francisco Airport. As I came down the escalator into the International Arrivals hall, I saw him standing there, gazing down at his luggage, looking noticeably disappointed. It made sense—he'd come all this way, made such an effort, and here I was, beginning our trial period of living together by showing up late. As we embraced, I felt his irritation, and when he asked me why I was late, I gave him a whole list of great reasons for not being on time. As I rattled them off, I realized they all sounded plausible—they were "the facts"—but we both knew it wasn't about the facts . . . it wasn't about my being on time at all. As I stood there watching other travelers arriving from international destinations, their families greeting them with flowers and giant hugs, I couldn't help but notice my glaring ambiguity. The truth was that, over the past few months,

Alessandro had become less and less the center of my world. It was so challenging for me to watch that happening, for here was the man who, less than two years ago, I was crazed for, the man whom I couldn't get out of my head if I tried. This was the man who had practically turned my prior life upside down. And now, standing in that airport terminal just a few minutes after his arrival, I didn't understand what had happened.

At the same time, another part of me scrambled, crying out, *No, our love cannot be diminished. It has to be real . . . otherwise everything I felt was a lie; Michael was right all along, and this might not have been love after all!* How could everything have changed in such a short time? The passion for Alessandro that had once held me tight had loosened its grip over the past months, leaving me in mid-air, with nothing to hold onto anymore. Where was that sense of certainty that had taken me over in my proclamation to Michael, "I know he is THE one." Staring at Alessandro, still standing there holding his huge suitcase, ready to move into my house, I wondered if I could get that certainty back.

As we drove home from the airport, I reached out to touch his hand, and named the elephant between us in the car. "I am sorry. I can only imagine how hard this is for you—to leave your whole life in Italy and come here, despite my doubts and the uncertainty of our future. To be honest, one part of me is glad you're finally here, but another part is loaded with so much ambivalence about you living with Kai and me, and the plausibility of us as a long-term couple."

He nodded, as he gazed out the window, digesting what I had said. A slow and thoughtful reply came back: "Yes, it is very, very hard for me in this moment. But I also know it's important that I be here; it's necessary for both of us. We need clarity about our relationship, about our future. We've been living in a fantasy relationship long enough. We need to take this test, to try to live a real relationship, to see if that will work. I came here for that reason . . . to find the answer."

As I squeezed his hand, I came in touch with the other part of me that was not ready to give up on us. As much as the intensity between us had diminished, there was still a deep love for him, and a desire in me to understand: What was our relationship about? What was the purpose of our having met? And what was the soul mate thing that we had both felt so strongly at one time?

Arriving at my house in Novato, we settled Alessandro in, and began our experiment. After my morning routine with Kai, and dropping him off at preschool, I would crawl into bed with Alessandro. Those were often very precious moments of cuddling and lovemaking. When I wasn't travelling to teach workshops on the road, I worked with clients in my home or by phone, which gave me a certain amount of flexibility. I tried to make space in my schedule, especially at the beginning of Alessandro's stay, for us to be together. He loved food, and we spent tons of time in our huge sunny kitchen eating and cooking. If I had some free time, we'd go for walks during the day, or out to a café. Even though Alessandro had entered my everyday life, our relationship still had some semblance of "vacation" associated with it, perhaps because that was all we had ever known together. In the afternoons, when Kai came home, he'd hang onto Alessandro while I made dinner. Sometimes Alessandro would give Kai a bath, which was a delight for me to watch. After the bedtime ritual, when Kai was finally asleep, I would sneak back into my bedroom to cuddle up and watch a movie with Alessandro.

On the weeks when I didn't have Kai, I would often travel to teach a workshop, which, at times, caused a reaction from Alessandro. Although he knew this was my livelihood, he felt lonely when I was away, and began to question the purpose of his being in the United States if I weren't there with him. Thankfully, I lived in a communal house with great roommates, every one of whom loved Alessandro. They tried to engage him whenever I was on one of my trips, and this definitely helped bridge the gap.

Alessandro would witness me coming back from the workshops energized and deeply moved, and at times felt disconnected from my world. My experiences during those workshops were so profound that they were hard to convey in words. I tried sharing them with him, but in the end, it was a world he wasn't a part of, and might never be. This was painful and challenging for each of us to acknowledge. The world of teaching workshops and the Inner Journey seminar had been Michael's and my deepest meeting point, and I longed to have that same kind of connection with Alessandro.

Soon it was June, and almost time for him to head back to Italy. We hadn't made any decisions about our relationship, but I feared it was reaching its natural end. Alessandro felt differently, and wanted to see if that deeper love between us could be resurrected. He asked me to fly back to Italy with him, inviting me to spend ten days with him at his family's summer cottage, on a little island off the coast of Sicily. I agreed, hoping against hope that this trip could bring back my *yes* for us.

We travelled to a tiny island off the coast of Sicily, a precious little gem where time stood still. We took walks around the quaint town, imagining ourselves living in one of the charming houses that dotted the tree-lined streets. It was one of the Aeolian Islands, located in the Tyrrhenian Sea, just sixteen miles north of Sicily, and therefore benefiting from all the culinary glory of Sicilian food. Every morning, we could be seen at the bakery, our mouths open, staring at the pastries that had just been made. Gluttony took over, and we carried bags home in our arms, full of croissants, fresh bread, brioche, and chocolate tarts. One day, Alessandro took me to the far side of the island, to taste what he called the world's best cannoli. We arrived at the tiny shop, and he placed our order with an ancient Italian mama behind the counter, explaining that I was American and had never tasted their cannolis. She looked at me with knowing eyes and nodded slowly, as if I was about to be ushered into one of the great secrets of the universe. Within minutes, she presented us with cannolis that transported us to heaven. Other than enjoying good food, we spent our time relaxing, reading, and making love . . . with an occasional passionate fight. But, we never reached that elusive clarity we'd both hoped for, and on the plane home, I still felt so confused about how we should proceed.

Kai had turned four in May, and now he was enrolled again in a preschool program for special needs children, where he had thrived throughout the past school year. It was such a delight to see him sitting with other kids at the tiny tables and chairs that filled the bright and colorful room. Watching him in that environment gave me some sense of "normalcy"— that he was going to school, learning about numbers, letters, and colors—and maybe, just maybe, all would turn out fine. For Kai, the best part of going to school was the yellow bus that came to our house in the mornings to pick him up. He waited for it with eager anticipation, his whole body jiggling with joy when he saw it approaching. Kai had befriended Mary, the plump and cheery driver, and they hugged every morning as she loaded him inside.

At the beginning of June, Michael and I taught our first Inner Journey workshop together since the breakup. Almost two years had passed, and we both felt ready to take this plunge into facilitating together again. It was an incredibly healing experience, and an answer to so many prayers. No matter what craziness we had gone through in the previous two years, I had always felt we were a great team in our professional world of teaching workshops. Through the dark night of our divorce, I'd clung to the notion that this part of our relationship could be salvaged, both for ourselves and for our shared yearning to contribute to others. That Inner Journey workshop felt like a turning point—*Michael and I were really over the hump*, at least in that domain.

By the end of August, it became clear to me that my heart was much more *out* than *in* my relationship with Alessandro. I hadn't yet come to terms with *why* this was, but I could no longer live with so much ambivalence about my feelings towards him. I had examined my numbness pattern in therapy, and gleaned some insights about where this came from, yet it didn't change anything in the way I continued to feel. I took this as a sign that it was time to end things, and unfortunately, like many of my breakups, the way I ended it was not that skillful.

Often at night, after Kai was asleep, I would lie in bed imagining the scenario in my head—how I would tell Alessandro, what would I say, and how he would respond. Days went by, and still, it never seemed like it was a good moment to pick up the phone and do what I needed to do. One morning, while in my car on the way to jury duty, I suddenly felt overcome with courage to make the call. Afraid to lose the moment, I pulled over and urgently dialed Alessandro's number. Looking back, I'm struck that my very first phone call to Alessandro had also happened when I'd been feeling overcome. My pulling over to the side of the road that time, on my return from the trip to India where I'd met him (and just a few miles away from where I was to reunite with Kai and Michael) had changed my life. At that time, I'd dialed his number with the nervousness of a teenage girl. Now, almost exactly two years later to the day, I'd pulled over again with a similar urgency . . . but this time to *end* the relationship. The phone rang, and he answered with that very sweet way he always said my name. I winced with guilt, but forged on, launching into my speech, and ending with, "for the past couple of months, we've tried so hard, we've struggled through so many fights, and have poured so much of ourselves into this relationship. It's turned out to be just too much hard work, and I just don't have the energy for it anymore. I am worn down and need to let us go."

Alessandro immediately challenged me on this: "Relationships take work, Neelama, you know that!"

He was right, of course, relationships required work. And, in my heart, I knew he would have kept working, kept going, and done anything he could to keep us together, despite the many challenges. I was pretty sure he would not have given up on us, and that made what I had to say next all the more difficult. "Yes, I know, relationships are hard work," I replied, "But the bigger issue is that I am not in love with you anymore." There was dead silence on the other end, and I imagined my words travelling across the line to Italy, smashing any rays of hope Alessandro still had left. I knew that, along with his hope, his pride would be broken too. Then something astounding happened. After digesting my words, his attempts to save the relationship halted in an instant: there was no more contesting; no more trying to change my position; no more encouraging me to try to figure out why I didn't feel anything, or do more work on the relationship. In fact, there was no resistance of any kind—he accepted what I'd said—and somehow this amazed me. We were over.

After our call, we exchanged emails, and decided that we wanted to stay in close contact, and remain friends throughout the breakup. We'd both endured too much pain and guilt with our former partners to repeat this with each other. We committed to handling our breakup differently, and to my surprise, for the most part we did. We were able to talk and share our feelings, and to keep our hearts open to each other, despite everything. We even decided to meet in person to formally complete our relationship. In September, Alessandro flew to San Francisco, and we had a very sweet closure, sharing one last meal and magical night together before he left.

Looking back, I know that my relationship with Alessandro taught me a great deal. I realize that the feelings I felt towards him in the beginning, while strong and captivating, were not the significant markers for long-term love that I had so firmly believed at the time. I came to see just how much I had projected onto him at the beginning of our relationship, the biggest part of which was an idealized parent. This is an incredibly common phenomenon—science has discovered that so much of what happens during the "falling in love" phase is actually a chemical reaction in our brain. Inside my brain, it was as if my little girl was jumping for joy, saying, *Yay—I finally found "the one"* (i.e., the perfect daddy!) who is going to save me, protect me, and love me unconditionally. This produced a great surge of hope for the "happily ever after" I dreamed of. More than ever before, I really felt that I'd finally found my Romeo.

As time went by, and this huge projection diminished, Alessandro was toppled off the pedestal and smashed to the floor in a million pieces. He was not the idealized, perfect "parent" that I so desperately wanted him to be. He was a regular person, *just like me*. Through this relationship, I learned just how narrow my definition of love was. Up until that point, I had believed that love was that feeling, that high, that swept me away in the beginning of my relationships. Once that high faded, which it always did, I felt that the love was gone, and therefore it was time to end the relationship. Yet the high *itself* was never questioned, until Alessandro, because, with him, the high was so extreme—so much so that it led me to turn my life upside down and cause a lot of pain in its pursuit, firmly believing that *this was it*. The dissolution of our relationship finally forced me to really examine this high that I'd called love. In the end, I had to admit I knew much less about love than I'd thought.

(His: Lan: A Thai Flower)

In the spring, our community in the Bay Area urged Neelama and me to offer another Inner Journey seminar. It would be the first time since the Immersion workshop, about twenty months prior, that we would be facilitating as partners. In the end, we were confident that, in service to others, we would be able to "park" our issues. And we did just that, delivering a hugely insightful, enjoyable, and successful four-day course to our participants. Spending an extended period of time together, in both preparing and delivering the seminar, while staying focused on something bigger than ourselves, was the impetus that propelled us forward, in leaps and bounds, in our healing process and our friendship.

At the conclusion of the Inner Journey, we celebrated at the Broken Drum restaurant in San Rafael, surrounded by the many friends and volunteers who had supported us as staff. Many of these people had known us for a long time, and had seen us weather the unbelievable storm of our separation. They loved and cared for us deeply as friends, and honored us as teachers as well. We had sat together many times, in this very restaurant, toasting the end of another successful workshop. It was a precious moment when we all lifted our glasses for a toast. I looked at Neelama, my heart wide open, full of joy and the spirit of celebration. I had indeed lost my wife, but for the first time since that fateful day, I really felt that I had my friend back.

Neelama and I had truly turned a corner. The teeter-tottering ups and downs of almost two years of our separation dance slowly gave way to a decidedly more comfortable feet-on-the-ground connection of friendship—a new base for our continuing relationship as co-teachers and co-parents.

With the arrival of July, it was time for the Facilitation Training course. This nine-day course had always been my favorite workshop of the year. This year, Howard and I had sixteen wonderful men and women students with us, soaking up teachings and inner experience at a gorgeous retreat center in the lush countryside outside Gore, Virginia. A few days into the course, one of the students began attracting my attention, in a way that went beyond the usual friendly affection of a teacher for his students. Lan was a Thai beauty, statuesque and golden-skinned, and a project manager in a Fortune 500 company. She had been a participant at our recent Inner Journey seminar, and had been deeply fascinated by and drawn to our work. This prompted her to deepen her experience further by attending the Facilitation Training.

This particular training course always requires a good deal of close student-teacher interaction. But this time, I was surprised to feel something a little beyond that, as the energy between Lan and myself started to spark. Howard was quick to pick up on this, and during one of our ongoing clearings with each other, asked me to look at the projections I had on Lan in those feelings of attraction. With his encouragement and support, I kept a professional distance from her during the course.

As the last day of the training arrived, I conferred with Howard once again. The question was whether it would be appropriate for me to approach Lan after the course—for a date! We came to the conclusion that I could go ahead, because our student-teacher relationship would come to an end upon the completion of the training. During our group's last meal together, I pulled her aside, and with some butterflies in my stomach, ventured, "Lan, I don't want you to leave before I ask: Would you go on a date with me?"

Lan and I did have a date! We met for dinner at a restaurant in Washington, D.C. We were both still wide open from the recent deep processes, and had a beautiful time together, the conversation between us flowing easily and playfully.

During dinner, however, there was an internal background conversation going on in my head. The characters involved were "Mr. Fear of Rejection" and "Mr. Desire," who had opposing views as to how I should proceed from there. Towards the end of the meal,

I found the courage to share my feelings for her. "Lan," I said, "as you probably sense, I feel very attracted to you. I have to leave town tomorrow, so I want to be straight up with you: I would like to hug and hold you. Are you open to connecting more closely with me?"

Lan's eyes lit up, and her smile gave me the answer for which I'd hoped. I realized that I hadn't been this turned-on in a long time, and excitement filled my mind and body. We walked out into the warm summer night, strolling happily, hand in hand, through the lively and raucous D.C. downtown area, towards her place.

Once inside Lan's apartment, it wasn't very long before we found ourselves making out on her bed, which in my German culture is known as *schmusen*. The energy between us grew more and more intense and fiery, and moved quickly to passion and arousal. Our bodies were hungry, yearning for connection, and we both surrendered to one of the most basic aspects of human life—lust. Then, just when it seemed that the "gates of heaven" were about to open, my arousal disappeared. *"No!"* screamed a voice inside me, *"Not now! Please!"* Heat rushed through my body, followed by a wave of shame and embarrassment.

Between my ears, a voice screamed its recriminations at me: *Oh my GOD, what is WRONG with you! What a time to lose an erection! This is what you've been waiting for, and now THIS happens? She won't want to be with you now. It's over.*

Through grace, suddenly, another part of me came forward to silence this voice—the "higher aspect" of the mind, called the "witness" in Eastern spiritual language, which had been observing the whole drama as it unfolded. This witness saw the worry, the pressure, the embarrassment, the shame, the recrimination, and the fear . . . everything that was going on. This witnessing awareness somehow prepared the ground for me to speak with the voice of truth and just expose what was happening within: "Lan, I need to talk to you. I'm feeling embarrassed because of what didn't happen here just now. Now I feel pressure to perform, which is making it even worse. But I have no control over this; it either happens or it doesn't." I took a big breath, and went on. "And now I'm worried about what you think of me, and how you're feeling. You are so gorgeous, and things just went a little too fast for me. So, can we just relax, and wait a bit."

Again, the intuition that had led me to speak so truthfully was right on. Lan looked at me with her warm brown eyes and smiled understandingly. "It's okay, Michael, it really is." Her sweet and sincere assurance completely calmed me down. As we held each other tenderly, I focused on breathing deeply into my body. As I had hoped, this shifted me from the thinking and worrying of my mind into a state of relaxation.

It took no more than a few minutes for the magic to return, and as "the mountain and the valley" finally met, an inner voice shouted a triumphant, *Yeah!* The night was wonderful—sleep didn't matter, passion and intimate connection took over, and hours seemed like mere minutes. After I first reached orgasm, I did not allow myself to climb to "the point of no return" again, which kept my yearning alive to respond to Lan's beautiful and hungry body, and to take joy in her pleasure. Before I left in the early morning hours, we agreed to stay in touch by phone, and to find time in our busy calendars for a weekend together as soon as possible.

I left straight from our lovers' den and headed to the airport, still on cloud nine. Back in Marin, I went to pick up Kai from Neelama who, with her finely tuned feminine instincts, quickly picked up on what was going on. Maybe it was a subtle whiff of testosterone, or a gleam in my eye, or just that she knew me so well. No words were spoken, yet the message was conveyed through a knowing and teasing little smile.

Having found a lover was a powerful assistance in my retaining the inner expansion I'd experienced in the training. Everyone around me—my housemates, friends, and casual acquaintances—benefitted from my renewed spirit. Particularly Kai . . . his Papa was back in the saddle of manhood and energetically renewed. There was no way around it: great sex and feeling wanted by Lan made a big difference in how I felt about myself.

During the following months, the connection between Lan and me deepened beyond its hot and passionate beginnings to a lively and affectionate East Coast/West Coast long-distance relationship. Who was the happiest about this development? Neelama, of course! The tension in our relationship eased up considerably.

I remembered the comments of my male friends, who had not so jokingly suggested "getting laid" as a remedy for what had ailed me early on in the separation. With the timing now right for me, I definitely got their point. Having Lan in my life began to fill the gaping hole I'd felt after the loss of Neelama, and soothed that wound of abandonment. My budding new relationship gave my mind a new focus and direction. The deeper I went into my relationship with Lan, the more the friendship between Neelama and me found its feet.

By the late fall, communication between Neelama and me had a light-hearted and amicable style and tone, and was vastly more productive. Caring for Kai was always at the core of our conversations, but love and support for each other was re-entering the communication too. We began to schedule family time, at least once a month, where the three of us met for dinner, a picnic, or a visit to the beach. We sensed that our improved connection made Kai feel more safe and secure. We couldn't really measure that, because he still spoke in single words—Mama, Papa, peepee, wa-wa (water)—so his inner world was still somewhat of a mystery to us. But, by this time, Kai could walk, and even run a little, and he expressed his joy in movement. And, as limited as his speech was, just the excited sounds and assured tone of his voice were more than enough to express his delight in having his mommy and daddy together with him. On our outings together as a threesome, Kai was in seventh heaven.

I remember one particular afternoon we spent beside the ocean. It was early October, a time of year where the weather tends to be the best in the Bay Area. It was sunny and warm, with no hint of fog. The three of us ran along Muir Beach together, splashing in the still-cold shore waters of the Pacific, and stopping to dig in the sand. As Neelama and I sat down on our beach blanket, happy and exhausted, Kai squeezed in between us, smiling from ear to ear, and put his little arms around us, holding both of our necks as tightly as he could. It was our "Coming Out" moment—for the promising new post-separation friendship that was growing between us.

My relationship with Lan continued to deepen. She liked daily phone call updates, although this wasn't so easy for me. I had never been a phone person, and was accustomed to keeping calls short, fact-based, and goal oriented—which began to lead to the first tensions between us. I was also (and still am) not a small talk kind of guy, so we had differing needs and agenda for our phone connections.

Getting together with Lan in person took some serious planning, and it had to take into account four different schedules: Lan's, Kai's, Neelama's, and my own. I had, however, managed a trip back to the

D.C. area in September. For our second "date," Lan and I decided to rent a cabin on a wild river in the foothills of Virginia. During those three magical days, our bodies wanted no more than to be together as one, and even ached when we needed to pull apart. In the tradition of ancient Indian Tantra Yoga and the Chinese Taoist masters, it is recommended that, during love-making, men not be focused on orgasm, but learn instead to circulate the sexual energy throughout the body. That weekend, I was somehow able to live those teachings, which led to a state of ongoing sexual arousal. In recalling that weekend, the lyrics from the old Bachman-Turner Overdrive song *You Ain't Seen Nothing Yet*, come to mind, to describe the steady stream of electricity between us, breaking both our records for sexual engagement and stamina—not likely to be trumped in this lifetime . . . in my case anyway. These were the thought processes of my particular male mind, which couldn't help but think in terms of numbers, achievements, and conquests . . . and yet usually kept this tendency a secret.

My sexual attraction to Lan was surprising, because the beautiful physical Lan matched some but not *all* of the characteristics of the idealized woman who lived in my head, and had played a lead role in my sexual fantasies during the lonely nights of singledom. And still, the intensity of my physical attraction to her spoke for itself, blowing my mind. I realized two things: first, that there is a sexual turn-on, on a real-life energetic level, that actually surpasses the fantasy level. And secondly, that seeing each other for only a few days every four-to-six weeks, definitely kept the flame of passion alight to a much greater degree than sharing a bed every night.

As the months passed, and Lan and I chalked up more and more time together, the emotional, intellectual, and social aspects of our relationship naturally deepened, adding other dimensions to the sexual attraction. Lan, who was a professional in corporate America, travelled a good deal herself, often to Europe and Asia. Although of Thai origin, she had come to the United States at the age of twenty. After many years of study, she had completed her PhD degree at New York University. Lan's brilliant intellect and business experience added a whole new dimension to my more psychological and spiritually oriented world, and vice versa. I also realized that, in many respects—physical, cultural, social, and areas of interest—we were opposites. After our first connection had evolved to a steady relationship, I was introduced to her corporate world in D.C., to her colleagues, and to people in her social circles. And reversely, she was ushered into my world—diving ever more deeply into the study of personal growth and spirituality, and seeing firsthand the obligations of parenthood. The funny part in all of this was that she, the Easterner, was introducing me to the world of Western business, while I, the Westerner, was steeping her in the teachings and sacred meditations of the East.

At the beginning of December, the day came that I had once anticipated with so much fear and dread—the scheduled hearing in the Marin County courthouse to finalize the divorce between Neelama and me. Sitting on a hard wooden bench in the back of the courtroom, we watched as a few couples legally ended their marriages, mostly assisted by their lawyers. I couldn't help but ruminate about how the livelihoods of those professionals were enhanced by the degree to which their clients disagreed with each other. *What a set-up!* I thought. I had always wondered why more couples didn't employ mediators rather than lawyers.

As Neelama and I sat there together, observing the goings-on and calmly awaiting our turn, I felt very grateful for all the healing that had taken place between us. When it was our turn to approach the bench, we naturally, and unthinkingly, held hands. When the be-robed and bespectacled judge looked up at us from her paperwork, her glance shifted down momentarily to our clasped hands, her eyebrows lifted, and her grim expression morphed into an amused smile. Seeing the unspoken question in her eyes, I explained, "We still have love for each other, just not of the romantic kind."

"You two should teach workshops to people about divorce," she replied earnestly.

"We will!" we responded, in perfect harmony.

After Neelama and I left the courthouse, we held each other in a long and silent embrace, looked softly into each other's eyes, and then climbed into our respective vehicles.

Just before Christmas, I came down with a bad cold, and couldn't shake it off. It quickly developed into severe bronchitis. But help was on its way—Lan had time off for the holidays, and flew in from D.C. to take on the role of nurse. She took great care of the coughing, sweating, freezing, and sometimes *impatient* patient. In the end, being sick was actually a huge gift. Lan's tender love and care nourished me in a way I hadn't experienced in years. Since the birth of Kai, it was I who had been the caregiver. Having somebody care for *me* with such devotion was deeply touching and felt so nourishing.

During the first year of our long distance relationship "dance," one of the core dynamics between us revealed itself—Lan and I were into each other to differing degrees. We spoke about this at some point, and I acknowledged that I found myself holding back, compared to how she gave herself over completely to our relationship. There was something else going on with me, at an even deeper level, that was hard to detect, and even harder to admit—I felt something was missing between us. I believe Lan sensed this long before I did, and I can only imagine how painful this must have been. The inner world of feelings—in this case my own particular male psyche—is often a mystery to the owner himself. I asked Lan to give me time to work this through.

She agreed, and I came to appreciate all that we had in common. We were both professionals in our fields of expertise, had a shared love of intellectual pursuits, relished fascinating discussions about almost any subject in the world, and enjoyed a straightforward honesty with each other, and the mutual attraction of our bodies. And last but not least, she adored Kai. Although she had no children of her own, Lan was just a natural mother, and Kai enjoyed her sweet and loving affection. They were both mergers by nature, who loved to cuddle together—a delight for me to behold.

However, our central areas of interest—the work we devoted our very beings to—were very different. Later on in our relationship, Lan admitted to having felt that I was not as much interested in her world as she was in mine. Hearing that observation, I recognized its truth, and made a conscious effort to involve myself more deeply and authentically in her world of business. In spite of my tendency to still hold back a little, we continued our D.C./California virtual romance, and the pluses still vastly outnumbered the minuses. Because we talked openly about our challenges from time-to-time, we managed not to let things tip too far out of balance. In late July, we even embarked on a trip to Thailand together.

After meeting up with Lan at Washington's Dulles Airport, we boarded a direct flight to Bangkok. This was my third trip to

Thailand, but this time I had found a very special personal travel guide: Lan. We took a train north towards Chiang Mai, enjoying an abundance of historical, natural, and spiritual sights and touring Buddhist temples along the way. Eventually, we set out on our journey to our final destination in southern Thailand, to visit the tiny village outside Phuket, where Lan's mother lived, and where Lan was raised. With a great deal of pride, Lan took me to her family home, nestled on the side of a steep canyon overlooking brilliant green rice paddy fields—a delight to behold.

At the door of the large house, Lan introduced me to Bau, her mother—a small but somewhat tough-looking Thai woman—who welcomed me politely. Shortly afterwards, however, Bau pulled me aside for a private tête a tête. "Michael," she said in broken English, "I must ask you a question. Lan's father is dead, as you know. So, as her mother, it is my responsibility to watch out for her. What exactly are your intentions towards my daughter?" I was stunned! Here I had found my equal . . . no, my master! . . . in the art of directness. (Neelama had struggled mightily with that particular "gift" of my German conditioning.)

Caught unaware and flustered, I tried to gather my thoughts. What actually *were* my intentions? Bau had to wait patiently while I listened to what was really inside me, no doubt *not* taking my hesitation as a good sign. "Bau," I said, "I want to be honest and direct too. I can't actually give you any promises as to how our relationship will continue. I like your daughter very much, but cannot guarantee that the attraction between us will last." Bam! The cat was out of the bag, for me in particular, as I listened to my own answer. Maybe I imagined it, but I'm almost certain I saw a sign of relief, rather than disappointment, on Bau's face, and the subject never came up again during the week we spent together.

On our flight back home, I had time to reflect on our trip, and noticed a sense of emotional flatness inside me, as if I was left feeling unfulfilled. All my prior trips to Southeast Asia had been heart-driven pilgrimages, inspired by a thirst to travel deeper within myself, through immersing myself in the sacred rituals, the holy places, the spiritual ambience, and the profound teachings of these ancient cultures. This was the first time I had returned from the East with my thirst unquenched. What had happened? Then the insight came in, bluntly and honestly: it was impossible for Thailand's ancient soul to nourish me in the way in the way I longed for, because I had not come as a seeker, but as a tourist. Lan and I had shared the outer enjoyments of Thailand, yet the trip revealed something *more:* that we didn't meet as seekers. I realized that the worldly part of me enjoyed the relationship with Lan, yet the spiritual part of me didn't feel met. I was left wondering if there was a way to bridge this gap.

Chapter Eighteen:
What's Best for the "Boo?"

(Hers: Awakened in the Night)

Kai started a new school that August, and it was quite a change for us all. He had been in an amazing preschool program for special needs children, and was now officially entering kindergarten. Because of his diagnosis, he was lumped into a single classroom for children with all sorts of disabilities. I was taken aback on my first visit, because the classroom itself was rather ugly—it looked like a basement, with very little light. What was worse, it was completely chaotic. The nice but very small group of staff seemed outnumbered, and overwhelmed with the various needs of these unique kids. It was, from our point of view, a harsh contrast to the cheery and ultra-organized classroom he'd been a part of in the past two years. Seeing this environment, I was concerned that Kai wouldn't get the educational stimulation he needed in order to progress. As the months went on, I had a gnawing feeling that we weren't doing enough to help him advance. He was making progress, but at a snail's pace. Something didn't feel right about how we were going about things.

I had planned to stay single for a while, especially since I'd had no break between my marriage to Michael and my relationship with

Alessandro, even though the latter was largely by long distance. Although I terribly missed the affection and warmth that came with an intimate relationship, I didn't feel an urgent need to start looking for it again. But the universe, apparently, had other plans, and just a few months after my breakup, I met a wonderful man. Paul and I were introduced through mutual friends, but had never exchanged more than a hello. One weekend, we ran into each other at a movement meditation class, and our bodies suddenly found each other on the dance floor. I was attracted to the way he moved, and watching him dance really intrigued me. Paul had a level of ease and comfort in his own skin, which was a total turn-on. Afterwards, we talked and flirted a bit, and the thing that stood out most for me was his native English! After two years with an Italian, and seven before that with a German, I had forgotten the fluidity and humor that goes along with the ability to communicate in a shared native tongue. Paul was a Brit, and had that typical witty sense of humor I loved. He was strikingly calm and had an evenness about him, which I appreciated after the roller coaster my life over the last two years.

We began to date, and things sped up rather quickly. I spent a lot of time at his place that fall, as we had more privacy there than in my house. He lived in Mill Valley, at the top of a hill surrounded by trees, in a little forest sanctuary overlooking the bay. Winding my way up the road to his house became a ritual I treasured, an escape from my physically demanding worlds of work and parenting—a chance to just let myself go. He'd often cook me dinner, as I sat watching from a little perch in the corner of his kitchen, relaying the highlights of my day, and the challenges and joys of parenting Kai. Paul was a master in his kitchen, and I enjoyed watching him float around, as if the act of cooking were as easy as sipping a glass of wine. We enjoyed many a gourmet meal on his lovely wooden dining table, looking out the huge living room windows at the California sky.

This attraction was different for me—it didn't have the intense fire that I'd shared with Alessandro, yet there was a magnetic depth and sweetness in our connection that made my heart melt. Our bodies loved each other, and we spent hours merging in his bed, engaged in sleepovers whenever I had a free night. On the mornings when I didn't have Kai, my body surrendered to sleep, making up for the many hours I'd lost over the past four years. Paul was an early riser, and would quietly get up and prepare tea and toast, bringing it to the bedroom for me to have breakfast in bed, and waking me up with soft kisses. I cherished the luxury of those slow mornings, holding my warm mug, and looking out his bedroom window onto the sea of trees that engulfed us. Something about this gentle soul was so very nourishing, and my body soaked up his love like a sponge. Eventually our visit would come to an end, and I'd have to leave this refuge and return to reality. It was painful, but it became the norm in our yearlong relationship, as we fought to seize precious windows of time in both our incredibly busy lives.

The relationship with Paul felt like my favorite pair of jeans—familiar, comfortable, and something I always wanted to have with me. He was a great communicator, and it amazed me how quickly we entered into a depth of intimacy that made us both feel like we'd been together for years. It was also the easiest relationship I'd ever been in—we didn't fight or trigger each other into a fury as Alessandro and I had, nor did our personalities collide as Michael's and mine had. I had also matured over the previous few years, or so I hoped, and could only assume that I was a bit easier to be with too. There was a mutual respect and a shared vulnerability between us that created a safety and closeness that led me to wonder, even though we were still a fresh new couple, if Paul might be my life partner.

By late spring, however, one clear challenge began to emerge: our time together started to feel like a division from my real life. I longed to have Paul more connected to my world, and specifically to my life with Kai. The daily grind at home was still hard on me, especially when Michael was gone for more than a week at a time, and I craved more partnership. In the beginning of our relationship, Paul and I had consciously abstained from having any serious *future* conversations, to give us time to get to know each other, and see what we felt. Yet, as time went on, I began to feel fragmented from having to divide my time between work, Kai, and Paul, and wanted my life to be more integrated. We had many talks about this, and he shared his fears and ambivalence about truly committing to our relationship, and what it would mean for him to merge his life with ours.

One particular talk took place on a train in Spain. I had saved up enough frequent flier miles so that I could return to Spain that summer, to visit my Spanish family in Madrid. Luz, the daughter in the family, was exactly my age, and had attended my high school as part of an exchange program during our senior year. She and I had become dear friends, and she'd invited me to live with her family during my junior year of college. I had said yes to this generous offer, and spent five months in her family's home in Madrid. Luz's entire family took me in as one of their own, and we had remained in each other's lives ever since. Paul's family was in England, so we decided to make a joint trip to Europe to visit everyone. We took a train from Madrid, where my Spanish parents hosted us for a week, then proceeded up to Oviedo to meet Luz, who was now living in the north. Trains are a great place to talk, and Paul and I had a heartfelt discussion in the large booth in which we were comfortably seated for the five-hour journey. As the landscape rolled by our huge window, we came in touch with a shared desire to merge our lives. We discussed our concerns, and then began to brainstorm how we could make it work. We imagined where we would live, and how we could arrange the house so that Paul could still have his own space, if Kai's energy became too much for him. We even envisioned having a beautiful backyard, and all the fun we would have planting a garden. As the conversation went on, our bodies nuzzled up to each other, and our hearts cracked open with tears of joy. When the mountains of northern Spain appeared, engulfing the train, a sense of relief came over me, and for the first time since we'd been together, it felt like our relationship was really solid.

One night, in October, Paul told me to take a look at a magazine he had in his bathroom. I had been researching a new therapy for Kai, called neurofeedback, and Paul mentioned that the magazine had an article about this therapy. So I rushed in to find the magazine and check it out. Little did I know that this tiny article would be the beginning of a huge change for us all.

In addition to the information detailing neurofeedback, the article also mentioned a school in Georgia, called Jacob's Ladder, which was devoted to the neuroscience of helping children with brain disorders. As Paul went off to get ready for bed, I made a cup of tea, opened my laptop, and sat down at his dining room table to find the website for Jacob's Ladder. On their homepage was a video about the school and its founder, Amy, who shared a very emotional story about her journey with her own special needs son. As I watched the video, tears streamed down my face, forming a small puddle on my mouse pad. They were bittersweet tears of joy and relief. Watching Amy's video made me feel, for the first time since Kai's diagnosis, that somebody other than Michael and I truly understood what we were going through. It was so hard to describe to friends and family just what it was like having a special needs child, and so hard to put into words the daunting task of knowing how laboriously we had to work to help Kai accomplish basic everyday things, like chewing, making a sound, getting dressed, walking . . . so hard to get people to understand that even taking him to the grocery store or to a restaurant was virtually impossible, because nothing about our situation or our son's behavior was normal.

It was hard to admit, but at times Kai's special needs felt like an overwhelming burden to me. Listening to Amy talk, I realized that someone else had been through similar challenges, and had emerged hopeful, faithful, and victorious. Finally, I felt that real help was out there, for Kai and for us. But the school was in Georgia. *How would that work?* I sat at the table for a long time, sipping my tea, considering all that this might mean. It was very late by the time I made it to bed, where Paul was fast asleep. During that night I had an epiphany. In the middle of the night, I was awakened by the sound of a calm yet enormous voice whose message was, *You've been asking me for so long what my purpose is for you. I've given you a purpose. I've given you a child who has needs, and who needs you . . . but you've wanted a different purpose. I've handed this purpose to you . . . and you've wanted to exchange it for something else. You want to understand your life purpose? Look right in front of you . . . at your own son. This is it; Kai is it! He needs you, and it's up to you to give him the very best that you possibly can. And that means saying yes to your purpose, yes to My Will.* The voice disappeared, leaving me awed and intensely awake for the next few hours.

As I lay there in the silence of the night, I realized that, even after five years, I had not fully said *yes* to what God had put on my plate regarding Kai. The truth of this message rattled me to the core, and I prayed for the strength to surrender to what was being asked of me. By the time Paul awoke the next morning, I already had a plan in place to visit Georgia.

(His: For the Love of the Prince)

There is not much in life that beats sleeping in one's own bed after a journey halfway around the world. It was great to come home after a month of work and travel, and the reunion with the "Boo" could not come soon enough. I drove over to the Montessori daycare center to pick up my boy. "Papaaaaaah," he yelled excitedly, as he threw himself into my arms with joyful exuberance. Whoa, what an outpouring of pure love showered down on me!

When I told people that Kai was a special needs child, I sometimes got a sympathetic look in response, accompanied by an awkward "Oh, hmmm . . . what is his condition?" I understood why many people seemed to feel pity for us. Kai was hugely behind on the normal developmental curve. At the age of five, he barely spoke, was unable to dress himself, still wore a diaper, and demanded round-the-clock, one-on-one attention. But there was another side to this child that was an inestimable gift to a parent, and more than compensated for the challenges of his delayed development. Kai remained in the same pure and beautiful realm of innocence in which he'd entered the world—loving unconditionally, delighting in life, and overflowing with an essential sweetness and joy that "normal" children have usually lost by the age of five.

Kai's pure essential being, and untainted innocence, were the source of both my worst parental concerns and my greatest joys. Picking him up from preschool or daycare was at the top of the list in the latter category—a daily ritual infused with love and joy, such that Neelama and I both looked forward eagerly to our respective turns. Each and every time Kai spotted me coming to pick him up, a huge grin would appear on his face, and he would run towards me as if he hadn't seen me in months, flying straight into my open arms like a bee to honey. He liked to be held tight for at least five seconds, soaking up love and sharing his intoxicating happiness with every cell of his body. For me, those joyful greetings felt like a refueling of my parental gas tank with a high-octane mixture of love, joy, and gratitude. There were a myriad of other ways in which Kai, without ever knowing it, kept on giving to us, as all children give to their parents, and helped us remember how to be young at heart.

It was our teacher, Faisal, who pointed out to us that it was *because of* Kai's delayed development that he was able to stay connected to these inner essential states of joy, sweet merging love, and passionate excitement. Faisal reminded us that we all come into this world prewired with these inner states, as part of our human operating system—they are inherent in each of us. However, during the process of growing up, or "domestication" as Don Miguel Ruiz, author of *The Four Agreements*, calls it, we lose contact with these essential qualities to varying degrees. Kai's journey from birth onwards had been very different from that of mine and Neelama's, and he was, in a sense, *our* teacher—reminding us that his joy, his exuberance, his innocence were also *ours*, waiting to be rediscovered and lived again.

Labor Day arrived, an important marker in the rhythm of the school year, and Kai entered kindergarten. Throughout the month of September, Neelama and I became increasingly concerned. This public school classroom had only one teacher and two helpers to manage and teach some ten special needs children. When I dropped Kai off in the mornings, I was worried he would get lost amidst the clutter and intensity of this classroom. Some of the students were also quite loud, and Kai was sensitive to abrupt noises. In talking this over one evening, Neelama and I decided that, while waiting to see if there would be any improvements in the school setting, we would start looking for better alternatives for Kai.

A few weeks later, during a family evening at Neelama's place, and after Kai had gone to sleep, Neelama sat down and shared with me a series of surprising insights and happenings that had thrown her into a profound re-examination and re-prioritization of what was best for Kai. She had come across a private school for special needs children, and described to me the excellence of this school and the uniqueness of its approach. Just as she began to capture my interest, she delivered the big kicker: the school was located on the other side of the country.

Georgia? What? A school for Kai in the South? I was flabbergasted. "We live in Marin County, California. You're suggesting . . . what? Moving? To Georgia?"

Neelama tried to calm me down. "I just want to go and look at the school. After the workshop we're teaching in Virginia, we will already be on the East Coast, so I'd like to stop in Atlanta to at least *visit* the school and find out more. I'm really concerned that Kai isn't getting the support he needs for his journey. I've looked everywhere on the Internet for special needs schools, and can't find one anywhere near as promising as Jacob's Ladder."

As Neelama continued to describe the school, it's area of specialization, the credentials of its founder and teachers, and it's track record, my surprise turned to interest . . . although not quite to enthusiasm. I agreed that we needed to find a better option; I was not at all confident that Kai's needs were going to be met at his current school. Even his earlier preschool setting had given him more attention than he was getting now. But I assumed there would be something closer to where we lived. This was California, after all—a center of pioneering and cutting edge innovation! Surely that would extend to special needs schools, too. "I think we should keep looking closer to home," I said, "and if you really feel you want to check out Jacob's Ladder, then you should go, and we can share the cost."

In the middle of October, we flew Kai's Oma out to the Bay Area to look after him, while Mama and Papa left together to teach the "Journey into the Heart of God" program at the Land Celebration retreat site near Gore, Virginia. This was the new name for the Immersion workshop that Neelama, myself, and four other colleagues had designed and taught at the beginning of our breakup. The vision behind this course was to create a modern day monastery where, for nine days, the participants would leave the outer world behind and be initiated as modern day monks and nuns. One of the inspirations for this program had been my three-month meditation retreat ten years earlier in Myanmar, where I had become an ordained Buddhist monk. I had enjoyed my time at the monastery tremendously. What a wonderful opportunity the Buddhist monasteries offered: an ordinary person, or layperson as they called it, could take the vows and robe to temporarily become a monk or a nun and then, on leaving, remove the robe but be entitled to return at any time he or she felt called to. I had often wondered why Western orders didn't allow something similar.

Together with our friend and partner, Howard, and sixteen participants, we entered our "Mystic Monastery," leaving the world behind for eight days, knowing it would keep on turning without us.

One of the unique features of our monastery was its non-denominational approach. The root inspiration for bringing all major spiritual traditions together this way went way, *way* back to my first theological sparring with my father, when I was no more than six or seven years old. In a casual conversation, he had referred to Protestant worshippers as pagans, reflecting the orthodox Catholic exclusivity of his upbringing. "Papa," I asked, "do the Protestants have a different God then we Catholics have?"

He was silent for a moment, and then retorted with: "Our religion is older. They came later, so they have a different idea of God."

"That can't be right, Papa," I said, "Either there is one God or no God . . . no? How can there be two versions of God?"

I don't recall how my father responded to my child's logic, but I remember that something in me *knew,* from deep within, that somehow all religions and paths were actually about the same God. This sense never left me, and many decades later, manifested in our new program—eight days devoted to meditation, prayer, singing, dancing, praising, wailing, bowing, focusing within, and resting in peace—offering our temporary monks and nuns the opportunity for a profound deepening of their connection . . . to that which can't actually be named or described but, ultimately, only experienced within oneself. And that's what happened to all of us there, in those golden October days in Virginia.

After the seminar, I returned home, while Neelama went on her fact-finding mission to Atlanta. I awaited her return with both curiosity and apprehension.

Chapter Nineteen: To Move or Not to Move

(Hers: What is Love?)

I landed in Atlanta on a Monday afternoon towards the end of October. My first few hours were spent driving around the city to get a feel for the place. The air had a heavy moisture that stuck to my skin, even at this time of the year, reminding me that I was, indeed, in Georgia. To my surprise, there were some beautiful neighborhoods that gave this city a small town-feel. Huge trees dominated the streets, claiming the spaces between the houses as their own. There was a prevalence of red brick homes built with white columns, huge porches, and grand entryways, all of which oozed of The South. Those neighborhoods were sprinkled full of life expressing itself: people out walking their dogs; kids skipping home from school; and bikers dodging anything in their way. I had arrived just as the fall foliage peaked, and the sight of it stopped me in my tracks. The leaves, in their bright colors, were almost majestic, and yet undeniably familiar, reminding me of countless autumns spent in upstate New York as a child.

The next morning, I drove over to Roswell, where Jacob's Ladder was located. Roswell turned out to be an adorable little town, with a charming main street full of shops and restaurants, whose neighborhood vibe I loved. When I arrived at the school, I was greeted by Karen, the secretary, a warm Southerner with a smile as wide as the sky. She offered to show me around briefly herself, and as we walked through the halls of the small building that looked like a house, I was shocked to see the students working in individual cubbies—something she called a cornerstone of their program. It seemed a bit odd to me, to have those little kids in tiny cubicles with no windows, and I was, to be honest, a bit taken aback. Karen felt badly that she couldn't give me a more thorough tour, but encouraged me to return that evening, prior to the seminar that I was to attend. She told me that Amy herself, the founder, would meet me.

I returned later that night, and walking through the parking lot to the school, I noticed some anxiety arising inside. It suddenly hit me that I was in another world—Georgia. Suddenly, I felt so far away from home, and began to wonder, *what did this mean . . . for me, for us, for Kai?* My mind had found its way to the unforeseeable future, which no amount of thinking could control. I tried to take deeper breaths, and looked at the sky above, glistening indigo with some last hints of the sun as it said goodbye. This calmed me down and I was able to be in the present moment again, which was much more manageable than the perceived future. I took my seat in the waiting room, and within minutes, was greeted by Amy, a tall and beautiful blonde woman whose blue eyes sparkled with something palpable. We sat close to each other on chairs in this tiny lobby, and began a conversation that would change my life forever. She looked at me with a knowing that pierced through my eyes and into my heart. It was undeniable: this was a woman who, herself, had walked through the fire of parenting a child with special needs. She truly got it, both as a mother and as a professional, and spoke to me about the one-on-one aspect of their program, and her passionate conviction that this worked better than a group setting for children with significant brain delays. In that short meeting, Amy explained things to me about the brain that nobody had been able to articulate for me before, and with such clarity, faith, and inspiration. I felt the same ray of hope enter my body that I had on first visiting the Jacob's Ladder website just a few weeks previously.

After our meeting, I attended a three-hour seminar, which Amy conducted—designed to introduce people to the school and their unique methodology. I sat with about eight other parents around a few big tables in a quasi-conference room, which, by day, doubled as one of their physical therapy rooms. Colorful mats were stacked against the wall, and toys and books lined the shelves, giving off a feeling that kids played there, and were happy.

Amy went through an immense amount of detail in the span of that seminar, and I hung on her every word, writing it all down, and trying to keep up with what I was hearing. It was as if the pieces of the puzzle were finally being put together, by someone who had clearly mastered this domain. The school's philosophy was simple:

first, the brain has an unbelievable capacity to change, and second, the brain *changes,* based on the stimulation it receives. Their entire program centered around exercises designed to stimulate the brain in a variety of ways, depending on the child's deficits. The seminar presented me with much-needed explanations about Kai's condition, as well as actual solutions. Bittersweet tears streamed down my face; I felt as if somebody was holding my hand, relieving some of the burden that Michael and I had been carrying all these years. They were tears of gratitude at the prospect of finally finding an answer— a place that could truly help Kai's little brain grow. I was moved and inspired, and by the end of the evening when Amy and I spoke again, I declared to her that, if Michael could get on board with this, I saw no reason for us not to bring Kai here. Together, we decided that the best approach, before uprooting all our lives, would be to bring Kai in for a few months on a trial basis, to make sure the school was a good fit for him. We hadn't discussed finances, but I already knew that this was going to be a huge hurdle that Michael and I would have to overcome, as the tuition for Jacob's Ladder was as high as the quality of care provided.

The day after I returned home to California, Michael came over and we sat together on my little couch, looking out onto the sweet backyard in the house in Terra Linda where I'd recently moved. It was still October, which, in Marin, is often classified as summer. The view from my sliding glass doors captured all that I loved about this county, except a view of the beach. The sky was that perfect blue, with no clouds in sight. There were fruit trees outside, oleanders in bloom, and the brightness and warmth of the sun was palpable even from inside the house. Looking out the window, I laughed to myself at the irony of life. Just a couple of months ago, my friends and I had been consumed with our move from Novato to this house in Terra Linda, just a matter of miles apart. At the time, that had seemed like such a big change. And now, sitting on my couch with my former husband, I realized that this was nothing compared to what might lie ahead.

Michael listened intently as I excitedly spilled out my experience of Jacob's Ladder, of Amy, of the pocketful of hope I'd come home with—all of which contained the possibility that Kai's brain could finally have what it needed to reach its full potential. At the end of my monologue, Michael turned to me calmly and said, "I need time to digest all of this." He suggested we do some more research and weigh all the pros and cons, before officially committing to such a huge change of direction.

Days later, we started to have the more difficult conversation—about money. We wondered how we would be able to afford the cost of Jacob's Ladder on our salaries. Michael and I were deeply fulfilled by the work we did, but we didn't earn the kind of income we'd need to afford private school for our son. We actually lived quite simply. We both drove used cars, and, other than our trips to

India which, for us, were part of our continued education and personal development we needed to support our work, and also paid for by the frequent travel miles we accumulated from our work trips, we didn't have extra money to go on big vacations, own a home, or save for retirement . . . let alone pay for a private school! With spreadsheets in front of us, we got down to the real business of seeing what we needed to do so we could afford this opportunity for Kai.

The more we contemplated leaving our familiar surroundings, the more I saw all that we had created here. Most of the time, I had taken it for granted. But now, looking around at all that we might leave behind: our housemates; our best friends; our spiritual community; the most spiritually cutting-edge place on the planet; our beloved ocean; Kai's wonderful therapists, I felt a mixture of gratitude, grief, and sheer terror.

The other hugely important piece in this decision-making process was my relationship with Paul. He and I had numerous discussions about how we might make this move work for us, but we always came up empty. Paul loved his life in Marin, and had major hesitations about leaving. One night, while we were sitting on his couch, talking, he told me with finality that, no matter how much he loved me, he wasn't coming to Georgia.

I challenged him, "How can you say you love me, but won't come with me?"

With certainty and practicality, he replied, "This has nothing to do with love; I just can't do it. I know myself too well; I don't have the capacity to do this."

It floored me. "I really don't get that," I said, "That is the *hardest* thing for my little heart to understand. It goes against the very grain of everything I grew up believing about love. I've made *love* the compass of my entire life. God, I've changed jobs, states, even religions. I blew up my entire marriage for love. And now you're telling me it just isn't enough? *Love* is not this medicine that can wake us from the dead, turn a frog into a prince, or make you come across the country with me?"

He couldn't answer those questions for me.

Paul's decision not to move, *despite* his love for me, shook my love paradigm and rocked my world. I sank into the couch, feeling betrayed, as if I'd been punched in the stomach and lied to my whole life. I resented the fairy tales, Hollywood, the countless love songs I'd grown up singing, Valentine's Day, and everything else I could remember that perpetuated the lie.

Thus began a slow and painful process of further deconstructing my tightly held ideal about this thing called love: *with love ALL things are possible.* This was not the case! Paul loved me, I was pretty certain about that, but love wasn't enough to compel him to turn his life upside down, and take a huge risk for Kai and me. This was a painful realization, and I felt as if I was being dragged, limb-by-limb, out of the biggest dream of my life. The truth was that love *wasn't* always enough. This forced me to ask, again and again, *What is love, what does it mean, what does it require of us, can it really conquer all, is it even real?* In grappling with these questions, I realized just how righteous I had been about love, believing that I knew exactly what it was and how it worked . . . as if it could be defined in simple terms. This experience showed me that, as much as I had learned, there was still so much I didn't know about love, about life, about anything.

The following week, Michael and I met again, to try to reach a decision. After going through our lists of pros and cons, Michael quietly said, "If you really think this is the best move for Kai, I trust you, and say yes to coming along." I looked into his eyes, and saw the man I had married, just seven years ago, and remembered why I had loved him so deeply. I still loved him, but the love had morphed into another kind of love. As stubborn and righteous as he could be at times, Michael could be just as quick to surrender in the interests of the bigger picture. And when it came to Kai, or the "Little Prince" as he called him, he would do anything. Regarding that little guy, we were fundamentally aligned. We hugged and cried tears of joy, and sadness, for a long time.

The next challenge we faced was the decision about where we would live. Michael and I had almost always lived with other people, and the prospect of each of us living in a separate apartment, alone with Kai, and in a new town, felt gloomy. We decided that, at least for the trial period, it made sense to share a house together, both for financial reasons, and to diminish the loneliness factor. We hadn't lived together in three years, and considering the storm we'd just weathered, it was with some trepidation that we decided to test this experiment.

We spoke with Jacob's Ladder, and decided to begin Kai's trial period at the beginning of January, which meant we'd need to leave right after Christmas, just eight weeks away. Thus began the hard work of preparing to move. For me, letting go of my relationship with Paul was heart wrenching and painful, and proved to be the most difficult task of all.

Looking around at all my friends, our wonderful community, the support structure we'd built for Kai over so many years, while now preparing to live in a faraway and unknown place, felt daunting. But something was pulling me—the hope of Jacob's Ladder, the ray of sunshine that had implanted itself in my heart, and the faith that we'd finally found a place that could really help Kai. This light carried me through the dark grief of leaving behind so much that I loved.

(His: A Father's Surrender)

As soon as I knew that Neelama had returned from her exploratory trip to Georgia, I dropped Kai off at school and headed immediately to her house. As we sat in her living room, she excitedly described her trip. "The good news," she announced, "is that Jacob's Ladder is what it claims to be. It's an incredible program, Michael." Neelama went on to describe all the ways in which this school was unique and how, in this setting, Kai would not fall through the cracks.

"You speak as if you're sold," I ventured.

"Yes, I *am* sold on the school", she said, "I really think it would be great for Kai. That's the good news. The bad news, of course, is it's in Georgia, when our lives are here."

We both went into silent and prolonged reflection, considering what it would mean if we pursued this further. "Let's take some time," I suggested, "We don't have to decide anything right away."

Over the next week or so, we mulled the situation over again and again, between the two of us, and with our friends and other trusted advisors. I had spent sixteen years living in Marin County, on and off, and had somehow never fully taken it on as my "home." Now, with the prospect of leaving, all that changed. Driving along familiar roads, hiking my favorite trails, and visiting my special places, I realized that Marin *was* my home. Although Neelama and I hadn't made an official decision to move, the process of grieving had already begun for us both.

There were some positive aspects to Atlanta, beyond the excellence of the school itself. A move there would bring me closer to Lan, who lived only an hour and a half away from Atlanta. Also, most of our Inner Journey work took place closer to the East Coast, so travel time would be drastically shortened and airline expenses reduced. For Neelama, however, moving away was much more problematic in the relationship department. I wondered what Paul would do. Would he come along, too?

Next we turned to the cons—having to move away from our lives and friends in Marin topping that list. We realized we were part of an extended community of more than a hundred people. The obvious second item on the list of cons was the looming question of how we would be able to finance an expensive private school for Kai.

I recalled that, during the time when Neelama was pregnant, we'd talked about potentially sending our child to a Marin Waldorf School, until we learned with a shock that tuition fees were in the range of $8,000 to $10,000 a year. After Neelama's recent fact-finding mission in Atlanta, she had revealed to me that the annual cost of enrolling a student in Jacob's Ladder was a minimum of $44,000. It took my breath away!

Neelama and I were deeply fulfilled by the work we were involved in, but we didn't earn the kind of income to afford private school. We didn't own a home, lived communally, drove used cars, and other than our trips to India—thankfully, paid for by the travel miles we accumulated during our work trips—we didn't take typical family vacations. The prospect of paying for a private school looked more than daunting.

During my own school years, I had rarely even heard about private schools. In the Germany of my youth, colleges and universities were virtually tuition-free. Paying for schooling was a foreign concept to me . . . and now our son was five years old, and we were considering a private school that cost nearly as much as Stanford. Life had me, metaphorically speaking, by the financial balls—having to spend money for education in the first place, and having to spend such a staggering amount of it, and probably for many years to come, in the second place. It was a huge stretch, beyond my imagination.

As Neelama and I continued to talk about this conundrum, and look at the numbers of our respective incomes, we realized that there was no way we could afford such a school, even with savings from all the years of our previous combined earnings. I had an idea. "What about creating some kind of philanthropic foundation dedicated to funding Kai's tuition?" I suggested. "Maybe with the help of others we could do it!"

Neelama was inspired, perking up, "Yes, perhaps with support from all our family, friends, and the people we know in our Inner Journey communities, it just might work."

"So you are leaning towards going for it, and enrolling Kai in Jacob's Ladder?" I asked.

After a long silence, and with a sigh, she replied, "Yes. Now that we know that a school like Jacob's Ladder exists, it's hard to consider not giving Kai this incredible opportunity."

"And Paul?"

"No," she sighed heavily, tears welling up in her eyes. "He's too attached to his great life here."

"That's unfortunate. I really like Paul," I told her, "I feel he and I would become good friends if we were to spend time together."

"I think so, too," she said, "You actually have a lot in common. What are *your* feelings about the move?"

"In all honesty," I replied, "I don't want to go. A move to the U.S. South does not attract me. Here we are in the most liberal and progressive place in the country. The Bay Area feels quite European to me, which I love. And we have so many dear friends we'd have to leave behind. California is where all the newest spiritual developments happen, and where so many teachers live and work. In comparison, a move to Atlanta feels like going into a spiritual desert. But what can I do? In a way, I feel I don't really have much of a choice. As far as I can see from their website, and what you've shared with me, Jacob's Ladder offers a unique opportunity for Kai—a real chance for him to learn to speak and function independently. And now, what really tips the scales, is that you're willing to give up your relationship with Paul for this—Jacob's Ladder must be a really good school!"

She nodded, with tears in her eyes, her heart obviously as heavy as my own.

We left each other that night feeling somber and sad, already anticipating the loss of our friends and our home base. The die had been cast; the decision was made.

Together, Neelama and I wrote an email to our friends and community groups, where we found the courage to make ourselves vulnerable, and ask for help for Kai's tuition. In response, some of our closest friends, Maria and Britta, stepped forward to organize a farewell/fundraiser event as a send-off party for us.

Bittersweet is the only way to describe that evening. Because of our imminent farewell, the part of our personalities that so often stops us from truly connecting with others went on the backburner. We found ourselves laughing hysterically, crying liberally, loving everyone openly and authentically, and expressing our huge gratitude and appreciation for our shared life with these beautiful friends.

We signed up our first eighteen "Angels for Kai" that night—friends who generously and lovingly committed to a monthly donation, which would give us reliable support in covering Kai's tuition. In the course of the following year, and coming from various communities of friends, we had some thirty-five people step forward to become monthly donors for Kai, guaranteeing us about one-third of the annual tuition. We were, and continue to be, quite blown away by the overwhelming support given to us for Kai. It felt, and still feels today, like a miracle.

The farewell party ended with our sitting in a circle with about forty of our friends, on the floor of the big living room in our beloved Upper Road house. We looked in silence and sweet connection at the candle burning in the center, reminding us of so many other circles we had sat in on this floor over the past decade. Many of us had a final cry, realizing and accepting that there will always be change, that every farewell is a small death, and that life always moves on.

Christmas came. Oma flew in from Elmira, New York, Neelama's dad, Bob, and his wife, Peggy, from Colorado, Lan from D.C., and Paul drove over from Mill Valley . . . to join our Christmas Eve dinner at Upper Road. For Neelama and I to have our partners with us, Paul and Lan, was a beautiful and important step in the normalization process of the friendship between us. As for Kai, he was happy as a clam—he had most of his favorite people under one roof.

Shortly after Christmas, Oma and Neelama packed up Neelama's car, and headed off on their journey to Georgia across our vast continent, from the golden hills to the green hills. Then, with the dawn of 2010, Kai and I said our final farewells to our beloved Upper Road community of friends. Looking out from our deck, holding him in my arms, I reflected on the many years I had lived here, and especially the event of Kai's birth in our downstairs bedroom. The waters of the North Bay below whispered its well wishes for our journey in the form of a light breeze, and tears streamed down my face as I gave thanks for the privilege of having lived on its shores. I looked back over the incredible life I'd had here, and as I glanced down at my wiggling and giggling son, I looked forward to what the future would bring, praying that the boy in my arms would be the benefactor of the adventure on which we were embarking.

Chapter Twenty:
Eastward Y'All

(Hers: Finding Meaning)

A few days after Christmas, Paul and I said our final goodbyes, and I drove one last time down the Mill Valley hillside, leaving behind all that had become such a refuge for me over the past year. I wept in the car, playing one of our songs over and over, as if to stab myself in the heart. It felt like everything was happening so fast, and there was nothing I could do to slow it down. The next morning, I packed up my car and drove to Sacramento, to pick up my mom and begin our five-day journey from California to Georgia.

We had a fun mother-daughter road trip, and laughed until our sides hurt. It was the best medicine I could have asked for to help get me across the country with a bleeding heart. We arrived in Roswell on New Year's Day, and my mom and I quickly got to work cleaning our rented townhouse, and getting it ready for Kai and Michael, who would be landing the next morning. It was great to have my mom with me; I cherished our relationship and the way we had become so close over the years. She helped ease the transition to this unknown place, for which I was extremely grateful. The next day we drove to Hartsfield Jackson Airport, in Atlanta, to pick up Kai and Michael, and were greeted by an exuberant little boy who really cared only about seeing his Oma. Driving home, we told Michael of our cross-country trip adventures, to his great amusement. As we entered our new "home town" of Roswell, he looked out the window, and I saw him trying to take in this new reality. We were no longer in California, and the look on his face showed both excitement and worry.

My mom stayed with us for that first week, to help us adjust to our new life and to be a witness to Kai's first day of school. A few days before he started Jacob's Ladder, we had taken him there to have an extensive evaluation with Amy. In a small room, full of toys, she observed Kai playing, talking, and interacting with us for a few hours. Then, with Kai being entertained by Oma, Michael and I sat down to answer a slew of questions from Amy about his development. When we returned the next day, she handed us a thick stack of papers that detailed her findings, and also described close to a hundred exercises that would comprise Kai's individualized program . . . which was to begin the next day. Amy went through the details of every single exercise with us and, about halfway through, when she saw from my face how overwhelmed I'd become, she, reassured me that we would not have to do these exercises at home—she just wanted us to know what Kai would be doing every day. The next morning, with anticipation and excitement, the three of us dropped the little prince off at his new educational home. Kai was greeted by Mark, a young and pleasantly outgoing teacher with

314

a beaming smile. Kai warmed up to him quickly, and then Mark whisked him away to begin their day. Oma, Michael, and I breathed sighs of relief as we walked out of this charming schoolhouse into the cool January air. The experiment had begun!

As the weeks went by, it became painfully clear that I needed to cut off contact with Paul. It was still so confusing, for my grieving heart, to continue our relationship by phone, prolonging the undeniable reality: he was not coming, and we were not going to be together. One night, while Michael was travelling, and Kai was snoring in my bed, I crept into Michael's room to have my last phone call with Paul. I couldn't help but feel the irony of the situation—there I was, sitting on my former husband's bed, the man I left and whose heart I'd broken in two, now having my own heart broken by this breakup with Paul. It was pretty odd. Paul and I stayed on the phone for hours, reminiscing about the good times in our relationship, sharing pictures together on our iPhones. We laughed and cried at the irony of what we were doing now— breaking up even though we'd been a totally happy couple.

As I hung up the phone, I realized that I hadn't really known the pain of heartbreak until that moment. It had been I who had left every major relationship in my adult life . . . except this one. This breakup was not of my choosing, and the pain was so intense I felt like my heart would explode. I began to pace around Michael's bedroom, just like I'd paced in labor with Kai. The pain overwhelmed me, and all I could do was pray to be able to bear what felt like an unbearable torment. When the agony felt like it would consume me, I dropped down on my knees and found myself begging for some mercy, for some grace to relieve this hurting heart. I wanted so badly for God to give me a sign that this was the right decision, and that I hadn't just put myself, and all of us, through meaningless suffering for no point. I prayed fervently that there might be a meaning to all of this—there had to be—and for God to please help me see that meaning.

Meaning arrived the next morning, when I came across a recent photo of Kai on my iPhone. It was taken just after he'd come out of the tub a few nights before, and he was standing wrapped in his towel, with his toothbrush in hand, wearing the most adorable innocent joy on his face. The look in Kai's eyes in that photo exuded a happiness most adults would never know. As I looked at that picture, I realized our little guy had no idea what Michael, Oma, and I had just been through to "fertilize" this soil for him. It struck me in that moment why parenting for many people is such a spiritual path. Here we were, all the way across the country, letting go of everything important and meaningful to us, in a place we would never have imagined ourselves choosing to live—all to support this little bug. We had been given a gift, and Kai had brought us to a place that none of us had been before—geographically, but even more so, internally. He had transmitted a happiness to us previously unknown, the kind of joy that intoxicates you. In exchange, we were given a specific purpose—to become the temporary stewards of this soul, the caretakers of a precious bud—and our job was to help him grow roots and blossom into the incredible flower he was meant to be. Most days, I couldn't help feeling as if I'd fallen short on that mission; I'm sure most parents feel that way at times. But on that day, looking down at this picture and the blissful look on my son's face, I knew I hadn't.

(His: Georgia on My Mind)

We had rented a townhouse from Esther, a warm and sweet Polish immigrant who had lost her job when the economic downturn had taken hold in the Atlanta area, and now lived with her son in order to cover her mortgage payment with rental income. For the short term, two bedrooms were fine for us because Kai still didn't sleep in his own bed. Kai adjusted immediately to his new home, which surprised us all. It seemed entirely normal to him that Mommy, Papa and Oma were all there together, living with him. There was no sign of the move having caused him distress—if anything, he seemed overjoyed to have all the love and attention in this small container.

On January 4th, the big day came for Kai. He would be joining a student body of about thirty special needs kids and almost an equal number of teachers at his new school. He was nervous and excited, and so were we. The whole household woke up early that day and enjoyed breakfast together, before jumping in the car for the twenty-minute drive to Jacob's Ladder.

We were warmly welcomed by Amy O'Dell, the founder of the school. Kai was holding on tightly to my body, as we were introduced to his one-on-one teacher, Mark, who welcomed the "Boo" with a giant smile. For occasions like this, I had created a little transition ritual. Dangling Kai between my legs, and to the count of one-two, I would swing him ever closer to Mark, who then caught him on the count of three. Matching my playful energy, Mark carried Kai around, showing him all the new and exciting things to see and touch. It was with a renewed optimism that we left our son in the capable hands of this wonderful team of professionals, trusting that whatever was in store for him at this school had to be significantly better than what had been available to him back in California.

In my whole life, I had never lived in a small townhouse and so, particularly after the beauty and spaciousness of the home I'd just left, it was quite an adjustment for me to live in a space not much bigger than our old garage. Nonetheless, soon after Oma left on her trip home, Neelama, Kai, and I found our rhythm as a family again. In what seemed like no time at all, he had created a new wake-up ritual. As Neelama and I were peacefully sleeping in our respective bedrooms, we'd become aware of little bare feet trampling across the hall coming towards one us. Kai would storm into the bedroom, screaming "wake up, wake up," ripping off the bedcovers and pulling that parent roughly by the arm into the other's bed. There he'd carefully position Neelama and me, like pawns on a chessboard, with himself right in the middle, putting his arms around each of us, and beaming happily—bringing to life his picture of an ideal family: Mama–Kai–Papa, all of us together as they should be. Someone else—me, in fact—soon grew very fond of this not so gentle but oh-so-heartwarming morning ritual. I had "my family" back, and realized just how much that meant to me. For me to have Kai around almost all the time was a joyful treat, and I didn't miss the "week off" I'd had when he visited Neelama in our old 50-50 childcare arrangement.

Mornings with Kai were particularly sweet for me, but mornings for Neelama were another thing entirely. More than a few times, Kai and I had come in to wake her up, only to find a weeping Mommy in her bed. She was heartbroken to be without Paul. I could truly get what Neelama was going through, and I felt a great deal of compassion for the pain and loss she was enduring.

There were also times when another part of me couldn't help reflect on the "what goes around comes around" law of karma. In the early '70s, John Lennon wrote the song "Instant Karma," which brought a broad awareness of the concept of karma, and karmic consequences, into our modern western culture. The move to

Georgia for Kai's sake had caused Neelama to lose her mate. Paul's choosing to prioritize his work and community over his relationship with her, plunged Neelama into the same dark underworld of rejection and abandonment with which I was so familiar.

To be radically honest, there were a few moments when, in addition to my care and sympathy for her, another feeling arose, for which my native German language has a specific term that, amazingly to me, doesn't exist in English: *schadenfreude*. This German word has no direct English translation but, in its literal sense, means to take pleasure in *schaden* (damage)—another person's pain or misfortune. It was the Beast in me that couldn't help but feel that Neelama was finally getting a taste of her own medicine. The fact that a German word exists for this phenomenon demonstrates a cultural awareness of the shadow side of personalities dating back many centuries. Just by being human, we can be sure of *schadenfreude* visiting us from time-to-time from the underbelly of our psyche. The eleventh century Persian mystic, Rumi, wrote a poem called "The Guest House," which describes how I attempt to live life when an invasion of shadow parts, activated by life's situations, reveal themselves in my psyche:

The Guest House

This being human is a guesthouse.
Every morning a new arrival.

A joy, a depression, meanness,
some momentary awareness comes
as an unexpected visitor.

Welcome and entertain them all!
Even if they are a crowd of sorrows
who violently sweep your house
empty of its furniture,
Still, treat each guest honorably,
he may be clearing you out
for some new delight.
The dark thought, the shame, the malice,
meet them at the door laughing and invite them in.
Be grateful for whatever comes,
because each has been sent
as a guide from beyond."

— *Jelaluddin Rumi*
  (trans. Coleman Barks)

Notwithstanding the occasional encounters with my shadow side, I could not help but feel compassion for Neelama during her painful journey through "the dark night of the soul."

As for me, that first month in the deep South had turned surprisingly into a time of joy and happiness. The shuffling back and forth of Kai between us, which I dreaded, had ended, and I felt his development was in extremely good hands at Jacob's Ladder. One of the many miracles was that Kai stopped needing a diaper. Six years of diaper changing, and our financial support of the diaper industry, came to a sudden and surprising end. Somehow, his teachers at Jacob's Ladder were able to get him potty trained. It confirmed again one of the major teachings in our journey with Kai: Everything happens in "Kai Time," not our time."

Chapter Twenty-One:
The Trial Period

(Hers: What Does God Have To Do With It?)

Don't surrender your loneliness so quickly.

Let it cut more deep.

Let it ferment and season you,

as few human or even divine ingredients can.

Something missing in my heart tonight

has made my eyes so soft, my voice so tender.

My need of God

Absolutely

Clear."

— *Hafiz* (Trans. Daniel Ladinsky)

It was the end of January, and snow was falling in Georgia. The skies were grey and I was perplexed—this was the South after all; Florida was practically down the road. Where the hell was the sun? One month had passed since Paul and I had our last hug, and my body still wept to think of it. Winter dragged on for what seemed like an eternity, full of dismal days and buckets of rain and loneliness. Michael and I returned to our routine of work, where one of us would usually be home alone with Kai while the other was on the road. Those were the hardest times for me—Kai and I alone for several days on end. There was nobody to talk to; we had no friends, and this kind of life felt so foreign. For the past sixteen years, I had lived communally with groups of people who were my closest companions. There was always someone to chat with, someone in the kitchen, someone for Kai to bother, someone around making noise. No matter how many days and weeks passed, I couldn't get used to opening our apartment door to find just quiet emptiness. Stepping back inside, seeing that tiny living room with it's dismal view onto a parking lot, knowing it would just be Kai and I alone all weekend, created a huge sense of isolation.

Some days, after picking Kai up from school, I would just drive around Roswell. How I longed to be able to take him for a walk in our cute downtown. But Kai was not that kind of kid—he could not just go for a stroll along the sidewalks, or sit down with me for a meal in one of those darling little restaurants, where so many other families were eating. Those experiences were foreign to him, and thus to me. So I would just drive up and down the streets of our quaint town, watching people through the restaurant windows as they laughed, dined, or toasted to some occasion. And there I was, driving slowly by in hopes of soaking in the sense of life that was going on around me. After a few rounds of this, I headed back towards our house, welling up with salty tears, and aching at the loss of what I had left behind.

It occurred to me one cold night at the end of February, which happened to be my birthday, that I was a thirty-nine-year-old woman with a special needs child, living in a condo complex in Georgia with my ex-husband! I laughed out loud, thinking this was not at all how I thought my life would turn out. I'm sure many people have similar thoughts at times in their lives, especially as they get older, and maybe especially so on their birthday. Birthdays have a way of demarcating phases of life, for better or for worse. Looking at where I was now, I realized I needed something bigger than myself to pull me through that cold and depressing winter and so, one Sunday morning, I found myself at St. Michael's church, just a few miles from our apartment.

Part of me thought it was crazy to put myself back in a church setting, with all the dogma and rhetoric that often entailed, not to mention countless scriptural reinterpretations with which I vehemently disagreed. At the same time, I kept hearing the voice of Osho, one of my spiritual teachers, in my head. He always said that it wasn't the institution, or even the teacher, that really mattered on one's quest to find God. Even if the teaching or teacher themselves had been corrupted, the student could still succeed on their path. The structure itself didn't have to be perfect for the path to work—it was the purity of the student's heart, and the totality they brought to their search that mattered most. Somehow I trusted that, if I were willing to deepen my connection with my Higher Power, then it didn't matter if I was sitting in a church, a temple, a mosque, or on top of a mountain.

As the winter months went by, I attended more church services than I had attended in my entire adult life. I knew that what I was experiencing at Mass had less to do with the outer form of church and more to do with a deepening relationship with a presence inside me. Out of my loneliness, a deep longing arose to connect more fully to that presence which felt to be within me . . . and greater than me. It was that presence that I called God, and that presence in which I put my hope and faith to get me through the lonely heartbreak and sense of desolation that had become my reality. It wasn't church I wanted, or even religion. What my heart longed for was an unbroken connection to that unconditional love I'd tasted before. By participating in the structured practice of prayer, ritual, and Holy Communion, something in me reconnected, bit-by-bit, to that Divine Presence that was always with me.

The church had a comforting feel. Sun streamed in through the colorful windows, sprinkling rainbow speckles on the wooden pews, where strangers sat shoulder-to-shoulder. Music filled the space with love, entering my body and shaking up my heart. There were some inspirational priests. One, in particular, gave a powerful sermon one Sunday about the Eucharist, known to many as the Holy

Communion. The teaching of the Catholic Church is that Christ is not just symbolically present in the Eucharist, but that the bread and wine are literally transformed during the Mass into His Body and Blood: "transubstantiation." I could never quite wrap my head around that one, but could understand, from my studies in religion, that many spiritual and religious traditions down the ages have used the process of transmission to transfer Divine energy to us humans. That was how I came to understand communion: a sacred opportunity for this transmission to take place within me. During that same homily, the priest said, "There's no question as to whether Christ is present in the Eucharist. The real question is, are YOU present?"

That question struck me to the core. I realized in that moment that God was always present. It was me who had been out of touch. I'd been so focused on Paul, the move, the loss of what I'd left behind, and my aching heart, that I had forgotten the most important relationship of all. Communion was an opportunity to re-establish that relationship. Since the structure of church was helping me do that, I didn't want to throw the baby out with the bathwater, and so could appreciate the gifts, while setting the rest aside. I came to realize how much I needed structure, even in my spiritual life. Left to my own devices, *that* inner relationship was the first to go on the back burner. Without a daily practice, I reverted to my usual coping mechanisms of laziness, distractions, or filling myself up with anything external. I came to see that, for all the issues I had with organized religion, and there were plenty, I couldn't deny that the deeper meaning behind the structure itself, whose ultimate purpose was to reconnect the individual to God, to help us reorient our compass needles towards our true nature, *did* work for me . . . especially if I committed to it.

The brightest light amidst all of this was Kai. His trial period at Jacob's Ladder was going better than either Michael or I could have hoped. The school exuded such love, joy, and, positivity to every student, no matter the disability. I was in awe watching parents wheeling in children who couldn't move any part of their body, and how those kids were greeted with such sacred regard by their teachers. It moved me to tears, and the very same kindness was shown to Kai. His teachers were amazed at how quickly he progressed in such a short period of time. Seeing him settled at the school warmed my heart, and after so many months of worry, something in me finally relaxed. It was the first time, since Kai had entered kindergarten, that I could sleep soundly, knowing we were doing *everything* we could to help our boy.

By the time late February rolled around, I had decided to take on the practice of Lent. It wasn't something I'd planned, but a series of events brought me to the National Shrine in Washington D.C. on the eve of Ash Wednesday. I had come to D.C. to teach a workshop, and there, in those very days, Josh, a dear friend, was dying. He and his wife, Susan, had been my clients for almost four years. Josh had been suffering with cancer ever since I knew them, and one of the tragedies was the timing of it all. Josh was my age—so young, too young. Yet they had faced this storm together with such fierce grace, and I was honored to have been part of their process over the past years that we had worked together. Susan asked me to be with them in Josh's final days, and it was a bittersweet experience that touched me more than I ever could have imagined. I arrived at their apartment on Wednesday, to find Josh nearing the end of his life. While I held his hand, as I watched Susan care for him in unimaginable ways, I heard him speak for the very last time, whispering, "I love you" to his devoted wife. It had been a heavy and difficult day, and, as I walked out onto Sixteenth Street in the heart of D.C., the deep blue sky and cold air felt so precious to me. The imminence of death was present, not only Josh's but mine too. Everything felt incredibly fragile. In that moment, I remembered it was Ash Wednesday, and drove directly to the nearest church, figuring there must be a few more services left.

I ended up at the largest Catholic Church in America. The Shrine was stunning, especially at night, its outline illuminated like a European cathedral. The massive structure was potentially overpowering, but on that night during the mass, I felt transported into another time, another place, a world without cathedrals. I was back in the desert, envisioning the forty days Christ had spent in what I have always imagined to be the most transformational journey of his life. And somehow, that opportunity for transformation was available to me, here and now, through the invitation of Lent. It was an invitation to spend forty days putting the inner world above all else, honoring my bond with God as the priority of my life. Forty days? My answer was yes. Forty days seemed do-able.

It was a very different approach to Lent than I'd ever taken. Throughout my Catholic youth, Lent had mostly felt like punishment—I felt forced to give up something I loved, usually chocolate. In the light of Josh's death, Lent took on an entirely different meaning. I hadn't been around death all that much, but I felt that the gift of witnessing death was a tremendous wake up call. Most of the time, I was numb to the fragility of my time here. Sitting in that church, with Josh dying just a couple of miles away, made it easy to see what really mattered. I remembered that, in almost every spiritual tradition on the planet, the practice of abstinence is used to strengthen the individual on their inward journey. By letting go of my "crutches," even for just a period of time, I was hoping to reorient my compass needle towards the source of peace and strength that I knew resided at my center. Abstaining from my various forms of addictions forced me, in many ways, to turn towards another kind of sustenance—my own soul, and its connection to that which was infinitely greater than me. I attended daily mass during that Lenten season, and felt that what I yearned for was finally happening: the forging of a more sustained connection to the Divine, a connection that would carry me through one of the darkest periods of my life.

Michael and I were doing incredibly well in our experiment of living together, and I felt a true partnership begin to emerge on our journey of co-parenting Kai. Every so often, our tempers would collide and sparks would fly, but for the most part, it was an enjoyable time of newfound friendship. He was there for me many times during those difficult winter months, and would frequently provide a compassionate ear in my moments of grieving Paul. I was often struck by the hugeness of his heart. I wondered how he was able to hold me in my heartbreak, given that just a few years earlier it was I who had broken his heart in two. Yet he managed to dig deep within himself and find a place big enough to listen to my monologues, which always ended in puddles.

Perhaps the greatest gift of all came at the end of one of those sessions together, when Michael reminded me of the teachings on which all of our Inner Journey work was based—teachings I had given countless times to participants, but teachings that were harder to give than receive, and even more difficult to put into practice now that it was my own heart on the line. Michael guided me back to myself, and into the pain that the Paul situation triggered in me, which was, of course, much deeper than just the relationship. In the breakup, I felt as if I'd lost love itself. Having gone through this process himself just a few years earlier, he was able to help me realize that most of the grief I was feeling was mine alone to deal with, and Paul was not to blame. Michael was a great friend to me in those months, and another level of healing happened between us, as we grew to understand each other a bit more deeply. I was shocked at the ease and closeness of our new living arrangement. We had clearly arrived at another place in our relationship—we had transcended our bitter divorce, and were well on our way to forging an even deeper bond. This made my heart very happy.

That spring, Susan asked me to perform the funeral ceremony for Josh. I was honored to be part of such a sacred event. It was to take place in at a chapel beside a cemetery in D.C., where Josh had loved to ride his bike. Little did I know how much this ceremony would give to me. A small group of family and close friends gathered in the tiny chapel at the entrance to the cemetery. As I watched Susan stand up at the podium, brimming with unending love and tears for Josh, something clicked in me. I had been trying to wrap my head and heart around the Paul thing for all those months and realized, in that moment, that love didn't necessarily mean "being together forever." Love actually meant many things, and on that day—in the middle of Oak Hill Cemetery in beautiful Georgetown, with the birth of spring all around us—love meant letting go. And Susan did that with such grace that it inspired me to think a bit differently about love.

There was still a piece of me that was holding on to the hope that Paul's life would be so miserable that I'd find him at my door one day, begging to join me after all. The night I landed in the airport in Atlanta, after Josh's funeral, I even felt a faint sliver of hope that Paul might be waiting there for me . . . perhaps he would just wake up, turn around, and "make the change," the words to one of my favorite Michael Jackson songs. But he wasn't, and he didn't.

I had collected my bags from the airport area, and knew that Michael and Lan were minutes away from picking me up. Suddenly I wavered, and felt that my body didn't want to go out those doors and get into the car. Going out those doors meant so many things. It meant really being in Georgia, and letting go of love and friends as the center of my life. It meant learning to face and be comfortable in my aloneness. It meant growing up more, standing on my own, earning more money, entering a new phase of motherhood, and claiming this place as my new home. I felt the sheer weight and immensity of everything that lay beyond those doors, and I just stood there for a several moments . . . frozen . . . waiting . . . fighting my last fight . . . and then my tiny sliver of hope extinguished itself. Something inside me relaxed. A surrender happened, and I walked through those doors—finally ready to move on.

Hours later, I was back home, lying on the couch in the condo complex in Georgia. Upstairs, my mom was fast asleep with Kai, and I was told that she was still his favorite. In the next room, my ex-husband was asleep with Lan, his girlfriend, whom I adored. This was nowhere near the life I'd imagined for myself, but as I fell asleep that night, the last prayer on my lips was, "Lord, thank you for taking me on the ride of a lifetime."

Later that spring, we decided that we would indeed stay on in Georgia. Kai was thriving at Jacob's Ladder, and it was time to turn our trial period into a reality. One afternoon, while Kai was at school, Michael came upstairs to my bedroom, which doubled as my office. It was a beautiful day, and my room had a huge window that looked out over a sea of trees sprinkled by the afternoon sun. He sat down on my bed, and slowly broached the subject of us needing to move, come August. Our lease would be up then, and we both felt cramped in the tiny apartment. With some trepidation in his voice, he began: "Neelama, what about us continuing to live together, but getting a bigger place, perhaps renting a house together? Kai loves this arrangement so much, and with all of the travel we both do, and the high tuition bill, it just makes so much sense."

I had to agree . . . it made a ton of sense, and yet my body tensed up with ambivalence. As much as I loved having Michael around, and felt so lonely when he was gone, I was concerned that continuing to live together would, in some subtle way, box me in. I voiced my concerns, saying, "I'm just worried that us living together could somehow block me from getting into my next relationship." He listened intently, and then nodded . . . which immediately helped to relax the stiffness that had begun in my neck. "My concern is not pressing in this moment," I confessed, "but it's something I'm worried about down the road." My mind trailed off to consider the alternative of us *not* moving in together. *We would have to get two apartments, maybe in the same condo complex. I'd be living alone in another tiny apartment.* I dreaded even thinking about it. "Yes I'm willing to move together," I continued, "but ask that we check in with each other from time-to-time about how this arrangement is going for each of us. And, if it does seem to prevent me from moving forward in my romantic life, then I'd like the freedom to move out." He nodded his head, and looked at me compassionately with his clear blue eyes. I could tell from his gaze he understood the complexity of this for me, and that was enough.

(His: Nothing Lasts Forever)

Kai's trial period at Jacob's Ladder was impressively successful. It truly was a boot camp for his brain, and we both felt he was getting so much support for his growth and development. Each day began with one of us entering a hyperbaric oxygen chamber with him—a vertical tube-like structure. We were to sit or lie down in the enclosed tube for one hour, while breathing in the oxygen pumped out by this machine. Its loud noise frightened Kai, but we turned it into a rocket ship in our imaginations, and that made it fun. The rest of Kai's day consisted of a series of exercises done one-on-one with one of his teachers, whom he loved. These included: physical movements, to stimulate activity between his brain hemispheres; oral motor therapy, to exercise the muscles in his mouth; hearing and speech; object recognition; pronunciation; and auditory and visual processing. There was also a listening program designed to stimulate his brain activity. And finally, he underwent a neurofeedback routine three days a week, a form of biofeedback that measures brain wave activity and teaches one how to self-regulate. Self-regulation was one of Kai's biggest challenges, so we were looking forward to getting support with this.

Lan and I spent five days on the Mayan Riviera at the end of February. The gorgeous sunsets and beautiful sand beaches created an ideal ambience for romance and intimacy, but I realized that my feelings of sexual attraction for her, and the usual yearning of my body to merge with her, had diminished somewhat. Lan was a total "yes" for our relationship and even hinted, in some sunset dinner conversations, at her willingness to come to Atlanta to join our unorthodox divorced couple "family experiment." Inside myself, I couldn't help but notice the subtle ways I was withholding my feelings from her, but I just wasn't ready to broach the subject, so I avoided any serious look into the "relationship mirror" that might have allowed me to admit and share with her what I saw.

Upon returning to our respective home bases, our relationship dance continued with my visiting Lan in April, during a teaching weekend engagement in D.C. The following month, on the day after Kai's May 20th birthday, she joined me in Florida, to assist me in the Family Constellation seminar I was leading in Royal Palm Beach. Since our trip to Mexico, I had become less and less engaged with Lan, and was holding back more and more in our long distance connections via phone or email, making it almost impossible for her, single-handedly, to keep our boat from sinking. When she began to talk about relocating, so as to be closer to me, I realized that I had to confront and expose what was going on for me: I did not want Lan to move down to Roswell to live with us. At the end of the workshop, I finally shared with her what I had so desperately been trying to avoid. "Lan," I said quietly, "you must have noticed that I've been holding myself back over the last few months. It's because I was trying to avoid hurting you by talking authentically about my feelings. To be honest, my feelings for you are not strong enough for me to want to move into a more serious relationship, such as you moving down to Atlanta to be with me." As her face fell, I paused for several moments before continuing. "I admit the possibility that, for me, you were a 'rebound partner,' and if that's true, I am so sorry. Over our two years together, I really hoped that, at some point, I would begin to feel towards you what I knew you were feeling towards me. I saw your willingness to fully commit and give yourself—and I'm sorry that it just never happened for me. I truly did hope for that. But it may be that our differences were just too big." It was out. Lan was visibly upset, and she cried quietly in bed. I went to the bathroom and showered, just to give her some time and space to herself. We had an awkward and uncomfortable night, sleeping in the same bed while knowing it was for the last time.

Restless and wired, we got up early the next morning for the drive to the airport, where we said gentle goodbyes and parted; Lan, with visible hurt in her eyes, and me with a mixture of relief and guilt in my conscience. On returning home and sharing with Neelama what had happened, she was both astonished and saddened by my decision. She said she would have loved to have had Lan live with us in our communal arrangement.

For Neelama and me, another important decision was looming. Should we stay in Roswell? If so, we would need more space. Should we get two apartments, or rent a house together? Over the past five months, Kai had done well at his new school, and had proceeded from level one to level two in his development program, an indication that the customized and intense ""Kai curriculum" was working. Our boy was very much loved by the teachers at the school. Because he was so very willing to do his best, his teachers had a much easier time with him than they typically had with their students. Kai's sweet and loving personality drew everyone towards him, and often people were lined up at the school to get a hug or kiss from him. All of this sealed the decision for us: Neelama and I agreed that the trial period had proved fruitful. Jacob's Ladder had actually worked out better than either of us had expected.

I initiated a conversation with Neelama about continuing to live together. We decided that, as long as we were honest, we could work out almost anything. After this talk, we started to look for a house to rent, as close as possible to downtown Roswell, with its appealing coffee shops and restaurants. By the end of June, we had found a local family who needed to move to Texas, for their children's schooling, and were happy to rent us their home in a nice residential neighborhood in Roswell. The great move into 2155 Federal Road happened, with a big truck transporting all the furniture and belongings we'd left in storage in California across the continent to Georgia. Oh my God . . . we had finally arrived!

I felt immense gratitude. A part of me couldn't believe we had made this move, and were able to carry the financial load we'd taken on. I knew that we could not have done that without the generous support of our friends and communities, "Kai's Angels," as well as the support of Neelama's family and my brothers in Germany. I felt how truly blessed we were. It reminded me of a song lyric by Donna De Lory that we had used many times in our workshops: "Blessed always, blessed always, for the love of God surrounds us. Let our joy be so triumphant, that we rest in God and say, Amen."

Chapter Twenty-Two: Allies on the Path

(Hers: One Song)

"All these religions, all this singing . . . one song . . . the differences are just illusion . . . and vanity. Sunlight looks slightly different on this wall than it does on that wall . . . and a lot different on this other one . . . but it is still ONE light."

— *Rumi* (trans. Coleman Barks)

As I stood unpacking dishes in our new kitchen, residual tears of grief spilled out onto the coffee mugs that held so many memories for me, memories of California: faces of dear friends; times spent drinking tea in all of kitchens in which I had lived; meals shared; glasses of wine; funny stories; dance parties; meditation evenings; communal house meetings; countless walks on the beach; meaningful conversations . . . tearful goodbyes. The loss of it all still hurt, and I slid down onto the floor, feeling the full weight of the decision we'd made . . . this was no longer an experiment—this was it. This was our new life, and Georgia was now our home. I looked outside the kitchen window and watched Kai and Michael running through the backyard like wild monkeys. The landlords had left behind a trampoline for our use, and Kai rushed towards it with gleeful abandon. Little could I know the countless joyful hours that were to be spent on that trampoline in the two years we were to call Federal Road our home.

Michael went back to India that August. The same spiritual university that we'd both attended before was now offering a training that he hoped would greatly enhance our work with others. Neither of us had been back since 2007, but we both continued to feel deeply indebted to the teachings and the processes that had healed the anger and pain of our divorce, and given us this chance at a newfound friendship. The transformational work we'd done at this center had undeniably made us better parents, better teachers, and better human beings—contributing to our lives, and to our work with our own students, in unpayable ways. Yet over the years, I'd become somewhat disconnected from the work, and my hope was that Michael's trip would help me to discern if there was still more for me to learn from this spiritual source.

Michael returned with a heart shining like the sun, beaming with excitement and inspiration about the new teachings and processes in which he'd immersed himself. On his first day back, we drove Kai to school together, and on our way home, he began to explain the immensity of his experience. It wasn't so much *what* he said, but *how* he said it, that touched me. I had known Michael for fifteen years by then, and would call him a healthy skeptic over an optimist any day. Yet he was glowing with something palpable. His description of what had occurred in India far transcended belief, or even faith. This was a man who had clearly tasted something remarkable, and was inviting me to taste it too.

I flashed back to a time in 1997, when I had called Michael from a small makeshift phone booth in the middle of Rishikesh, India. I was 26 at the time, and halfway through my yearlong sabbatical of backpacking around Southeast Asia. I had come to India in search of one thing: an enlightened teacher. Through my religious studies, I had learned that most of the great spiritual and wisdom traditions on our planet started because something tremendous had *happened* to its original founder: Buddha, Jesus, Mohammed, Lao-Tzu, and others . . . those individuals had been awakened to a much higher level of consciousness—truth and love. They were a living light on the planet in their time. I wanted to find a living light on our planet *now*, to learn from someone who had awakened to another level of consciousness, and someone who was alive and breathing—not dead and gone, whom I could only read about in a book. I had called Michael from this small phone hut in a moment of desperation, to see if he could point me in the right direction. Of course he could, and recommended I go to meet Brahma Vedant, a seventy-year-old enlightened farmer on the coast of Gujarat, in Western India. Michael hadn't actually been there himself, so wasn't aware that he was sending me to an authentic Indian ashram, not the commercialized Guru-villes that come complete with beds, running hot water, and spoken English. This was the real deal, and I was deeply blessed that Michael had guided me there.

I stayed in that tiny ashram with this ordinary yet wise being for the next three months. We lived simply: sleeping on concrete; working in the fields; eating vegetarian food with our bare hands; and once a day coming together for Darshan. There, we would meet Brahma Vedant—not as a farmer, but as a transmitter of that very light I so longed for. Because he spoke in Gujarati, I did not have the usual mental distraction of having to process words, clouding my experience. That was perhaps the greatest blessing of all. In the past I'd depended upon my mind to know. Yet there, in that little room painted the most brilliant shade of turquoise, with a gentle breeze relieving us from the stifling heat, all I had to rely on was my being. And my being received his transmission loud and clear: a silence and stillness that permeated every part of me, leaving me thirsty for more.

Here we were, Michael and I, nearly fifteen years later, and I was again thirsty . . . and Michael was again supporting my quest to quench it. We sat talking in the car for at least another hour, at the end of which it became abundantly clear that I would be going back to India as soon as possible. Some of my friends asked me if I thought this would derail my reconnection to Christianity, which had become the center of my spiritual life over the previous year. I had continued to delve ever deeper into the Christian tradition of my past, a tradition which I had spent the better part of my adult life mocking. But I was not the least bit concerned that going back to India would weaken this new connection. If anything, I was pretty certain it would enhance it. I had always felt, somewhere deep inside, that there was only one God. Maybe it came from the Judaism of my childhood, and the line I'd heard repeated so many times in Temple during the Shema, the central prayer from that tradition, *"Sh'ma Yis'ra'eil Adonai Eloheinu Adonai Ehad (Hear, O Israel, The LORD is our God, The LORD is One)*. *The Lord is One* had stuck with me all through the years. Since I was pretty certain there was only one God, it made both logical and heartfelt sense to me that there would be many different ways to find Him/Her/It.

In the middle of October 2010, I bid a tearful farewell to Kai and Michael, and headed off again on the long journey to India. I arrived on campus in the middle of the night, and tiptoed into the dormitory, so as not to wake my roommates. I was amazed how familiar it all looked, even though it had been three years since I'd last visited. The dorms were simple and quite austere, with about sixteen beds to a room. Our program began the next morning, and we were greeted by a row of monks and nuns who ceremoniously placed sacred powders on our third eye, and sprinkled holy water on us. As I made my way up front to the altar, I was touched and surprised to find that this was no ordinary altar, for on it were images from all the religious and wisdom traditions of the world. An ancient Rumi poem entered my heart: "All these religions, all this singing . . . one song." I had always felt at my core that God was so vast that no way could He/She/It fit into any one box. It saddened me that we humans spend so much wasted time arguing about which box was the *right* one. I realized then, that my returning to India was another opportunity to expand beyond anything that kept me limited in my relationship with the Great One, that which is beyond all names, all forms, all religions. As I bowed down, my heart broke wide open. Out of me flowed tears of gratitude: for my parents; my life; Kai; Michael; my family; my friends; my work—all I'd been given, and all those who had loved me and contributed to me . . . but most of all, for The Great Creator in all its forms before my eyes, and the mysterious and formless ways It had gifted me with a most blessed life. I lay down on the prayer rug in front of the altar, and wept with tears of love for God, knowing I had come home again. This trip reconnected me both to my own spiritual quest and my desire to help others, and it set the stage for the years to come.

One of the greatest gifts of that trip was another fundamental shift regarding Kai, who, I realized during that week, had *made* me a mother. This was best expressed in a letter I wrote to him that I hope, with every fiber of my being, he himself will read someday:

My beloved Kai,

It is my deepest prayer that you will read this letter one day, and understand the full weight of what you have given to me in this life. Thank you, my sweet son, for the sacrifice you made for me. You taught me another kind of love. It was through you that I finally grew up. When I became your mom, my life was suddenly about something bigger than just me. How did that happen? Bit by bit, you eroded me, and I'll be honest . . . it was an excruciating process. I think of it now like the mortar and pestle: you ground me down, and stretched me to the deepest and widest edges of my human self. So much for the grandiose ideal of "a mother's unconditional love." No, my love, for you I had countless conditions, and at no time did you yield. There they were, all of those parts of me, throwing their individual tantrums as their needs were asked to take a back seat to yours. There were so many times when I felt utterly trapped—backed into the corner of my heart's limited capacity to love—and again, there you were, demanding me to stretch more, to find more, to become more. And when it seemed like there was nothing left, out of the ashes of that erosion, another love was born. It's a quiet love— not the dazzling kind that gets the hungry crowd's applause. It's the love that poured itself into my heart, bringing with it both the clarity and strength I needed to let go. I've come to realize that this is the love that sustains me, when all the other loves come and go. It's another kind of love entirely—the one that finds its fulfillment in hearing you say your own name.

I landed back in Atlanta on Halloween night, and was greeted at the airport by an excited little boy already dressed in his skeleton costume. We made the hour-long trip home from the airport with Kai repeating "trick or treat" with sheer bliss for most of the ride. The moment we pulled into our driveway, he and I set off through our neighborhood, the streets full of excited kids dressed up for the occasion. I laughed at the juxtaposition of where I'd been just twenty-four hours earlier. It was a very quick and painless re-entry into life as Mommy.

Over the next year, Michael and I grew even closer spiritually. Our house on Federal Road had a huge finished basement that served two equally important purposes. After school, and on weekends, the room was Kai's domain. There was a sound system down there, and we would put on children's music and dance wildly around, singing and laughing our heads off. Kai laughed so hard that it choked off any sound from coming out of his mouth; he was contagious to be around, and had a way of bringing out my own silly child like nobody else. His favorite activity was marching around the periphery of the room, banging plastic water bottles together. Anytime a guest came to visit, Kai promptly handed them their own set of water bottles and dragged them downstairs to initiate them into our marching band ritual.

When Kai was not using it, this room was our sacred place, where Michael and I did our spiritual practice. On the far end, in an alcove, we had created an altar, replete with images and symbols of the Divine in many forms. Often, when Kai was at school, we would meet down there to do our meditation and devotional practices together. At some point shortly after I returned from India, Michael and I declared to each other that the coming year, 2011, would be a year in which we would both focus on our inner growth and awakening. We spent countless hours at that altar during the course of the next year and a half, and went through quite a deep process of what I can only call an inner purification. One of the core teachings from India was that is was important to *be with* whatever life was presenting. This was an age-old spiritual precept, so simple and yet so damn difficult to put into practice in real life. Michael and I often held space for each other in what we called "Inquiry" sessions, where we took turns supporting each other in staying with what was *now*. That *now* could be a difficult experience that one of us was having at work or with family, or a deep fear that life had churned up. Sometimes it had to do with our challenges in parenting Kai, or one of us feeling lonely down in Georgia. Whatever the issue at hand, it was a great gift to feel our shared love for transformation, and to be partners in that domain again. I felt a true peace at last.

The year 2012 was coming to an end, and with it, our planet was seeing an even greater surge of people focused on personal growth. This phase, in many spiritual traditions, represented a global rebirth. I reflected back on myself as a pregnant woman, afraid of the birth I was about to undergo, and experiencing the huge resistance I had to having Kai. I vividly remembered how, at the time, he had seemed like such a threat to my perceived idea of freedom. As I gazed at the altar where Michael and I had spent so much time in the past few years, I realized that I felt a freedom inside of me that was deeper than I'd ever known. This freedom had nothing to do with free time per se, or the ability to pick up and go away on a moment's notice, as I had once defined it all those years ago. This freedom was of another quality entirely. There was a spaciousness within me, as if I'd been widened out: by life; by love; by heartbreak: by moving across the country . . . but mostly by Kai. Over the recent years, my heart had been stretched, and I'd been *made free* by the very circumstances I'd feared would constrain me. Somehow along the way, a surrender had happened to me. It wasn't one particular moment, but rather a happening that snuck up on me, whereby, bit-by-bit, I realized the totality of what God had put on my plate, and was finally able to say Yes.

(His: Love, Serve and Remember)

It was primarily Neelama and Oma who made the house on Federal Road a "home" during August and September. As the women were "nesting," I was diving inward again. In the '80s, singer John Astin wrote a song, called "Love, Serve and Remember," that had always inspired and guided me. The second word in Astin's refrain, "serve," drew me back to India. The ashram now offered a new course to train people to teach some of the core principles and processes outside of India. The moment I heard about this course, I felt drawn to it—I wanted to share some of the blessings I had received. I felt that, without the experiences and the healings that happened at the ashram, Neelama and I would not be living together, nor co-parenting Kai as we were now.

Having to travel so frequently for my work, I continued to enjoy the ongoing benefits of accumulated frequent flyer miles, which now found me, courtesy of Lufthansa, being flown from Atlanta via Frankfurt to India. The course was filled with wisdom, and took me on a profound personal journey, from which I returned spiritually renewed and committed to my inner path. I felt like a well, overflowing with presence and love, and this had a significant impact on Neelama. She decided to participate in the upcoming October course. In front of our altar in the basement, Kai and I gave her a ceremonial send-off, and away she went on her modern day pilgrimage.

Upon Neelama's return, our inner spiritual compass needles were aligned like never before. I remembered our wedding vows, which we'd written independently of each other, and how amazed we were to find that the core of what each of us wrote was the same: a vow to each other's personal transformation. Now, after this latest spiritual infusion from Mother India, we had returned, not as a couple, but as loving friends and allies, deeply committed to each other's spiritual journey. A quote from the founder of the ashram confirmed the value of what was happening between us: "Friendship is the highest form of love." Since that time, friendship has remained the foundation of our relationship. Of course, because of Kai, we would always be connected with and bound to each other. Yet our unique closeness has allowed us to create a nurturing "divorced family home" for Kai, operate a business, and continue to teach workshops together.

As in any relationship, there is a garden to be tended and cared for. Or, as the fox tells the little prince in Saint-Exupery's precious book, *The Little Prince:* "To be friends, one needs to 'tame' the other, and one tames by being very patient. First you will sit down at a little distance from me like that—in the grass. I shall look at you out of the corner of my eye, and you will say nothing. Words are the source of misunderstandings. But you will sit a little closer to me, every day. . . ."

Part of our "taming ritual" was doing "Inquiry" work with each other. At its core is a simple yet elegant process whereby we hold space for each other, with an exchange in which each of us gives our silent presence, while the other explores and expresses their inner world. This practice is a profoundly useful tool for creating more intimacy in any relationship. Whenever we neglected this, our friendship weakened and our personalities took over, invading the relationship. As in any relationship, in ours as divorced friends and parents, there were ups and downs, and times of closeness alternating with times of distance.

What we were not able to manifest in the Atlanta area, was a circle of close friends. In California, we were on and off the center of social activities, parties, celebrations, and feasts. One explanation might be our intense travel schedule. The gift to us of our extensive travel is that, when we teach in the different Inner Journey cities, we are surrounded by a large number of students and friends, so that our need for human connection is fulfilled. Back at home, in Georgia, we often experienced a sense of isolation, partly self-imposed and partly based on quite different cultural values than those we brought with us from California.

Neelama and I lived almost as a married couple, yet were not romantically involved, so what did I do with my sexuality? For the first years, with the more inward focus, it was less of an issue. Self-love through masturbation was the natural way to respond to sexual fantasies and dreams. Also, sleeping with Kai fulfilled some of my cuddling needs. When our boy was asleep, his feet or arms, or some other body part, always reached out for some physical contact. Although every year Kai lost a little more connection to what is called the "merging essence," he continued to radiate a sweet, honey-like nectar that, admittedly, both of us drank from regularly. And, occasionally, Neelama and I would watch a movie together, where we cuddled in a nonsexual, yet physically comforting and nourishing way.

In April of 2012, Neelama and I found ourselves teaching a course in Ottawa called "Journey into Love." Right from the beginning, we acknowledged the fact that we were a divorced couple teaching about love and that, because of our experiences, we actually had a lot to share about what worked, but even more so, what didn't work, in the intimate dance of relationship. On Sunday, the third and final day of the workshop, I looked to my right at Neelama, looking lovely in a skirt and, for the first time since the separation bang of 2006, I suddenly felt a strong physical attraction to her. I was stunned: Neelama had become a "woman" again for the "man" in me.

For a while, I didn't want to admit this, even to myself. It took a few months before I confided to Howard one afternoon. We were teaching together that summer, and had gone for a swim in the pond at the retreat center during one of our breaks. As we sat on the dock, I shared with him that my attraction towards Neelama had returned. Howard looked pensive, and asked, "What are you going to do about it?"

As the dock swayed us back and forth, I felt my own ambivalence about the situation, "I don't know. A part of me doesn't want to rock the boat of friendship we've built. It's taken us *years* to get to this place. Our relationship is working amazingly well right now, and I'm so happy to have our little family back. I don't want to threaten this," In the end, I decided not to do anything about it, not even to share it with Neelama, but to just wait and see what would happen.

With the completion of 2012, I felt the longing in me for a refueling of my spiritual gas tank. I arrived back at the ashram on New Year's Eve. Hundreds of us from around the world gathered under the night sky on the beautifully manicured lawns to enjoy a multitude of Southern Indian dishes. Unexpectedly, I ran into friends from prior visits, and together we toasted each other with fruit punch at midnight. Some of us meditated in front of the altar in the session hall in silence, to welcome and pray for our planet and global healing in the coming year. A yearning in me, to contribute in my own ways to a shift in consciousness, is what had attracted me six years ago to this ashram. This same yearning had brought me back here once again.

Chapter Twenty-Three: The Proposal

(Hers: A Curveball)

Kai's progress at Jacob's Ladder is what kept me going in Georgia. I still terribly missed our community in the Bay Area, and nothing had replaced the close and intimate friendships we'd spent almost fifteen years building there. In the beginning of 2013, I began to feel my longing to be in an intimate relationship again. Over the past few years, to my great surprise, I'd come to relish being single. Having been in a series of back-to-back relationships most of my adult life, being alone for a time had actually been a great gift. It had thrown me back into myself in an amazing way. Before that, it had been much easier to blame my partners for my not feeling good, not feeling loved, not feeling loveable. As a single woman, however, that option was off the table—there was nobody else to blame. I was asked, time and again, to confront myself, to dig deeper inside, and to find another source of love within me. At first it had been difficult.

Like many women, I had been programmed to look for my source of love and worth on the outside. Yet, over time, it became more and more natural to seek that sense of fulfillment within myself. The process had matured me in a way I never would have expected, and I now felt ready to bring that fullness into a new relationship in my life. One day, at the little altar in my bedroom, I declared my plans to God . . . and, well, He laughed.

Michael and I usually tried to go out for dinner about once a month, just to have a night out and a break from our usual routine. It happened to be Valentine's Day, 2013, and we wound up at a little tapas restaurant that was overflowing with couples, candlelight, and live music. Our table was practically in the piano player's lap, and we had to scream to hear each other. It was a fun night . . . that ended with a giant curveball. Just as our dessert was arriving, Michael handed me an envelope. As I started to read the card inside, an enormous weight came over me . . . I froze. Seeing my reaction, Michael took the card from my hand. With a booming voice to counteract the piano, and brimming with inspiration, he compared our relationship to a chair, saying, "A chair has four legs. That's what gives it a solid, stable foundation. Our relationship has three of those legs: we are deeply aligned spiritually; we are best friends; and we have a shared love for Kai. We almost have four legs again, and I'd like us to see if we can get that fourth leg back."

The Valentine card was an invitation to do just that: to go away together for a few days to explore the possibility of resurrecting our "fourth leg." Michael explained that, about a year ago, he had become attracted to me again, and wanted to see if we could restore that part of our relationship. At this point, I had turned cold with shock, and didn't know how to respond or what to say. Plus I'd had a couple of cocktails at dinner and didn't want to speak from a place that lacked clarity. In his Michael way, though, he pressed me for an answer, to which I responded, stuttering, "W-w-wait a minute. You've been processing this for almost a year now? And this is the first I'm hearing about it? I need time, and some space, to get clear about what it is I feel."

He quickly replied, "Yeah, that's what this weekend would be: going away to get space to explore this, to get clear. . . ."

I couldn't help but interrupt. "No, you don't understand. I need space to get clear about *if* I even want to do *that*! Just because you want to go away and explore this, doesn't mean I do." Those words were so painful to say, but I couldn't keep them inside. One of the things Michael and I valued most in our relationship was a level of honesty I'd never known with anyone else. We could tell each other anything. And, as much as I didn't want to hurt him, or rub salt into his old wound of rejection, I needed to be as honest as I could, both for him and for me. I told him I needed some time to process this, and I'd get back to him when I was ready.

A few days later, I was rummaging through my purse looking for something, and came across his card. I quickly stuffed it into my desk drawer, where it was to remain for almost a year. In the quiet moments of my day, usually when putting Kai to bed, I reflected on Michael's invitation, but just couldn't come up with an answer. The truth was, we did have three legs. My work with countless people had shown me that what we had was indeed quite special, and that our three legs were actually qualities that many official couples did not possess. Yet I couldn't get past the problem of that damn fourth leg: attraction; romantic feelings; the *kind* of love I imagined between a husband and a wife. Over the past few years, Michael had become my spiritual partner, my ally, and my brother. The thought of kissing him made me cringe, as if I'd be making out with a family member. It seemed unnatural. And yet, we had conceived a child together—there had once been passion between us. Where had it gone? Was Michael right? Was it the wounding that took place for me in our marriage that was blocking my ability to feel attracted to him? Perhaps that was the explanation. Or was it something else entirely? At the end of the day, I didn't know for sure. All I knew was, no matter how much work I had done on healing all that had happened between us, I still was not attracted to him in a romantic way. I decided to do nothing until more clarity arrived, and thankfully, Michael did not bring up the invitation again for a long time. I didn't want to sink the boat of our friendship by dropping a bomb of rejection. For nearly a year, there was an unspoken agreement between us not to revisit the subject.

Since I had known him, it had always been a huge dream of Michael's to own a home. That spring, he took the initiative and began a search for a house that was affordable and close to Kai's school. We looked at tons of homes, but didn't find anything that was a total *yes*. One day, while browsing online, we came across a house that looked great: it was at the end of a cul-de-sac; it backed onto open space; and it had plenty of room for a trampoline—a key requirement. I was out of town working, but Michael went to see it, and within days put in an acceptable offer. His dream had come true: he was a homeowner. I myself still had some ambivalence about moving together again, particularly after the Valentine's Day incident, but the thought of living alone with Kai in some tiny apartment was still so disheartening—I couldn't bear it. In the end, I decided to move, with the same conditions as before. I had asked Michael to look for a house that had an additional room he could rent out if I decided to leave. He had stuck to his end of the bargain and so, that July, we moved together for the third time in three years.

Over the next few months, I saw another part of Michael come alive. He loved his garden, and even more so, the new fruit trees he bought, ruminating over where he would plant them. He lugged up big stones from the nearby creek to build a rock wall, installed a water filter in the kitchen, and took great care of things that were now "his own." I also loved the house. It was almost brand new, clean and bright, and had the same spacious feeling as our home back on Federal Road. We now had a backyard, and Kai's Grandpa bought him a new trampoline, to replace the one we had to leave behind. The only thing missing was our basement. We were able to put our altar upstairs in the hallway but, sadly, lost our basement marching-band ritual.

The following December found me in my office, packing for a trip to India. I hadn't been back in two years, and had saved up enough frequent flier miles to take me across the oceans again. This trip would be a combination of my own personal sabbatical, as well as training in some processes we could bring into the workshops with our own students. As I was zipping up my luggage, Michael came into the room and closed the door. He knelt down at my desk and said, "It's been almost a year since I gave you that Valentine's card, and opened up a conversation about the possibility of us exploring a potential new kind of future relationship. All I ask is that, when you are in India, you pray for clarity about this. When you come back, I'd like to have an answer." I welled up with tears— we would be leaving for the airport in under an hour, and goodbyes always made me wax nostalgic. Through my sniffles, I replied, "Michael, yes, of course . . . I will do that. You know you are my best friend; you're the closest person to me. No matter what happens, I want you to know that I do love you." He nodded and cried, and we embraced each other for a moment . . . before Kai came barreling into the middle . . . oh, how our boy loved group hugs. Kai patted us both on the back, saying, "Mama, Papa" and then cracking himself up with abandon. It was one of those precious moments that I hope flashes back to me at life's end, reminding me why this bittersweet adventure was so worth it.

Upon my return from India, we sat down at the kitchen table to complete the conversation we had started on Valentine's Day almost a year before. I prayed for the strength and compassion to say what I needed to say, in the most loving way possible. The words spilled out of me, "Michael, I want you to know I did reflect and pray on this while in India. And what you say, about our three legs, makes so much practical sense and I wish, I really wish, that the fourth leg would be there you. It would be so much easier, it really would. But it's just simply not there, and I cannot give up wanting that in my life. Maybe you are right, that my attraction to you is deeply buried under all that transpired between us, but I don't think so. We've done so much work, so much healing—we've come so far. And I do love you, with my whole heart, just not in *that* way. So, no, I don't think I'm blocked. I don't think there's anything I can resurrect on that level of our relationship. I think my love for you has gone through the most wonderful alchemy possible: it's transformed, grown, and blossomed into another *kind* of love. You are my best friend, my family, my deepest spiritual brother, and I am so grateful for all that has recently happened between us. I think we both need to accept that gift and move on to what's next for each of us in the realm of intimate relationships. I'm feeling ready to share that part of my heart with somebody again, and I hope you will too one day."

It all came out in one fell swoop, after which there was a long and awkward pause. We sat there in silence. He was taking it in, chewing on it, starting to digest it, and slowly, out came his response. "Yes, I hear you . . . I really do. It's painful, but I get it. I understand, and I thank you for your honesty." It felt like my answer had gone inside—the arrow had found the bulls-eye—and it seemed he'd been able to truly accept all that it meant.

(His: No! Turned on again)

As Neelama read the Valentine's Day card, my heart was tense, there was a contraction in my belly, and I could sense my fear of rejection. The wound from the big "reject" was activated. A voice warned me, *"She will say no. You are crazy. You will get hurt."* I watched with anticipation as her facial expression changed, indicating she was startled by this sudden revelation and proposal. Unlike Neelama, I had been "pregnant" with this idea for the some months and, on and off, had felt an attraction to her over the past year. As I feared, she said, "No . . . I cannot do this . . . I need to think about it. . . ." Her words stung, and I tried to breathe. All I could do was let myself feel the sting in my body, to face the rejection, and try to keep myself together. I reached for my margarita, taking a few sips as she continued to explain her side. All the while, the piano man was serenading the room with love song after love song, rubbing salt into my reopened wound. I found myself becoming more and more protective, feeling an armor cloaking me, shielding me from further hurt. For the rest of the evening, I lived with a mask on my face, and a stinging hurt in my heart. Coming home, I took refuge at my altar, and shed some tears. There was no way around it: it was painful not to be wanted sexually. That's why it had taken me nearly a year to approach Neelama again with my proposal. Over the next few months, the Valentine's Day conversation caused some subtle changes between us. Neelama held back from our normal cuddling, which was understandable, and didn't bring up the subject again. The pull of my attraction waxed and waned, depending on the circumstances, with peaked during our teaching times together, when she was most in her expanded feminine beauty and radiance.

The months flew by, and Kai continued to make great progress at Jacob's Ladder, where he spent about seven hours a day in his individually tailored curriculum. Every evening, when we picked him up at five o'clock, he ran into our arms, full of joy and excitement, as if he hadn't seen us in ages. Kai's sweetness and innocence continued to make him one of the most beloved children at Jacob's Ladder, and for sure, the most hugged. His progression through the developmental levels, from level one to level five, took place in only three-and-a-half years—a triumph indeed, given the original prognosis for our son.

As wonderful as Jacob's Ladder was, we were still not seeing the progress we had hoped for in regard to Kai's speech development. We attended some workshops to gather more information about the diagnosis of speech Apraxia, and came to realize that the key to success for this condition was frequent therapy sessions. We found a new speech therapy center, which specialized in apraxia, and although it was very expensive, set up daily thirty-minute sessions with two wonderful speech therapists, Heather and Alyssa.

In the exploration of new possibilities for Kai, it was usually Neelama who took the lead, in her efficient and unstoppable way. It was she who discovered, and did the due diligence, that led us to the Cobblestone Therapy Center. Exposing this brings me to one of the most challenging aspects of our divorced couple relationship. As in most couple relationships, neither one of us felt fully seen or appreciated by the other. Yet I had to acknowledge that Neelama carried, and still carries, much more than I of the logistical handling that raising a special needs child requires. The world in which we live, in these times, seems to require unending red tape and paperwork to access agencies and services: government; medical; educational; insurance; and, in particular, the specialized doctors and therapists we needed for Kai. I had neither the skills nor patience required to navigate through the complicated labyrinths of bureaucracy, and as a result, I didn't step up to the plate in this essential area, leaving Neelama to carry most of that load.

Perhaps, to some degree, my commitment to taking care of all the maintenance for the house and garden, for which Neelama had little interest or expertise, helped balance the giving and receiving between us. We learned that, as long as we stopped to check in with each other, and clear the air by exposing our resentments, our divorced couple relationship boat cruised along in smooth waters. However, when we waited too long to do this, we could expect a fight to break out eventually, and repressed frustrations to spill out. Our friendship-based relationship garden, just like a romance-based relationship garden, needed to be regularly fertilized with appreciation and acknowledgement, and weeded by clearing out withheld resentments.

The "India bug" caught Neelama before Christmas 2013, and just before she was to leave on her pilgrimage, I tapped into my courage and stubbornness, and ventured into her office to name the elephant in the room: "It's been almost a year since I gave you that card on Valentine's day, and I would like you to pray about this missing fourth leg while you are doing your inner work. *Danke*! Please give me an answer when you get back." There . . . it was out . . . again. She nodded in agreement, with tears in her eyes. Getting it out on the table eased my inner pressure, and as Kai and I started

2014 with a "Papa -Kai Intensive," I felt fully present with him and with my life, and open to awaiting the verdict.

When Neelama returned from India, she lovingly took a metaphorical club and hit me over the head with it. "I love you," she said, "but like a sister, not like a woman. I'm not attracted to you in a sexual way." She felt that trying to experiment with this would actually just lead to more confusion, and get her off track in opening up towards a new mate. Neelama explained to me that she had recently started to put out "feelers" on some online dating sites, and that she was getting ready to be in a relationship again. Her inward time was over.

What initially felt like being hit by a club, eventually proved to be very helpful. Somehow the directness and clarity of Neelama's pronouncement—that she was not romantically attracted to me—released the air from the balloon of secret hope that I had resisted acknowledging. Suddenly, after that conversation in January, I found myself actively interested in women in general, and although nothing immediately manifested in that area, I began to feel that I was at least beginning the process towards finding another mate.

One more big change occurred in our Georgia adventure: I became a homeowner. The low mortgage rates made it a financially wise decision to buy a house and pay off my own mortgage, instead of my landlord's. On top of this, our home would also be an investment that I planned to leave Kai one day. In addition to the outer challenges and tasks of finding the house I wanted, and getting accepted for a mortgage, the house-buying process proved to be an internally rich and deep experience. It became a process of "incarnation" for me. When Kai arrived in my life, one of my two legs had finally taken root on planet earth. I felt that, with owning a home, my other leg was now firmly planted here too. To my surprise, I continue to thoroughly enjoy "my home" and "my garden" to this day, and the myriad of tasks surrounding it are still something to which I look forward, and which bring a balance to my "psychological-spiritual" life.

My most recent garden project involved building a wall with stones I found in our nearby creek. Dripping with sweat, I schlepped them up the hill and arranged them into a natural stone wall, marking the boundary between the groomed lawn and the wild hillside. As I worked on this, I felt a deep connection to my "Papa," Hugo, which was very sweet and heart-filling. My father was a mason, and supported by my mother, had built our family home, literally, with his own two hands. Doing stonework was a natural connection to his world. As I stood in my backyard, taking in the almost-completed wall, I imagined him looking up, or down, on me with a smile on his face, murmuring: *"I would never have thought that this boy of mine would own a house and build a rock wall. Lord, you are a miracle worker!"*

Conclusion

(Ours:)

It has been two years since we moved into our home here on Manor Lane. Some of the most precious moments have taken place at our altar upstairs, with Kai sandwiched between us, iPad in hand. He knows the words to some of our prayers now, and it is so endearing to watch him pray, and blow out the candles when it's all over—his favorite spiritual practice of all. Kai is eleven now, and this decade has devoured all three of us, as a fulfilling life tends to do . . . especially when it is well lived.

We've come through an unbelievable eleven years, and Kai has crucified and resurrected something more precious in us than anything we've ever known. He is the greatest of our spiritual teachers, our little Guru, from whom we continue to learn every single day. It dawned on both of us recently, as we sat huddled around the altar that has become such a sacred spot for our family, that we have truly come full circle. We met sixteen years ago, on the floor of a meditation hall—two hungry students seeking God and awakening. That was the beginning of our bond; that was what had survived through the years of our rough divorce. As we now sat gazing at the many faces of God in front of us, we knew, with the totality of our hearts, that this same bond would sustain us as we continued to grow together in spiritual friendship on the journey Home.

Recently, while working on a chapter for this book, we found our wedding vows, and realized, much to our surprise, that not a single vow has been broken:

I vow to open this heart to its utmost vulnerability.

I vow to give freedom to your soul.

I vow to be curious and willing to see through the veils of who I want you to be, so I can discover who you really are.

I vow to walk with you on this journey of relationship, even when it excavates the deepest wounds in our hearts.

I vow to travel with you through pain and joy, hate and love, and through the unwinding of our personalities into Being.

I vow to take care of you.

I vow to choose honesty and love over defense and pride.

I vow to seek the deepest truth of who we are, and to use our union as a vehicle to serve the truth.

We are still trying to live up to these vows today: in our friendship; in our work partnership; in our parenting of Kai; and in the way we support each other's spiritual journey. It's a blessing to read these vows now and realize that, although the form of the relationship has changed, the commitment our souls made to one another has not.

We are so grateful that the love between us not only survived, but was deconstructed and made anew. Through the strong winds of the pregnancy, the heavy tornadoes of our first years as parents, and the torrential downpours of our divorce, our love was transformed into another kind of love—one that is brighter, stronger, deeper, more resilient, and a much larger version of what we had previously known.

Hindsight's

(Ours:)

"For one human being to love another; that is perhaps the most difficult of our tasks, the ultimate, the last test and proof, the work for which all other work is but preparation."
— *Rainer Maria Rilke*

We have discovered that relationship is the most challenging and the most rewarding experience a human being can have in this life. Relationships allow us to grow and transform like nothing else. They give us an opportunity to see ourselves fully: our beauty; our depth; our brokenness; our defense; our pride; our compassion; our tenderness; our righteousness; our vulnerability; our love.

We have learned so much through the decades of our own relationship and, because hindsight is 20/20, and reflecting back on it with more objectivity and greater awareness, it's easier to look at what happened from the perspective of lessons learned. We can more easily identify our mistakes, our ignorance, our blind spots, and the choices we made out of our unconscious reactions.

Since the original writing of this memoir, we've returned to the beloved Bay Area, where Kai was born. We continue to be dear friends, business partners, and co-parents of our little "Prince".

Neelama now lives with her partner, David and Michael lives in a communal house with a few close friends and has begun dating again.

If you've come this far in our book, you likely agree that so many learning opportunities are described here. As we came to the end of writing our memoir, we couldn't help but ask how you—our readers—could benefit from our mistakes and the insights gained. The idea of an online course was born. We wanted to be a guide for you, and others, who are going through the challenges of a breakup or divorce. In this life changing course, we walk with you – step by step – through the very rough waters of separation and divorce into a profound opportunity for growth and new beginnings. Your breakup doesn't have to be a tragedy – it can be a powerful chance to transform your life, preparing you to live fully and love deeply. We know first-hand that it is possible for you to open your heart again to happy, healthy love. It is our sincere hope that this course will support you and many others on this journey. Many blessings to you.

You can find the online course here: Healing Heart Protocol: A 5-step cure for transforming the pain of a breakup or divorce into a profound opportunity for a new life. or using the link below: http://www.innerjourneyinstitute.com/programs/healing-heart-protocol

About the Authors

Michael Schiesser and Neelama Eyres are founders of *The Inner Journey Institute.* They have worked in the field of adult education and personal transformation since 1984 and 1995, respectively. Since 1999, Inner Journey Institute has delivered live workshops throughout the United States, Canada, and Europe. The curriculum includes over a hundred programs that offer strategies and solutions in the areas of relationship, separation and divorce, gender differences, family dynamics, conflict management, training and development, and spirituality. They have been called, "technicians of the heart," and their work has assisted thousands of people in personal, professional and spiritual transformation.

They have created an in-person *Healing Divorce Intensive* as well as an online course called *The Healing Heart Protocol* to help people who are navigating through a breakup or divorce. These programs provide the tools and techniques necessary to consciously complete the past, so that people can move forward into a new and brighter future- one that includes opening the heart to live and love again. Please visit their website to learn more

www.innerjourneyinstitute.com.

Made in the USA
Las Vegas, NV
19 December 2020